WOLVERINE
SOULTAKER

Writer: Akira Yoshida
Illustrator: Shin "Jason" Nagasawa
Colors: Guru eFX
Lettering: Virtual Calligraphy's Rus Wooton
Covers: Katsuya Terada

Assistant Editors: John Barber & Sean Ryan
Editor: Nick Lowe
Consulting Editor: Mike Marts
Special Thanks to C.B. Cebulski, Aki Yanagi and Mutsumi Masuda

Collection Editor: Jennifer Grünwald
Assistant Editor: Michael Short
Senior Editor, Special Projects:
Director of Sales: David
Production: Loretta
Book Designer: Carrie
Creative Director: Tom Marvelli

Editor in Chief: Joe Quesada
Publisher: Dan Buckley

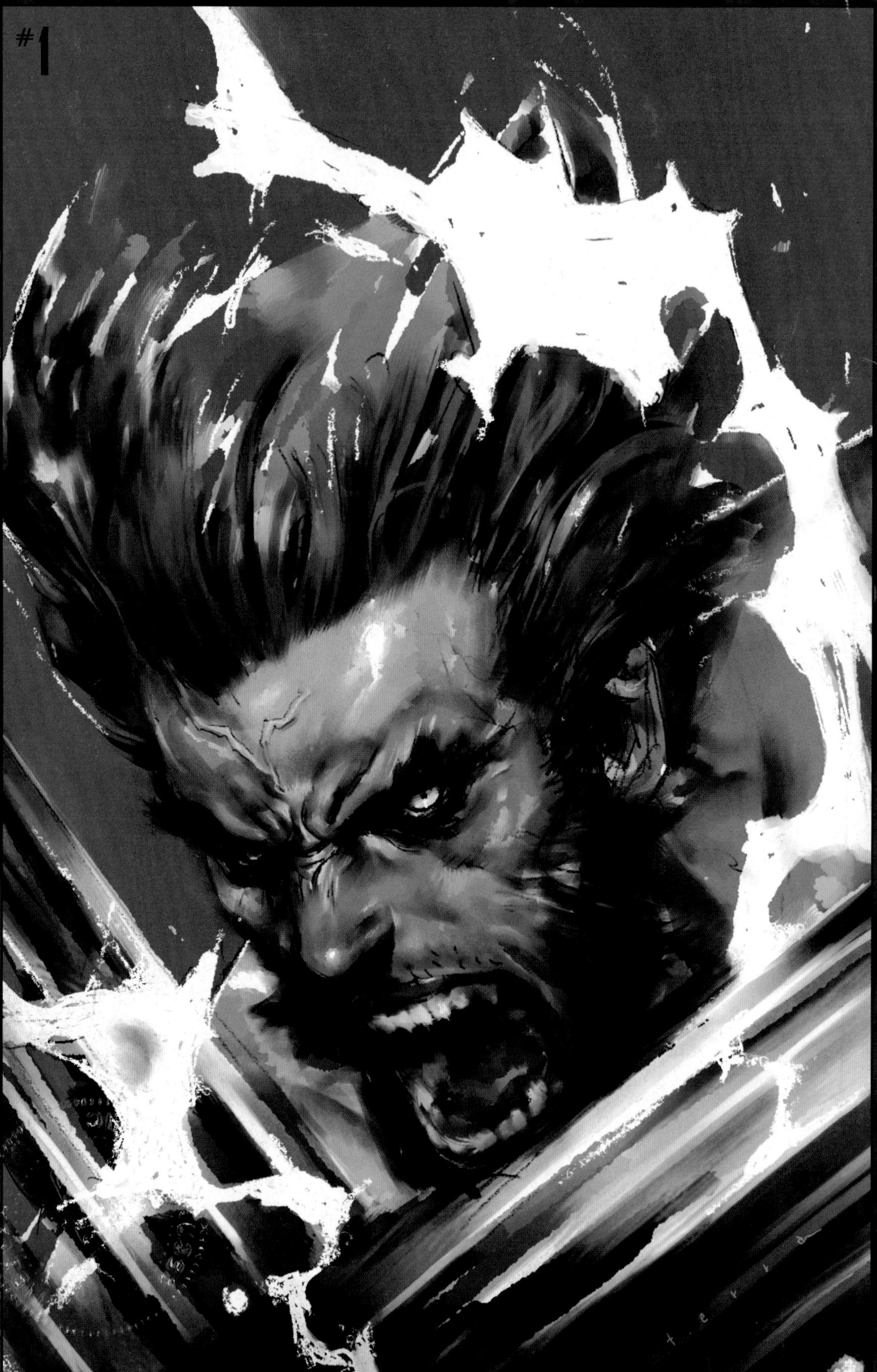
#1

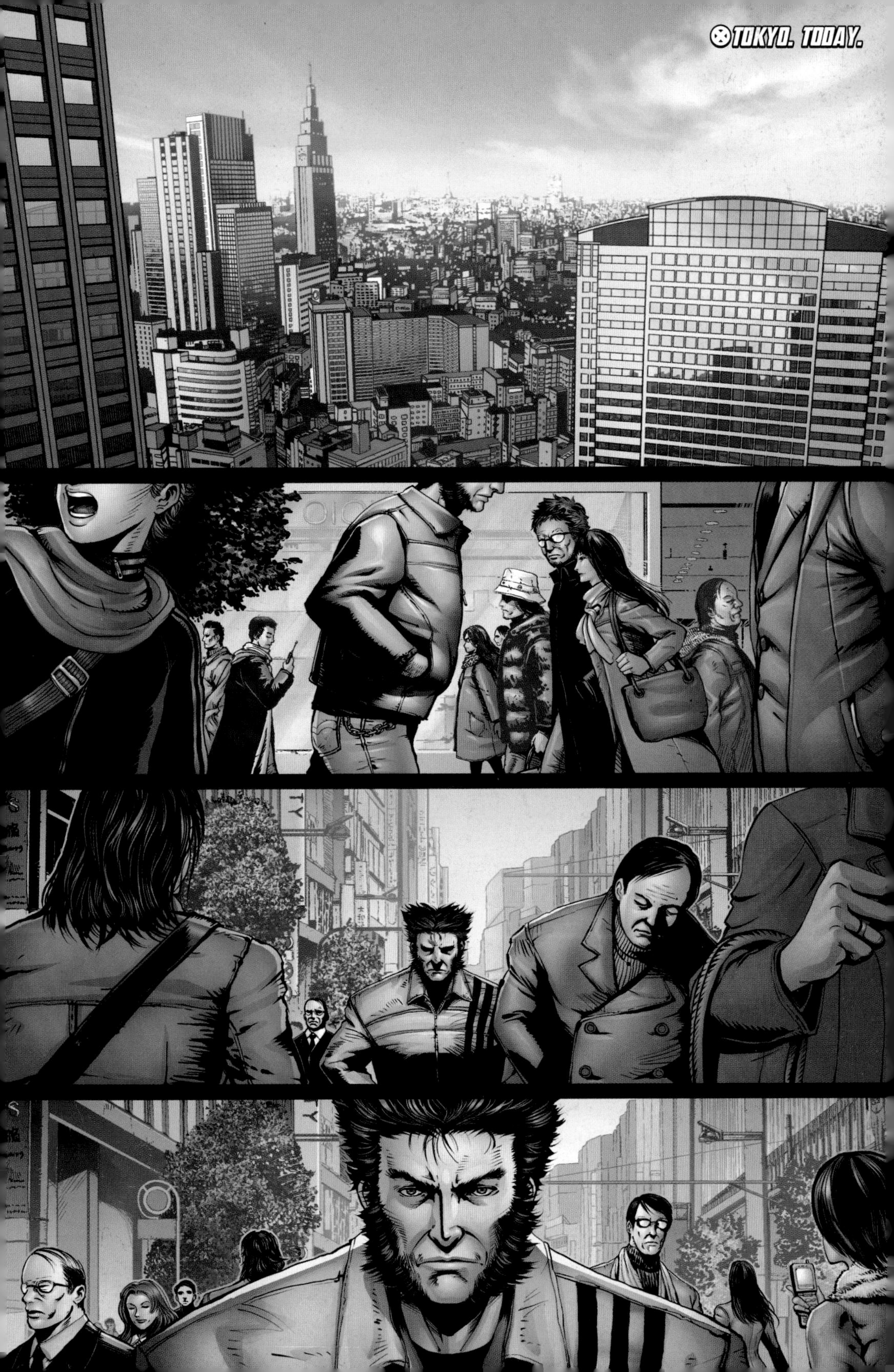
TOKYO. TODAY.

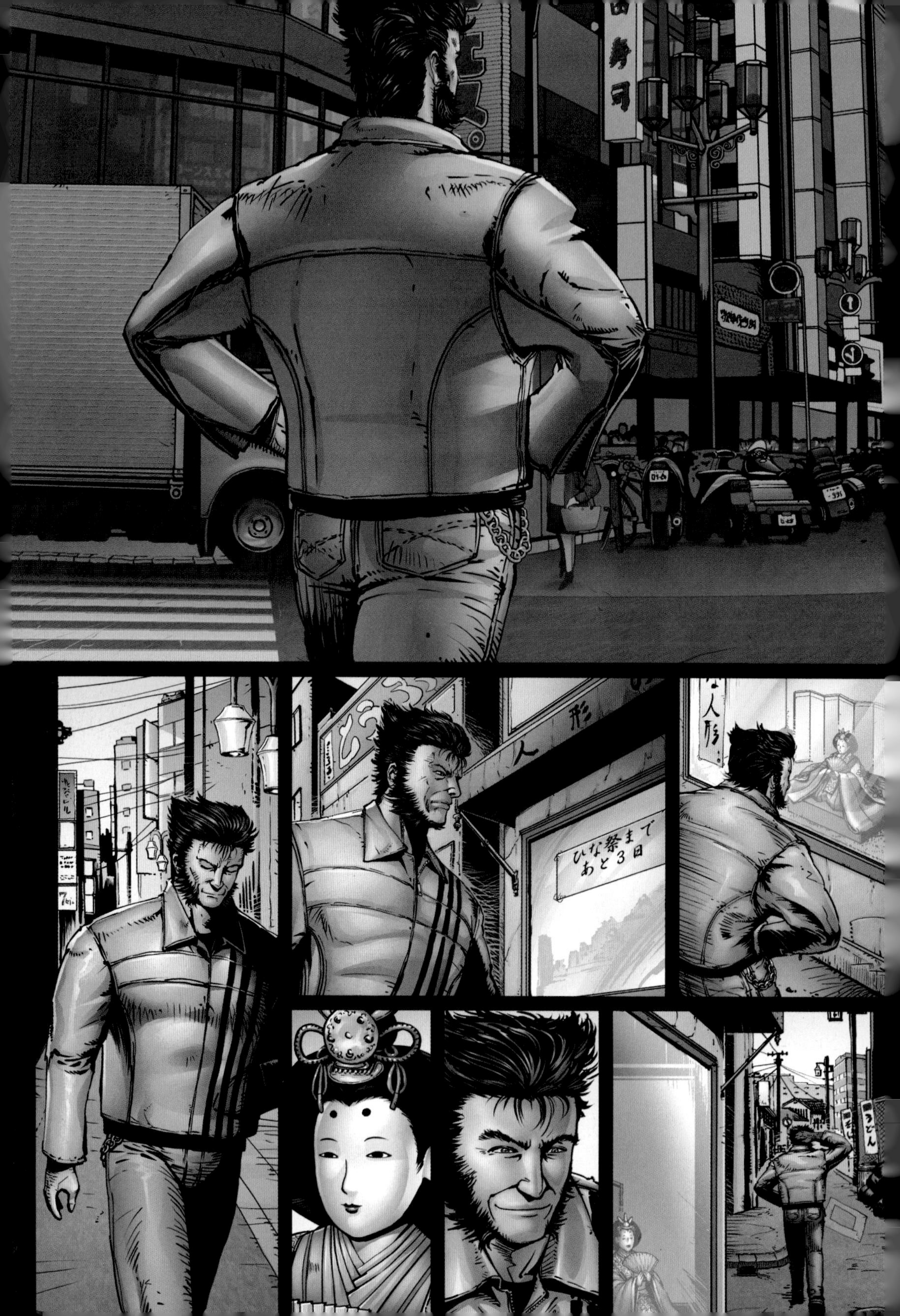
ひな祭まで
あと3日
人形
うどん

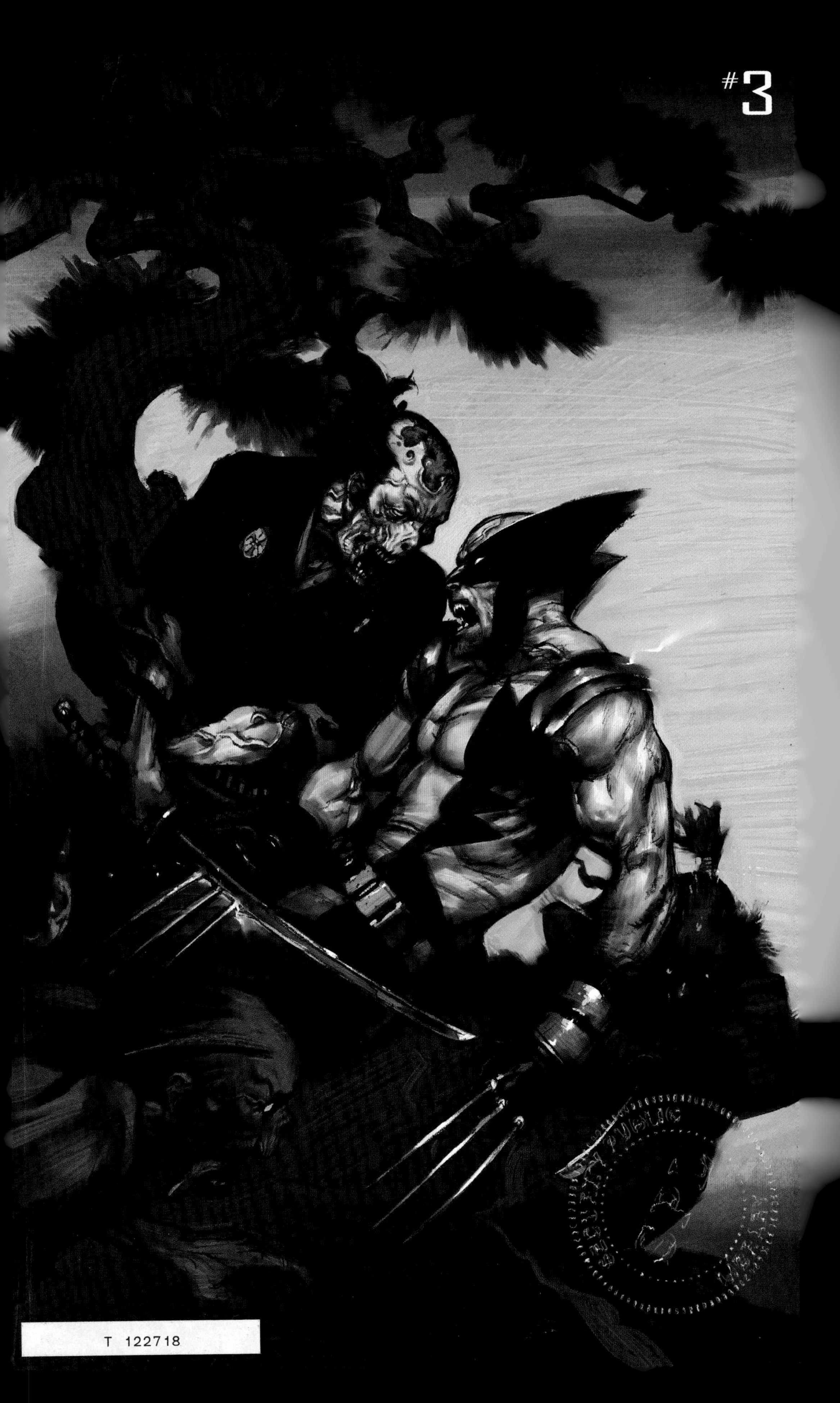
#3

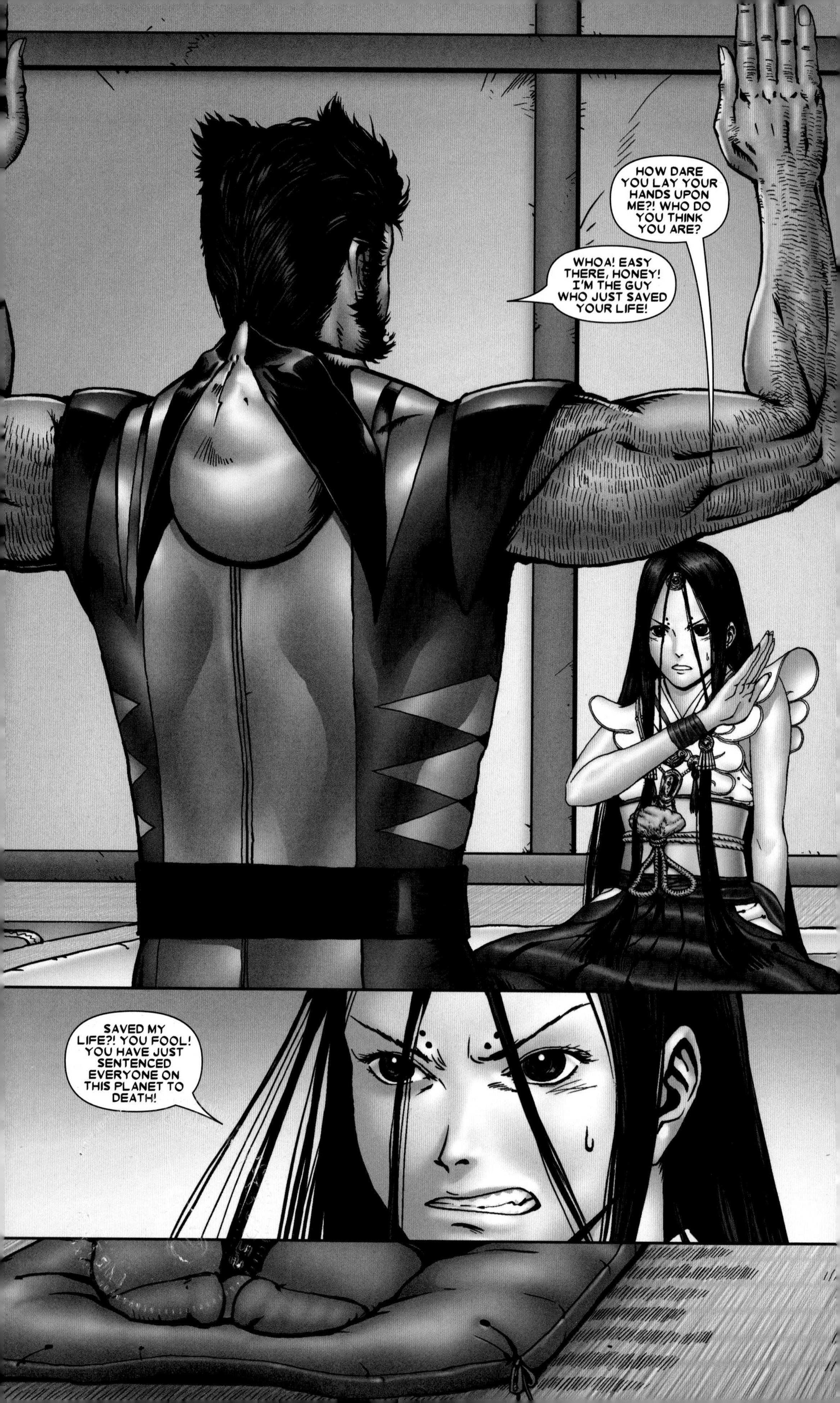
HOW DARE YOU LAY YOUR HANDS UPON ME?! WHO DO YOU THINK YOU ARE?
WHOA! EASY THERE, HONEY! I'M THE GUY WHO JUST SAVED YOUR LIFE!
SAVED MY LIFE?! YOU FOOL! YOU HAVE JUST SENTENCED EVERYONE ON THIS PLANET TO DEATH!

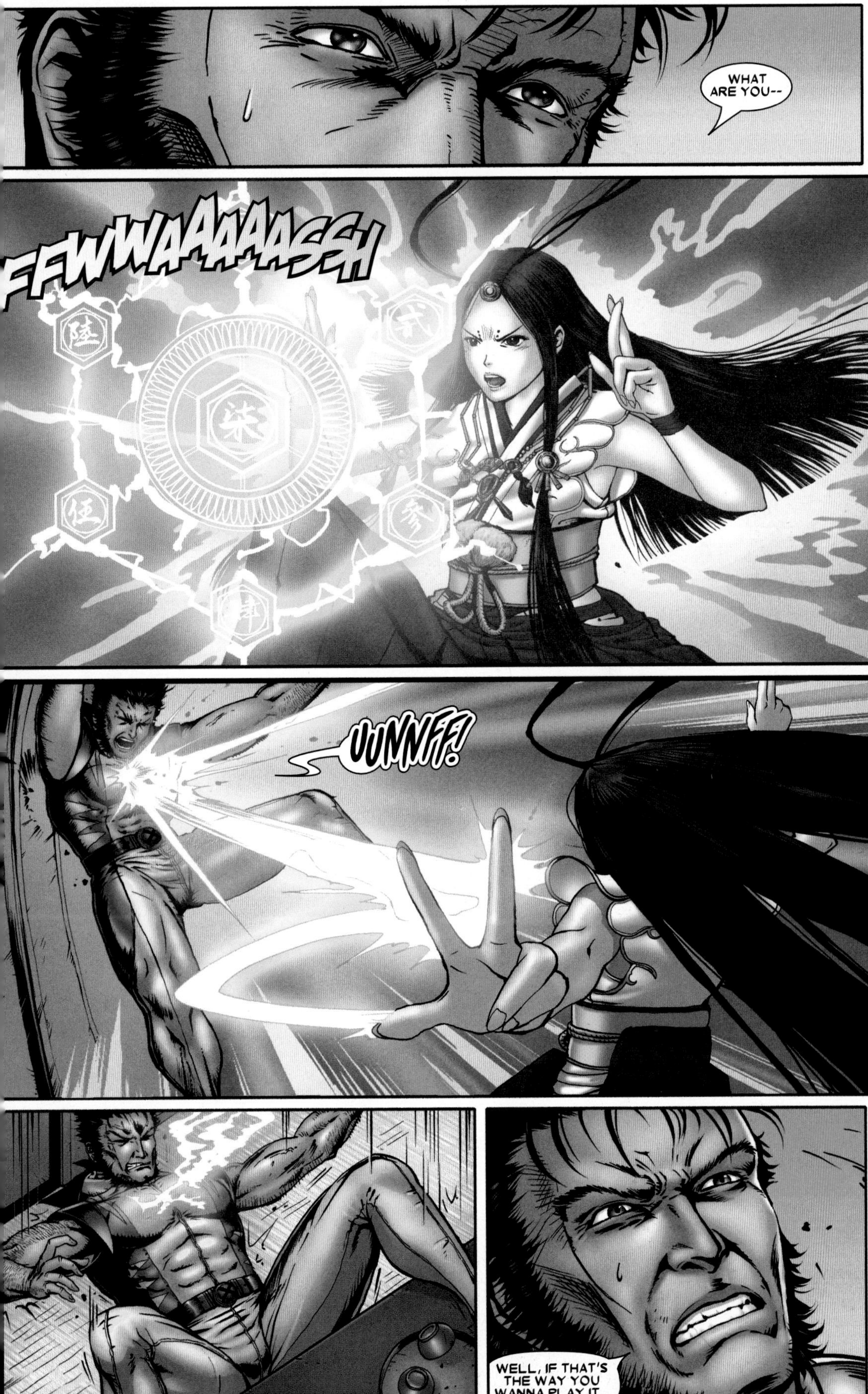
WHAT ARE YOU--
FFWWAAAAASSH
UUNNFF!
WELL, IF THAT'S THE WAY YOU WANNA PLAY IT...

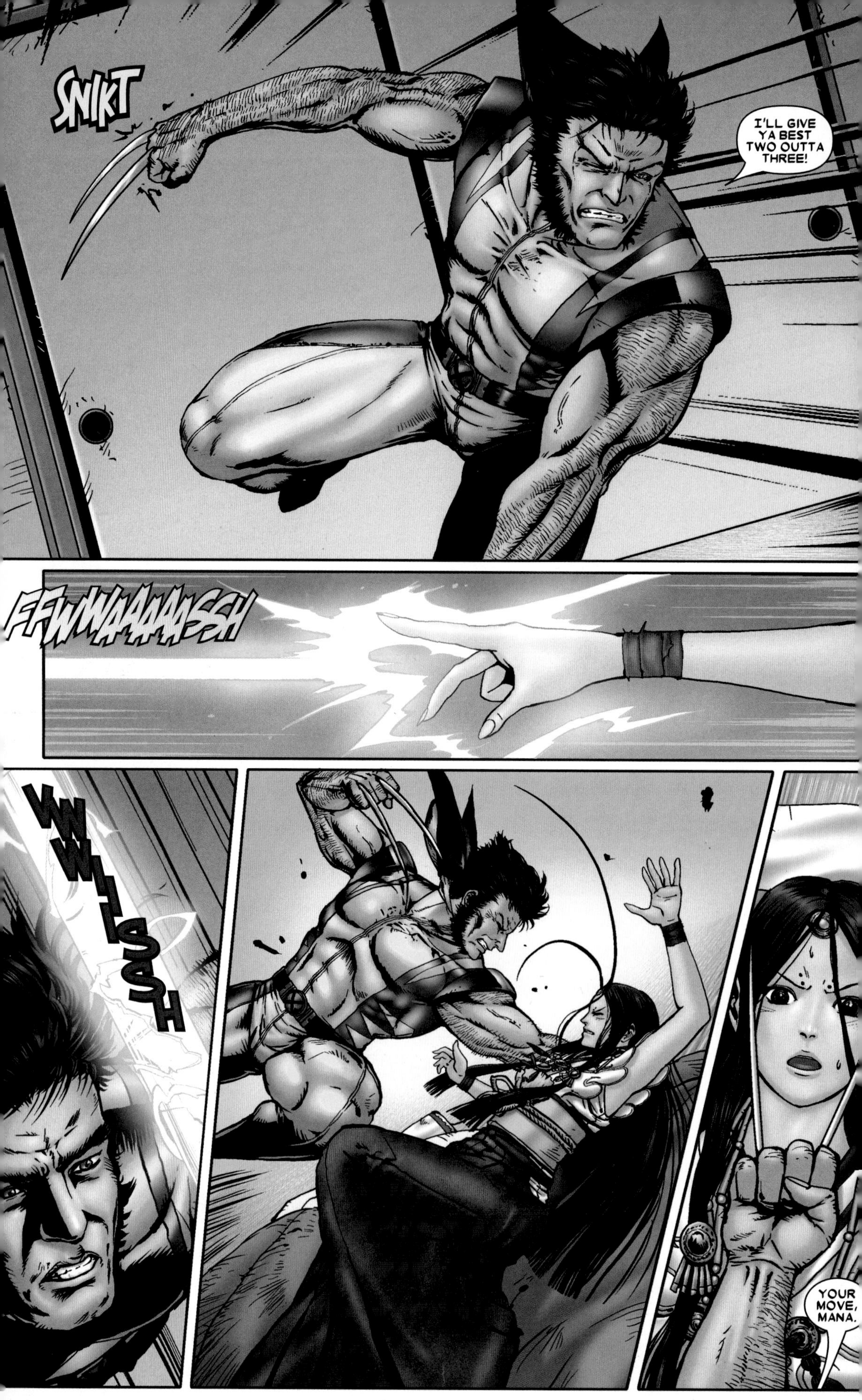
SNIKT
I'LL GIVE YA BEST TWO OUTTA THREE!
FFWWAAAAASH
VVWHISSH
YOUR MOVE, MANA.

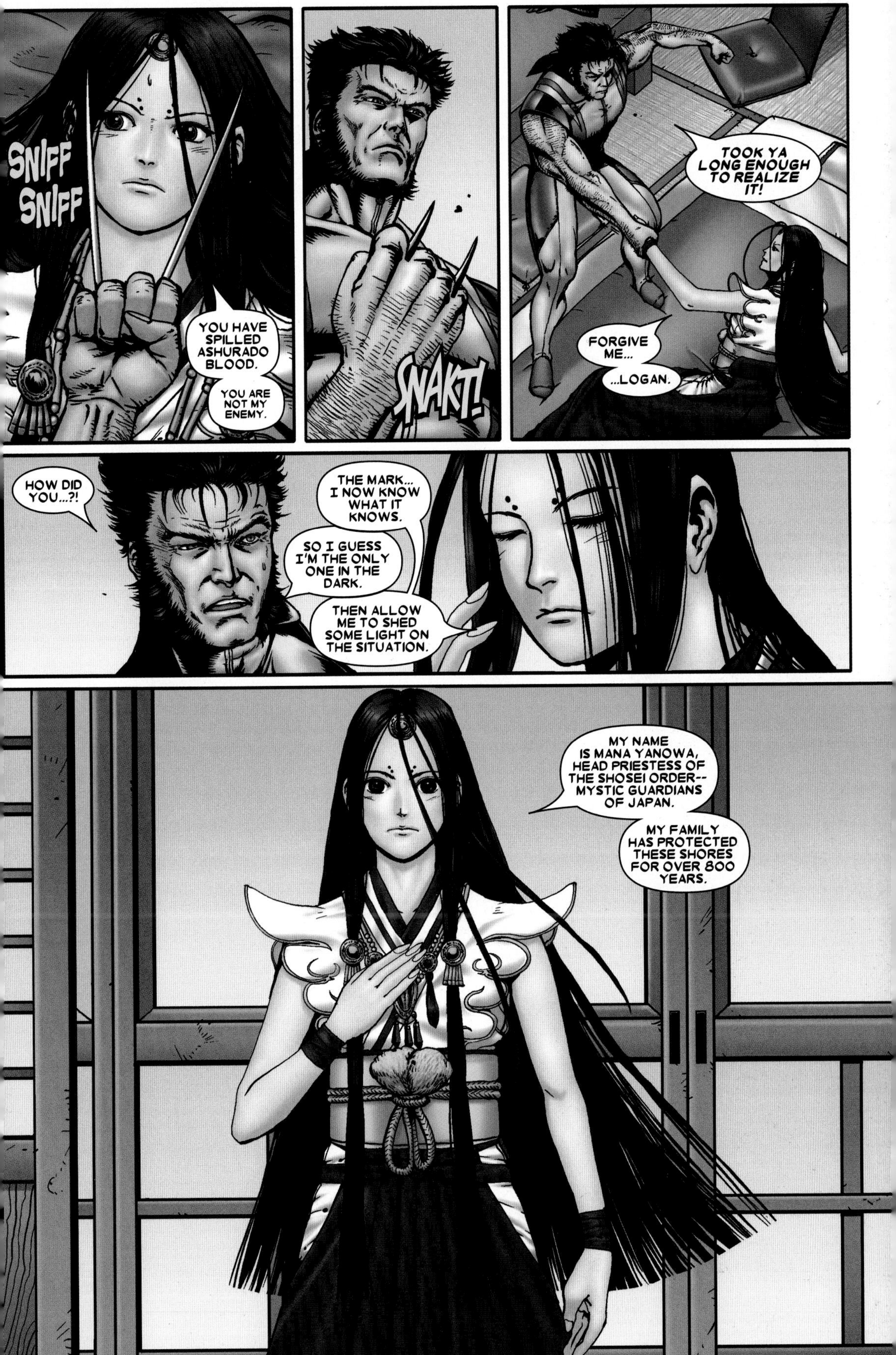
SNIFF SNIFF
YOU HAVE SPILLED ASHURADO BLOOD.
YOU ARE NOT MY ENEMY.
SNAKT!
TOOK YA LONG ENOUGH TO REALIZE IT!
FORGIVE ME...
...LOGAN.
HOW DID YOU...?!
THE MARK... I NOW KNOW WHAT IT KNOWS.
SO I GUESS I'M THE ONLY ONE IN THE DARK.
THEN ALLOW ME TO SHED SOME LIGHT ON THE SITUATION.
MY NAME IS MANA YANOWA, HEAD PRIESTESS OF THE SHOSEI ORDER-- MYSTIC GUARDIANS OF JAPAN.
MY FAMILY HAS PROTECTED THESE SHORES FOR OVER 800 YEARS.

"WHILE THE SHOGUN AND SAMURAI OF OLD FOUGHT OVER LAND AND POWER, IT WAS MY FAMILY WHO KEPT JAPAN SAFE.

"UNTIL THE DAY WE WERE BORN-- MY TWIN SISTER, HANA, AND I.

"TWO GIRLS DESTINED TO CLASH OVER LEADERSHIP OF THE ORDER.

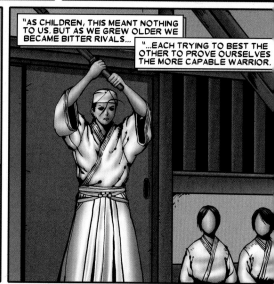

"AS CHILDREN, THIS MEANT NOTHING TO US. BUT AS WE GREW OLDER WE BECAME BITTER RIVALS...

"...EACH TRYING TO BEST THE OTHER TO PROVE OURSELVES THE MORE CAPABLE WARRIOR.

"I AM THE LATEST IN A LONG LINEAGE OF MIKO PRIESTESSES WHO HAVE SAFEGUARDED JAPAN FROM DEMONS, CURSES AND MAGICAL THREATS OVER THE CENTURIES.

"WHEN HELL COUGHED UP ITS EVIL INTO OUR PLANE OF EXISTENCE, WE PUSHED IT BACK.

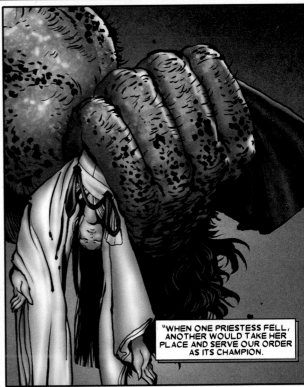

"WHEN ONE PRIESTESS FELL, ANOTHER WOULD TAKE HER PLACE AND SERVE OUR ORDER AS ITS CHAMPION.

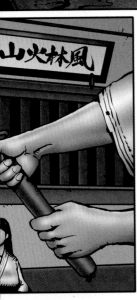

"WHEN IT CAME TIME TO DECIDE WHO WOULD INHERIT THE MANTLE OF LEADERSHIP, IT WAS I WHO EMERGED VICTORIOUS."

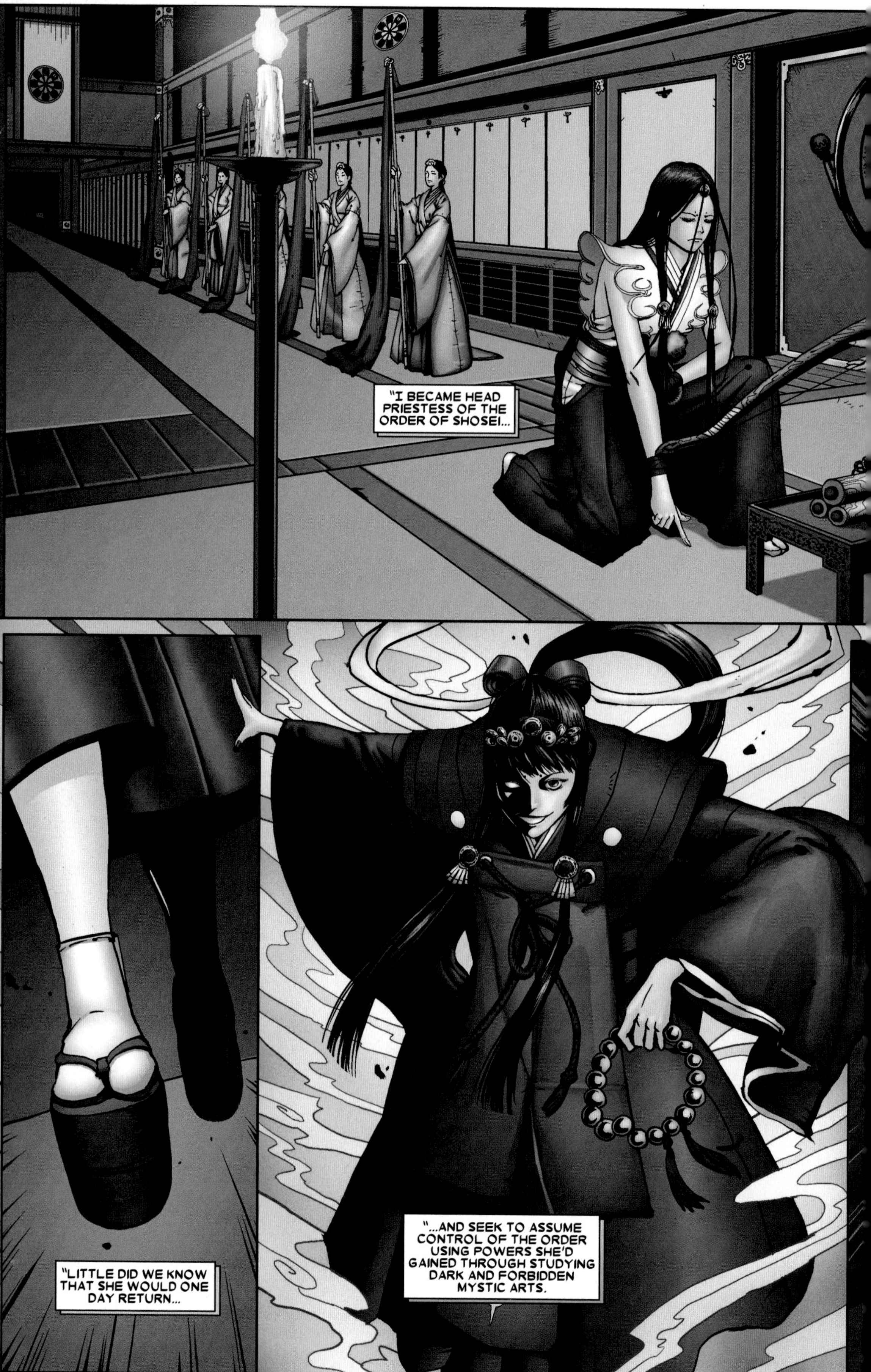
"I BECAME HEAD PRIESTESS OF THE ORDER OF SHOSEI...
"LITTLE DID WE KNOW THAT SHE WOULD ONE DAY RETURN...
"...AND SEEK TO ASSUME CONTROL OF THE ORDER USING POWERS SHE'D GAINED THROUGH STUDYING DARK AND FORBIDDEN MYSTIC ARTS.

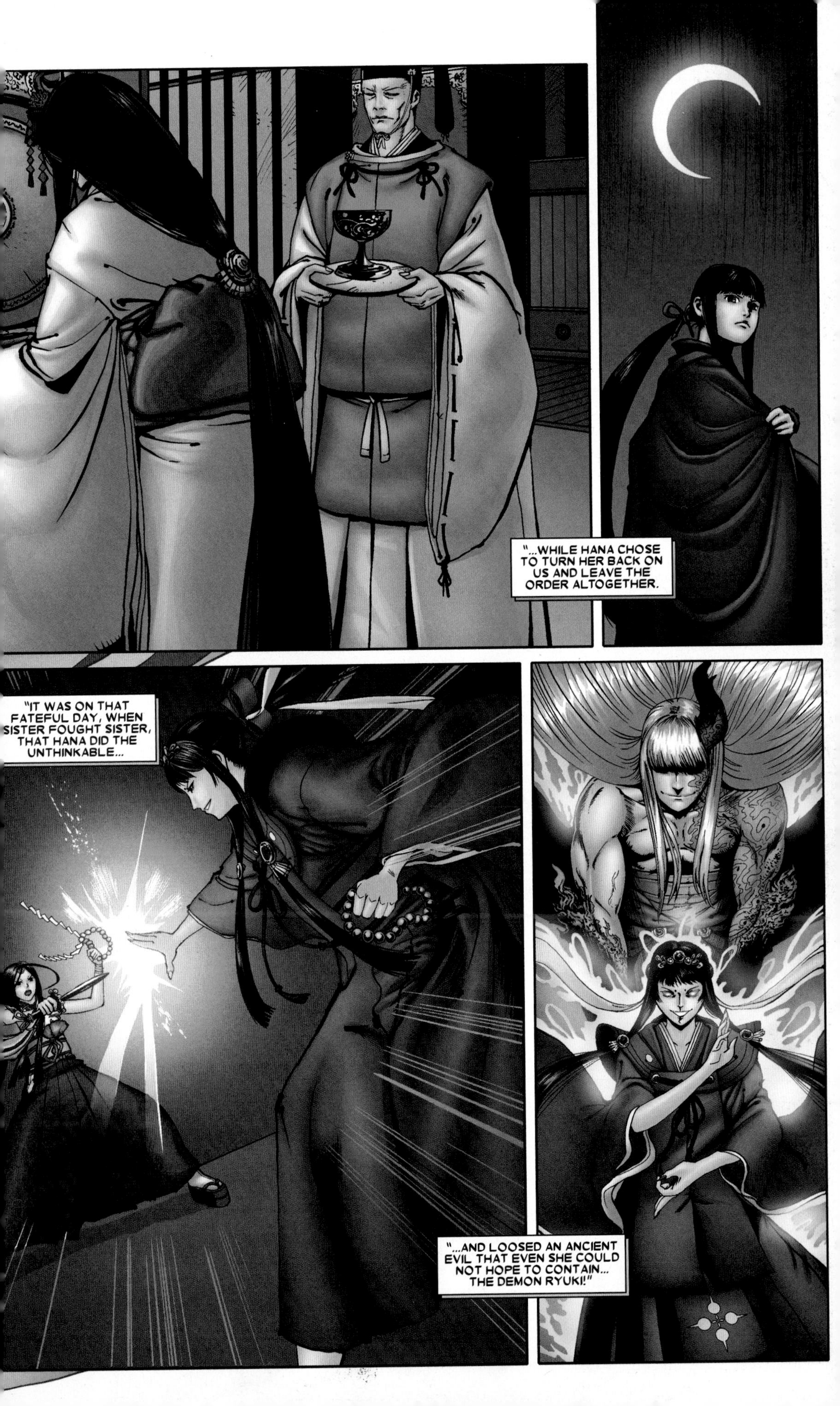
"...WHILE HANA CHOSE TO TURN HER BACK ON US AND LEAVE THE ORDER ALTOGETHER.
"IT WAS ON THAT FATEFUL DAY, WHEN SISTER FOUGHT SISTER, THAT HANA DID THE UNTHINKABLE...
"...AND LOOSED AN ANCIENT EVIL THAT EVEN SHE COULD NOT HOPE TO CONTAIN... THE DEMON RYUKI!"

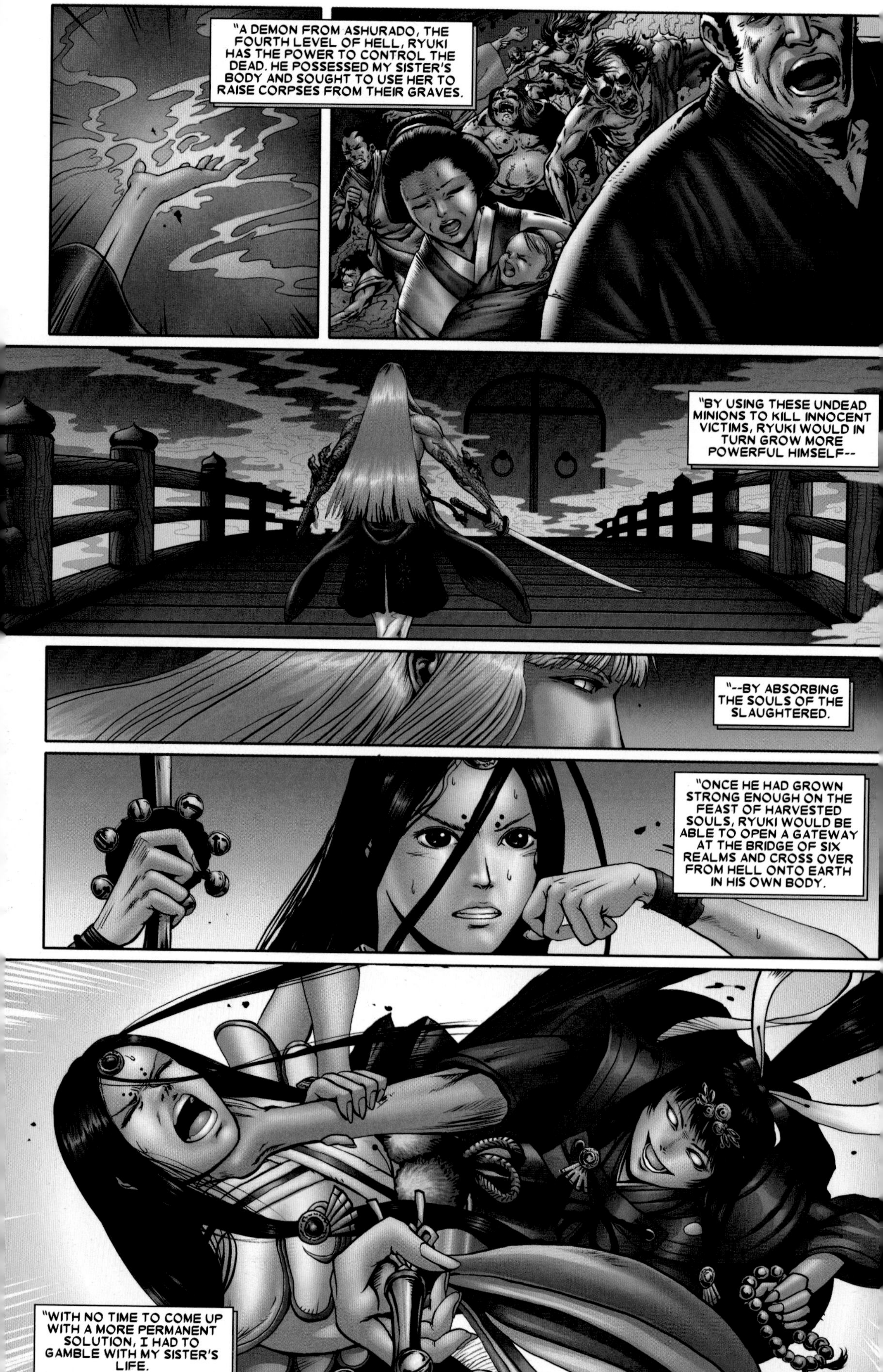
"A DEMON FROM ASHURADO, THE FOURTH LEVEL OF HELL, RYUKI HAS THE POWER TO CONTROL THE DEAD. HE POSSESSED MY SISTER'S BODY AND SOUGHT TO USE HER TO RAISE CORPSES FROM THEIR GRAVES.
"BY USING THESE UNDEAD MINIONS TO KILL INNOCENT VICTIMS, RYUKI WOULD IN TURN GROW MORE POWERFUL HIMSELF--
"--BY ABSORBING THE SOULS OF THE SLAUGHTERED.
"ONCE HE HAD GROWN STRONG ENOUGH ON THE FEAST OF HARVESTED SOULS, RYUKI WOULD BE ABLE TO OPEN A GATEWAY AT THE BRIDGE OF SIX REALMS AND CROSS OVER FROM HELL ONTO EARTH IN HIS OWN BODY.
"WITH NO TIME TO COME UP WITH A MORE PERMANENT SOLUTION, I HAD TO GAMBLE WITH MY SISTER'S LIFE.

"I HAD ONE HOPE.

NNNOOOOOOO!!!

"I SOUGHT TO TRAP RYUKI'S SOUL INSIDE THE JEWEL OF MY NECKLACE FOR ETERNITY.

"AND THOUGH IT WAS SUCCESSFUL... SACRIFICES HAD TO BE MADE.

"HANA'S SOUL WAS IMPRISONED WITHIN THE JEWEL AS WELL.

"AND MINE."

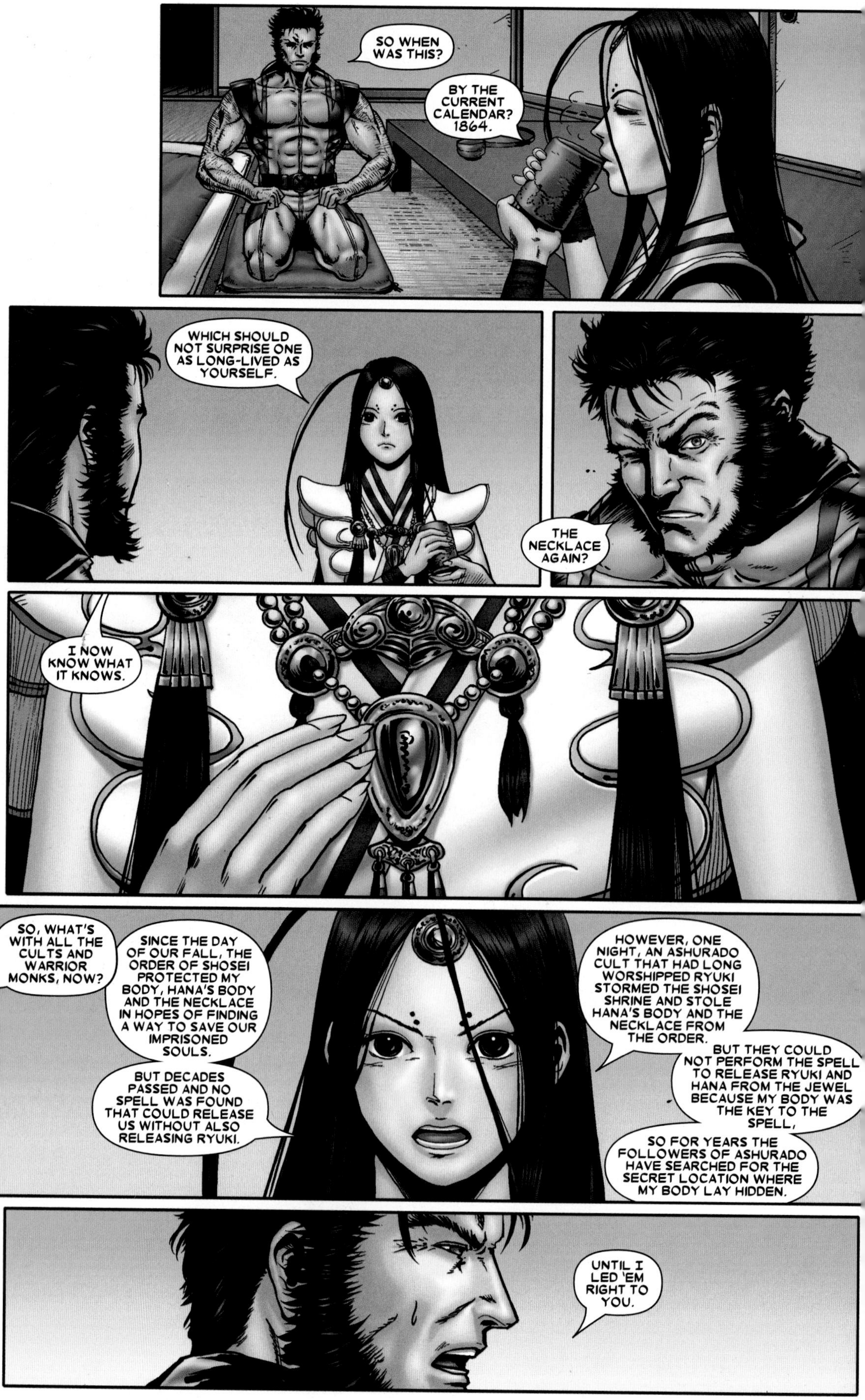
SO WHEN WAS THIS?
BY THE CURRENT CALENDAR? 1864.
WHICH SHOULD NOT SURPRISE ONE AS LONG-LIVED AS YOURSELF.
THE NECKLACE AGAIN?
I NOW KNOW WHAT IT KNOWS.
SO, WHAT'S WITH ALL THE CULTS AND WARRIOR MONKS, NOW?
SINCE THE DAY OF OUR FALL, THE ORDER OF SHOSEI PROTECTED MY BODY, HANA'S BODY AND THE NECKLACE IN HOPES OF FINDING A WAY TO SAVE OUR IMPRISONED SOULS.
BUT DECADES PASSED AND NO SPELL WAS FOUND THAT COULD RELEASE US WITHOUT ALSO RELEASING RYUKI.
HOWEVER, ONE NIGHT, AN ASHURADO CULT THAT HAD LONG WORSHIPPED RYUKI STORMED THE SHOSEI SHRINE AND STOLE HANA'S BODY AND THE NECKLACE FROM THE ORDER.
BUT THEY COULD NOT PERFORM THE SPELL TO RELEASE RYUKI AND HANA FROM THE JEWEL BECAUSE MY BODY WAS THE KEY TO THE SPELL,
SO FOR YEARS THE FOLLOWERS OF ASHURADO HAVE SEARCHED FOR THE SECRET LOCATION WHERE MY BODY LAY HIDDEN.
UNTIL I LED 'EM RIGHT TO YOU.

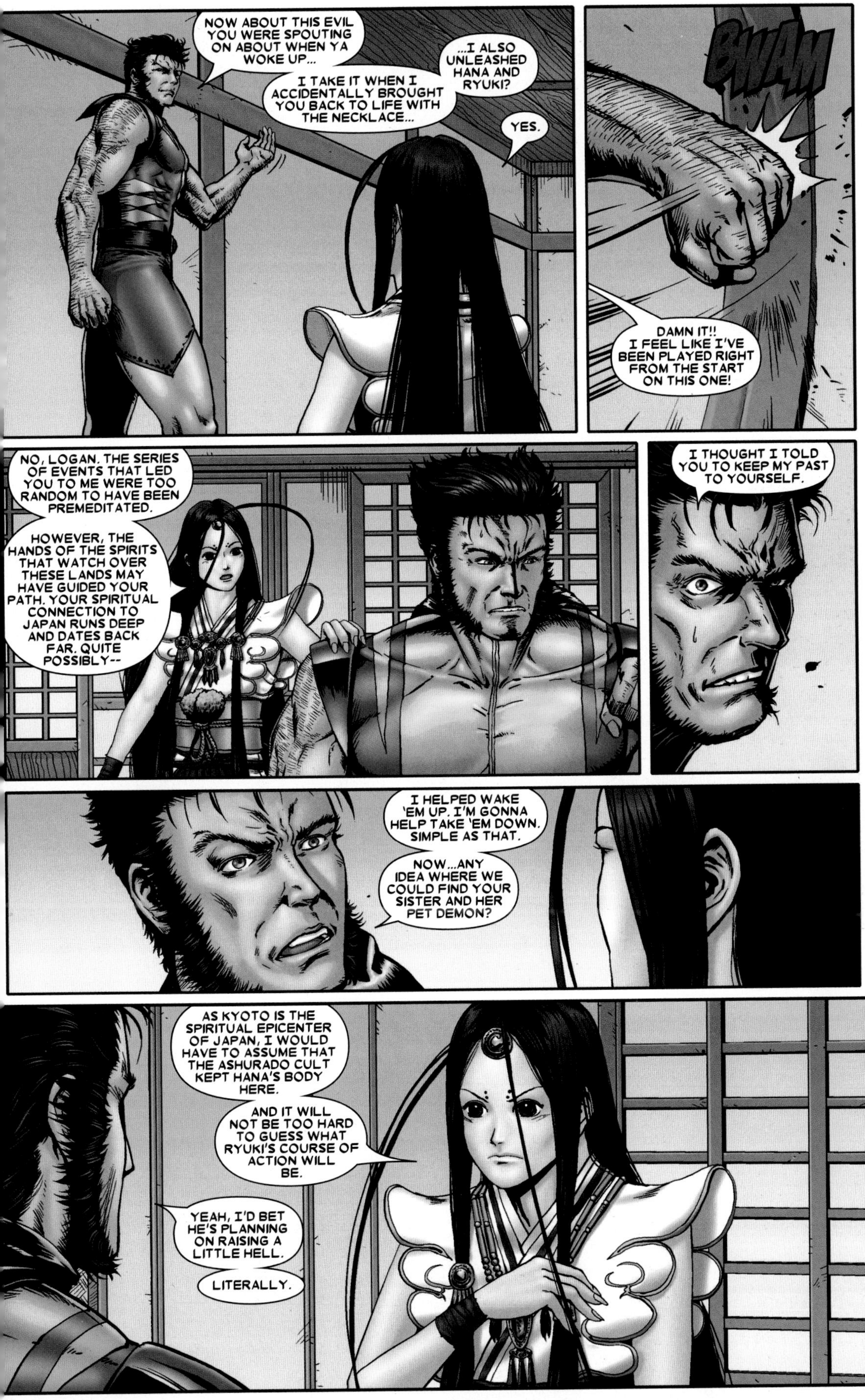

NOW ABOUT THIS EVIL YOU WERE SPOUTING ON ABOUT WHEN YA WOKE UP...
I TAKE IT WHEN I ACCIDENTALLY BROUGHT YOU BACK TO LIFE WITH THE NECKLACE...
...I ALSO UNLEASHED HANA AND RYUKI?
YES.
BWAM
DAMN IT!! I FEEL LIKE I'VE BEEN PLAYED RIGHT FROM THE START ON THIS ONE!
NO, LOGAN. THE SERIES OF EVENTS THAT LED YOU TO ME WERE TOO RANDOM TO HAVE BEEN PREMEDITATED.
HOWEVER, THE HANDS OF THE SPIRITS THAT WATCH OVER THESE LANDS MAY HAVE GUIDED YOUR PATH. YOUR SPIRITUAL CONNECTION TO JAPAN RUNS DEEP AND DATES BACK FAR. QUITE POSSIBLY--
I THOUGHT I TOLD YOU TO KEEP MY PAST TO YOURSELF.
I HELPED WAKE 'EM UP. I'M GONNA HELP TAKE 'EM DOWN. SIMPLE AS THAT.
NOW...ANY IDEA WHERE WE COULD FIND YOUR SISTER AND HER PET DEMON?
AS KYOTO IS THE SPIRITUAL EPICENTER OF JAPAN, I WOULD HAVE TO ASSUME THAT THE ASHURADO CULT KEPT HANA'S BODY HERE.
AND IT WILL NOT BE TOO HARD TO GUESS WHAT RYUKI'S COURSE OF ACTION WILL BE.
YEAH, I'D BET HE'S PLANNING ON RAISING A LITTLE HELL.
LITERALLY.

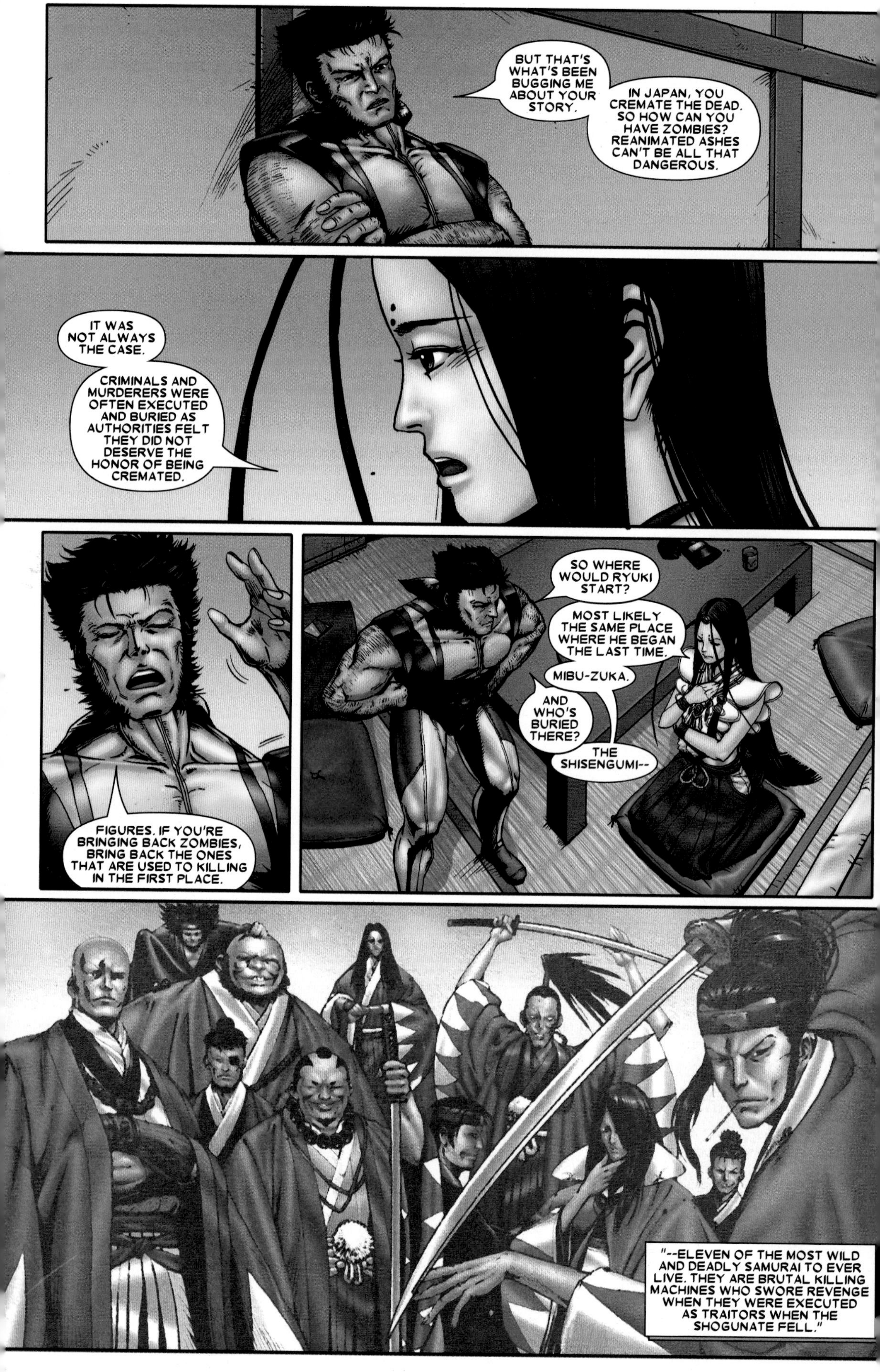

BUT THAT'S WHAT'S BEEN BUGGING ME ABOUT YOUR STORY.
IN JAPAN, YOU CREMATE THE DEAD. SO HOW CAN YOU HAVE ZOMBIES? REANIMATED ASHES CAN'T BE ALL THAT DANGEROUS.
IT WAS NOT ALWAYS THE CASE.
CRIMINALS AND MURDERERS WERE OFTEN EXECUTED AND BURIED AS AUTHORITIES FELT THEY DID NOT DESERVE THE HONOR OF BEING CREMATED.
FIGURES. IF YOU'RE BRINGING BACK ZOMBIES, BRING BACK THE ONES THAT ARE USED TO KILLING IN THE FIRST PLACE.
SO WHERE WOULD RYUKI START?
MOST LIKELY THE SAME PLACE WHERE HE BEGAN THE LAST TIME.
MIBU-ZUKA.
AND WHO'S BURIED THERE?
THE SHISENGUMI--
"--ELEVEN OF THE MOST WILD AND DEADLY SAMURAI TO EVER LIVE. THEY ARE BRUTAL KILLING MACHINES WHO SWORE REVENGE WHEN THEY WERE EXECUTED AS TRAITORS WHEN THE SHOGUNATE FELL."

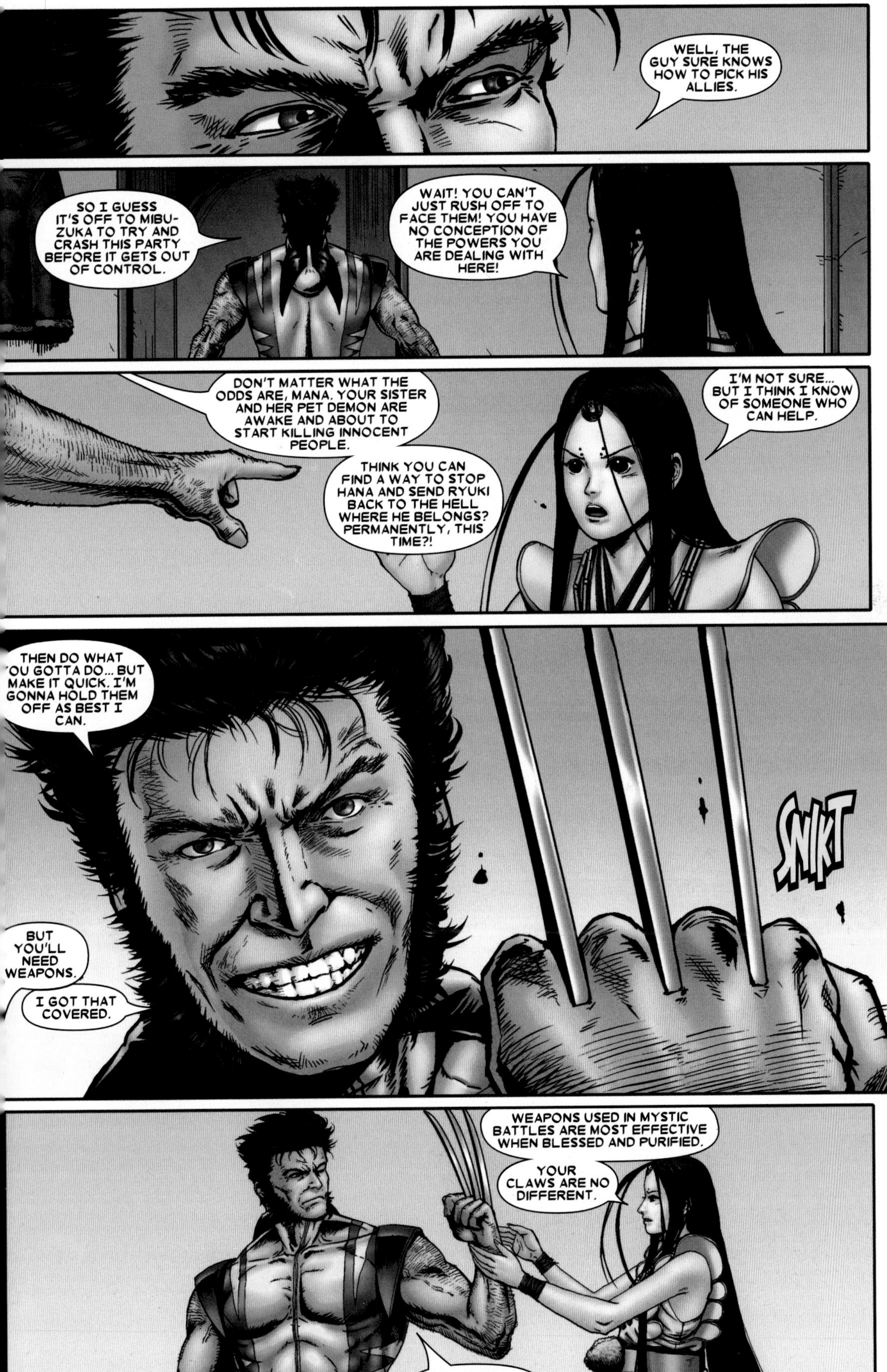
WELL, THE GUY SURE KNOWS HOW TO PICK HIS ALLIES.
SO I GUESS IT'S OFF TO MIBU-ZUKA TO TRY AND CRASH THIS PARTY BEFORE IT GETS OUT OF CONTROL.
WAIT! YOU CAN'T JUST RUSH OFF TO FACE THEM! YOU HAVE NO CONCEPTION OF THE POWERS YOU ARE DEALING WITH HERE!
DON'T MATTER WHAT THE ODDS ARE, MANA. YOUR SISTER AND HER PET DEMON ARE AWAKE AND ABOUT TO START KILLING INNOCENT PEOPLE.
THINK YOU CAN FIND A WAY TO STOP HANA AND SEND RYUKI BACK TO THE HELL WHERE HE BELONGS? PERMANENTLY, THIS TIME?!
I'M NOT SURE... BUT I THINK I KNOW OF SOMEONE WHO CAN HELP.
THEN DO WHAT 'OU GOTTA DO... BUT MAKE IT QUICK. I'M GONNA HOLD THEM OFF AS BEST I CAN.
SNIKT
BUT YOU'LL NEED WEAPONS.
I GOT THAT COVERED.
WEAPONS USED IN MYSTIC BATTLES ARE MOST EFFECTIVE WHEN BLESSED AND PURIFIED.
YOUR CLAWS ARE NO DIFFERENT.
PURITY'S NEVER BEEN ONE OF MY STRONG SUITS.

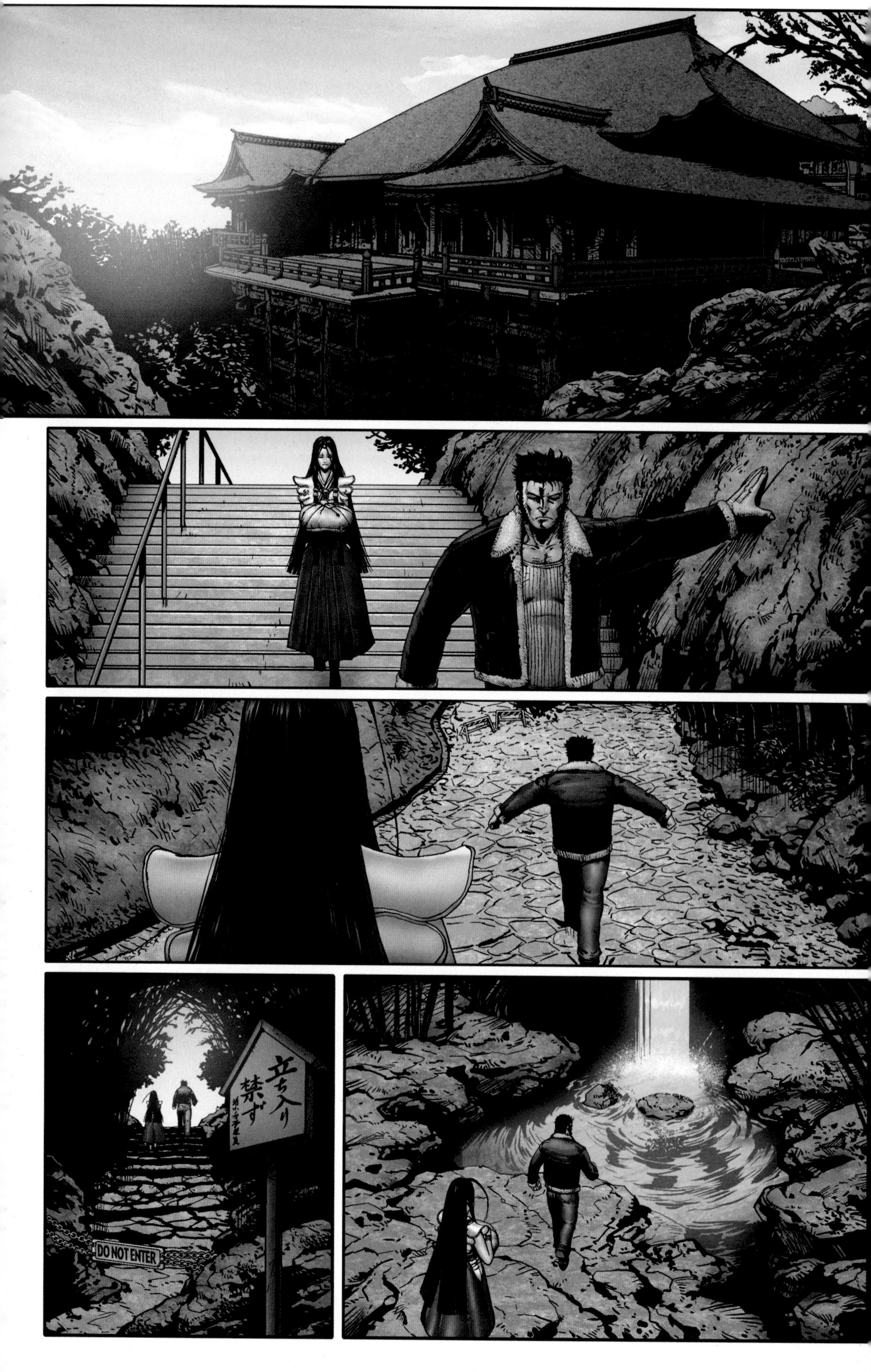
立ち入り
禁ず
DO NOT ENTER

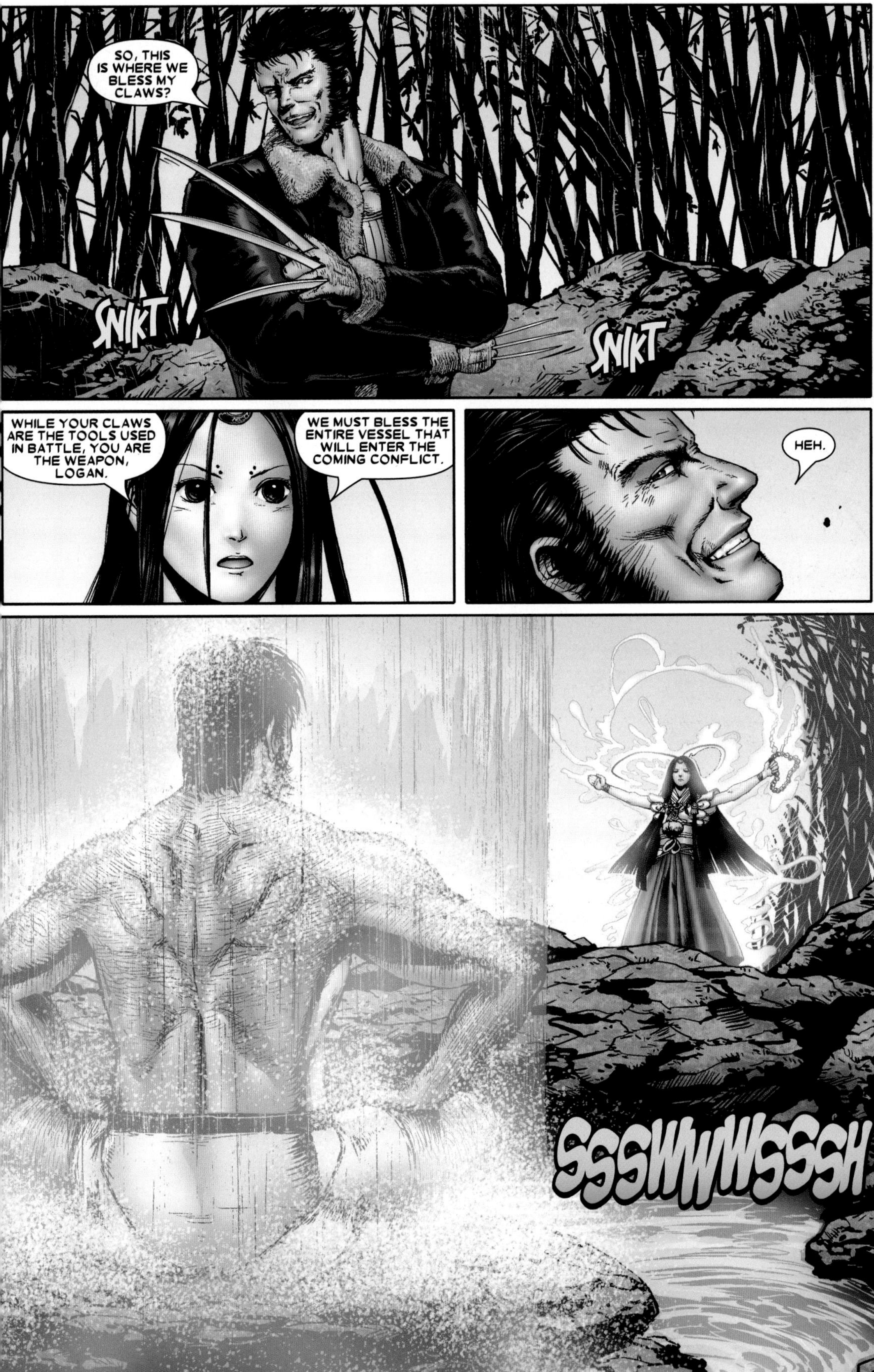
SO, THIS IS WHERE WE BLESS MY CLAWS?
SNIKT
SNIKT
WHILE YOUR CLAWS ARE THE TOOLS USED IN BATTLE, YOU ARE THE WEAPON, LOGAN.
WE MUST BLESS THE ENTIRE VESSEL THAT WILL ENTER THE COMING CONFLICT.
HEH.
SSSWWWSSSH

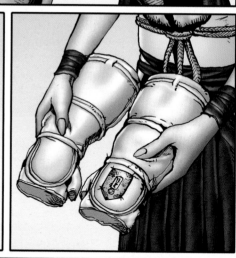

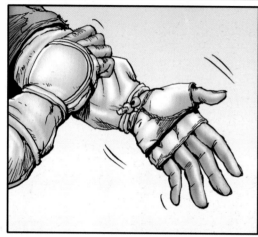

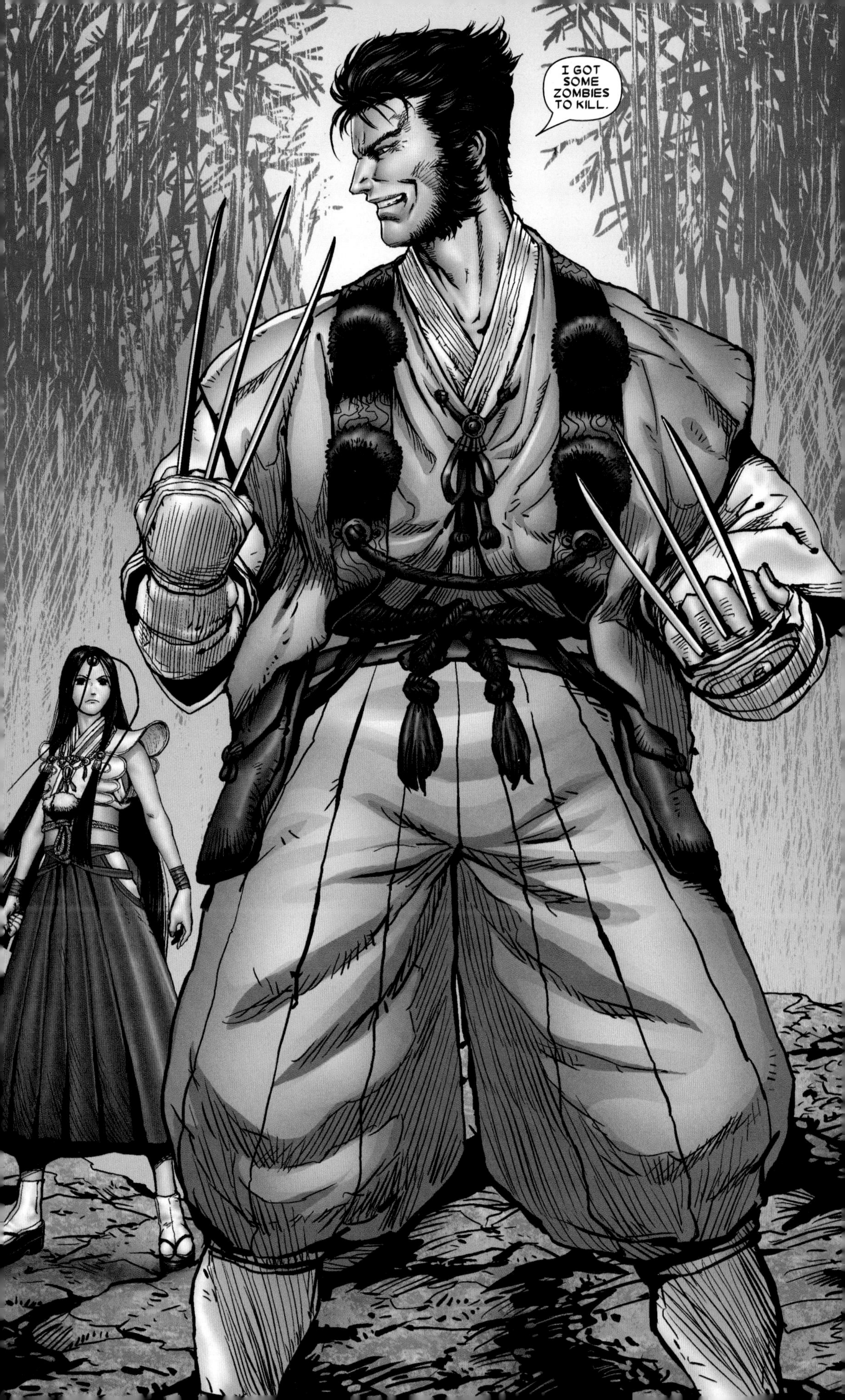
I GOT SOME ZOMBIES TO KILL.

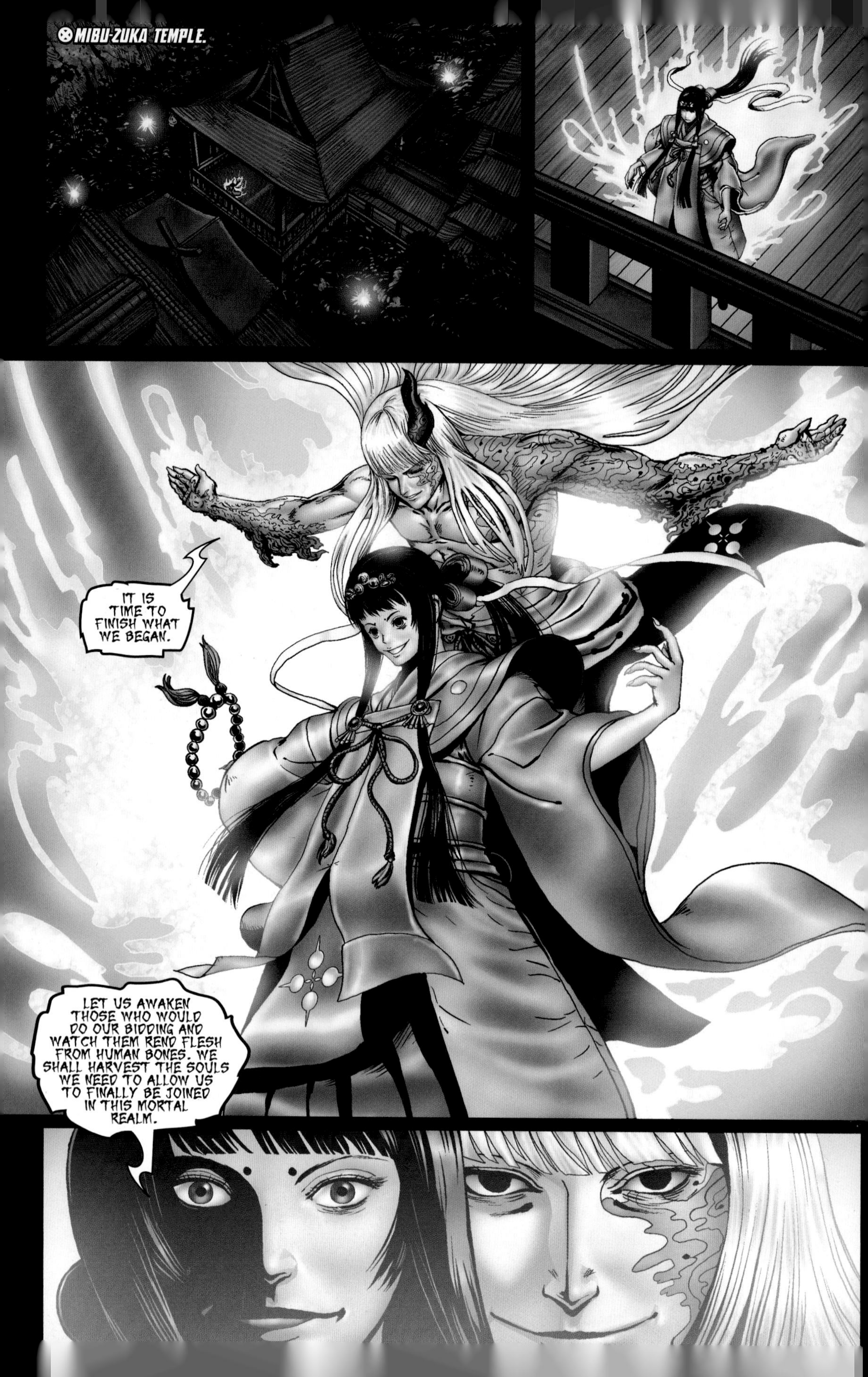
MIBU-ZUKA TEMPLE.
IT IS TIME TO FINISH WHAT WE BEGAN.
LET US AWAKEN THOSE WHO WOULD DO OUR BIDDING AND WATCH THEM REND FLESH FROM HUMAN BONES. WE SHALL HARVEST THE SOULS WE NEED TO ALLOW US TO FINALLY BE JOINED IN THIS MORTAL REALM.

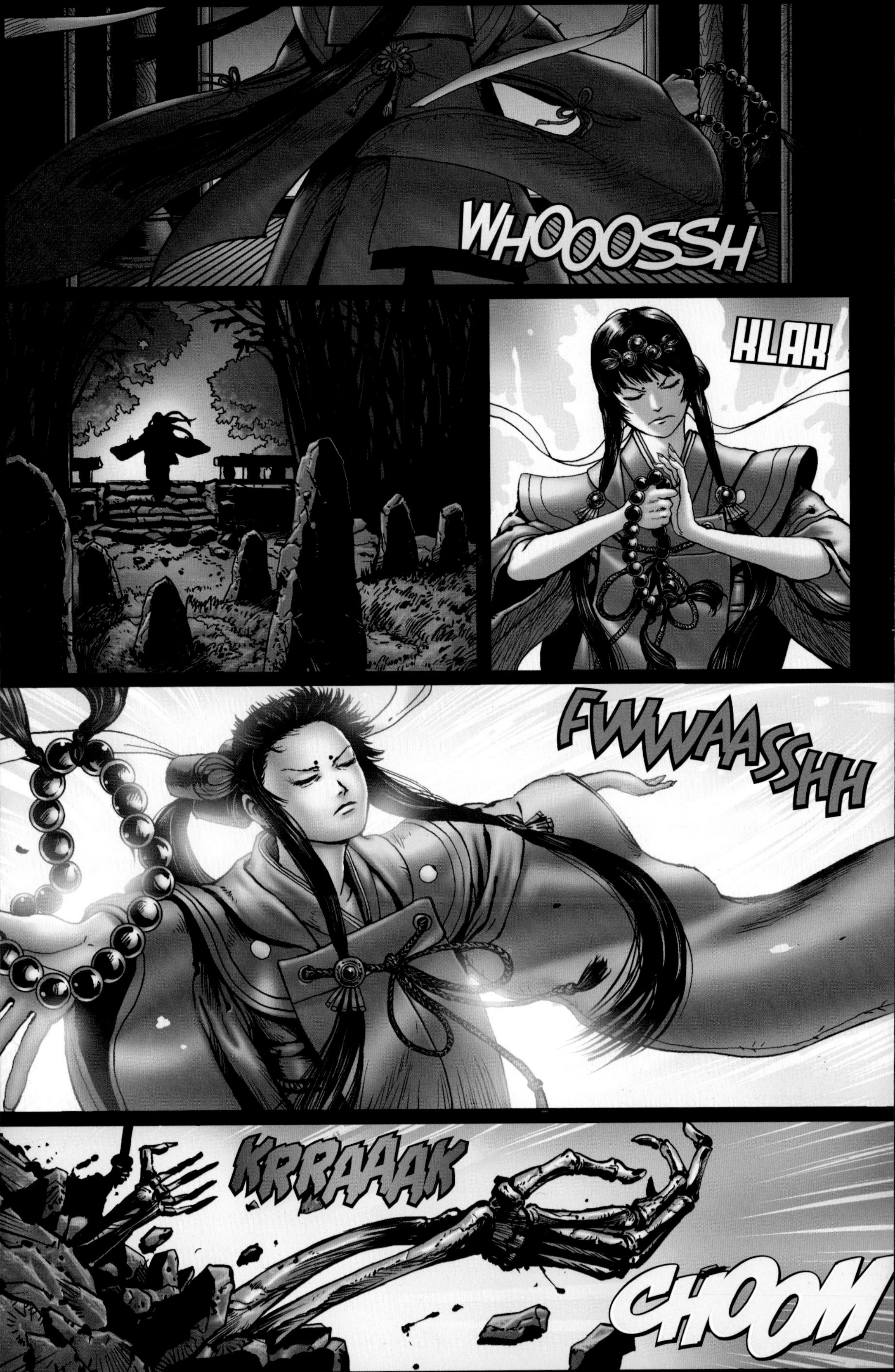
WHOOOSSH
KLAK
FWWAASSHH
KRRAAAK
CHOOM

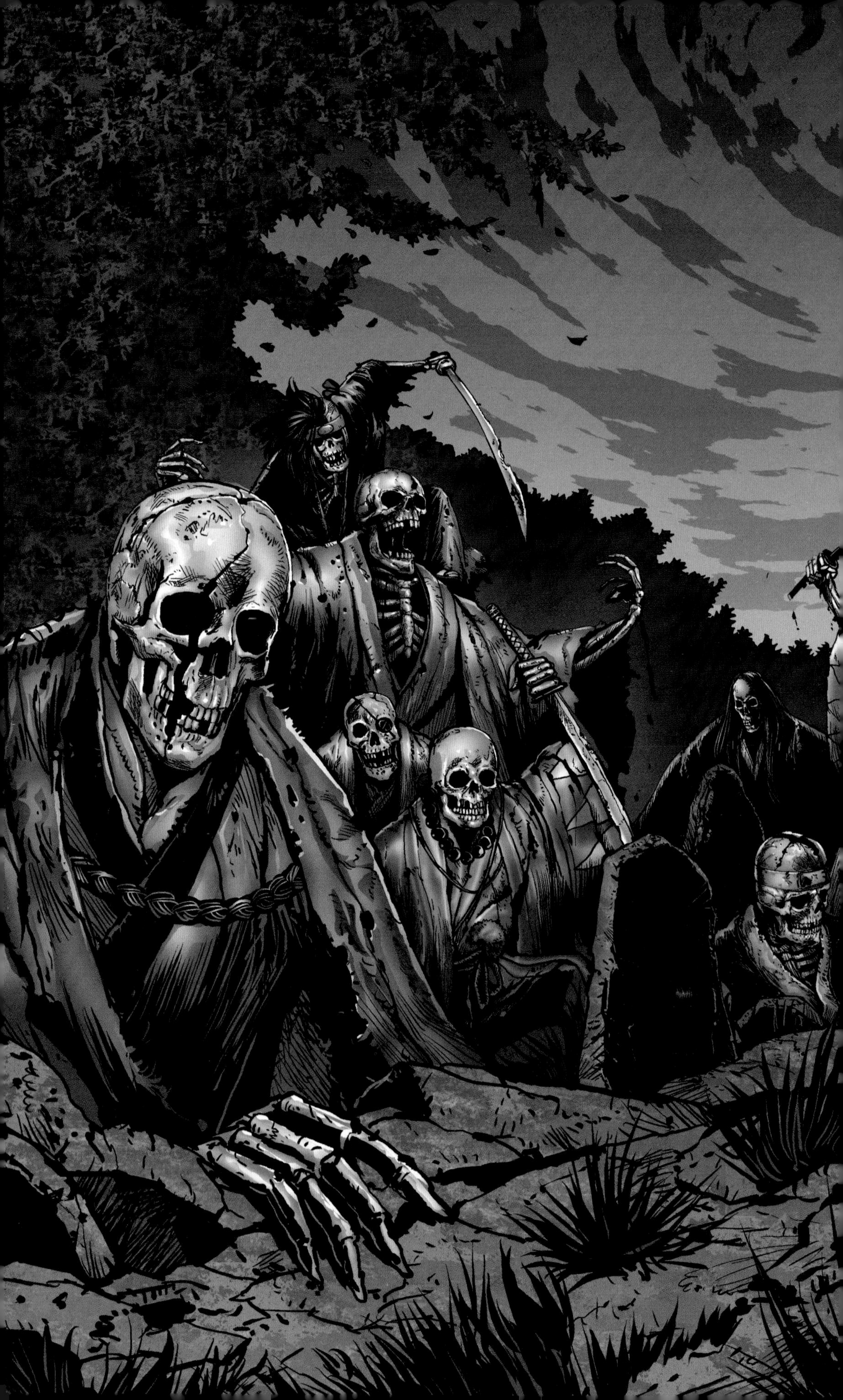

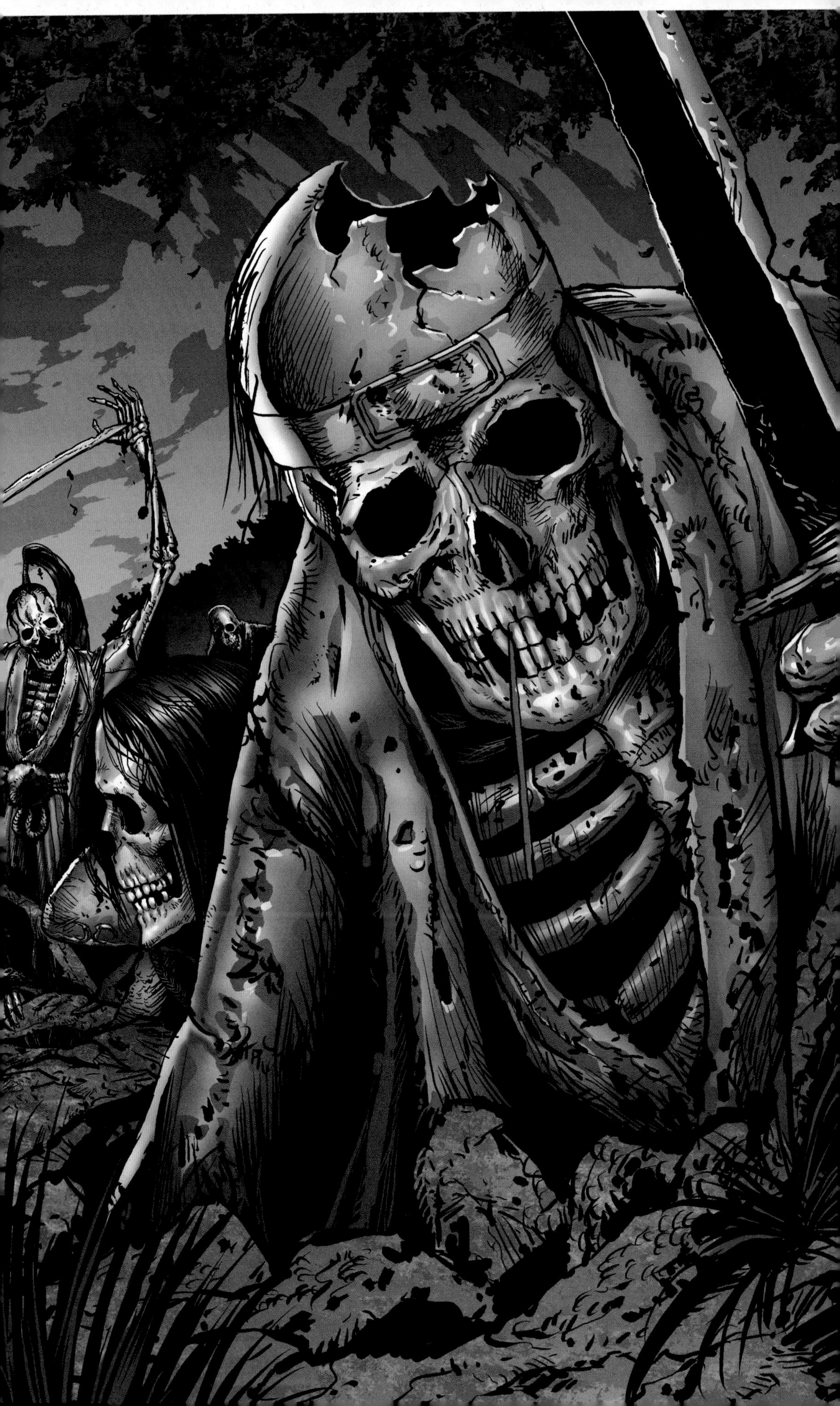

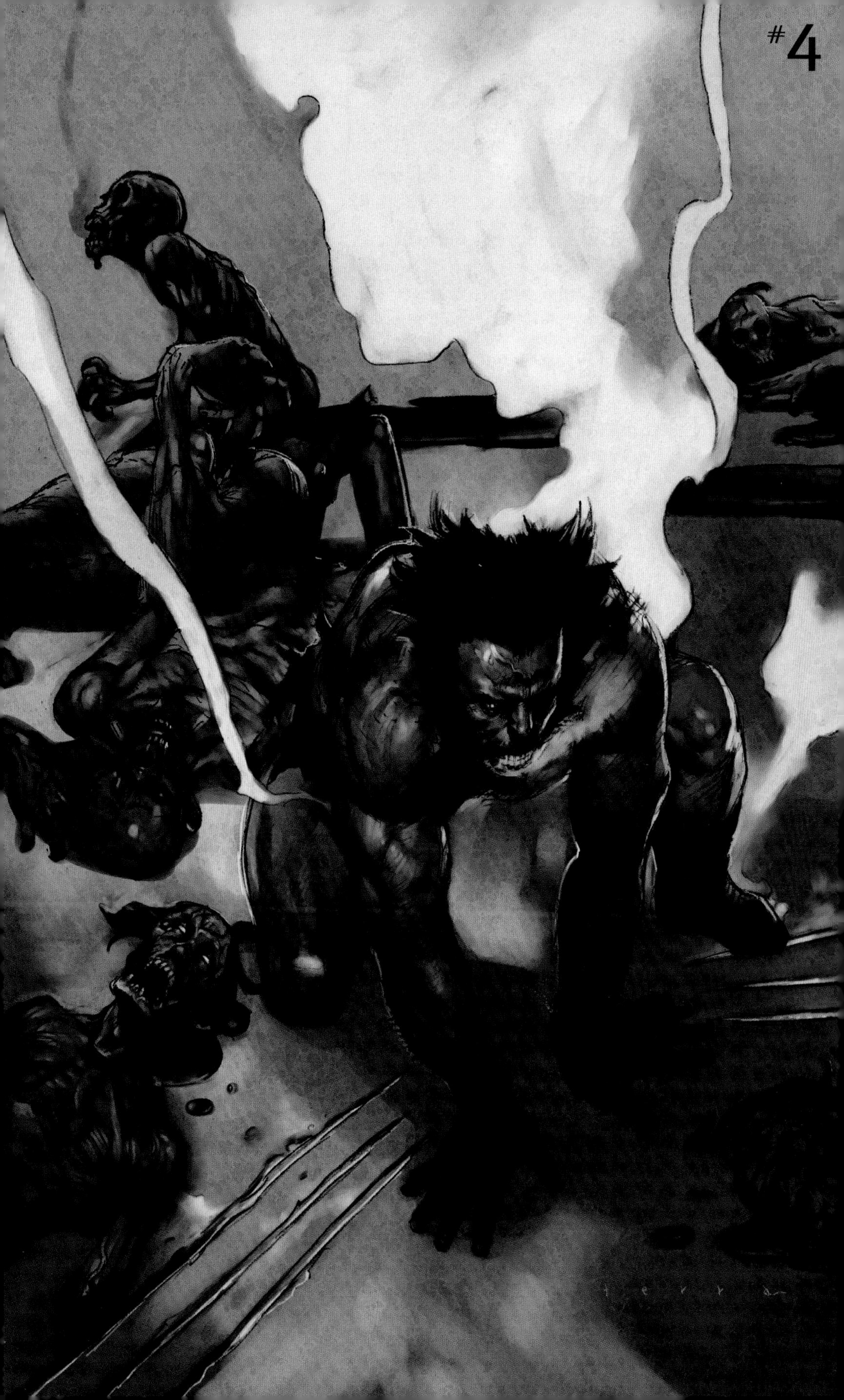
#4

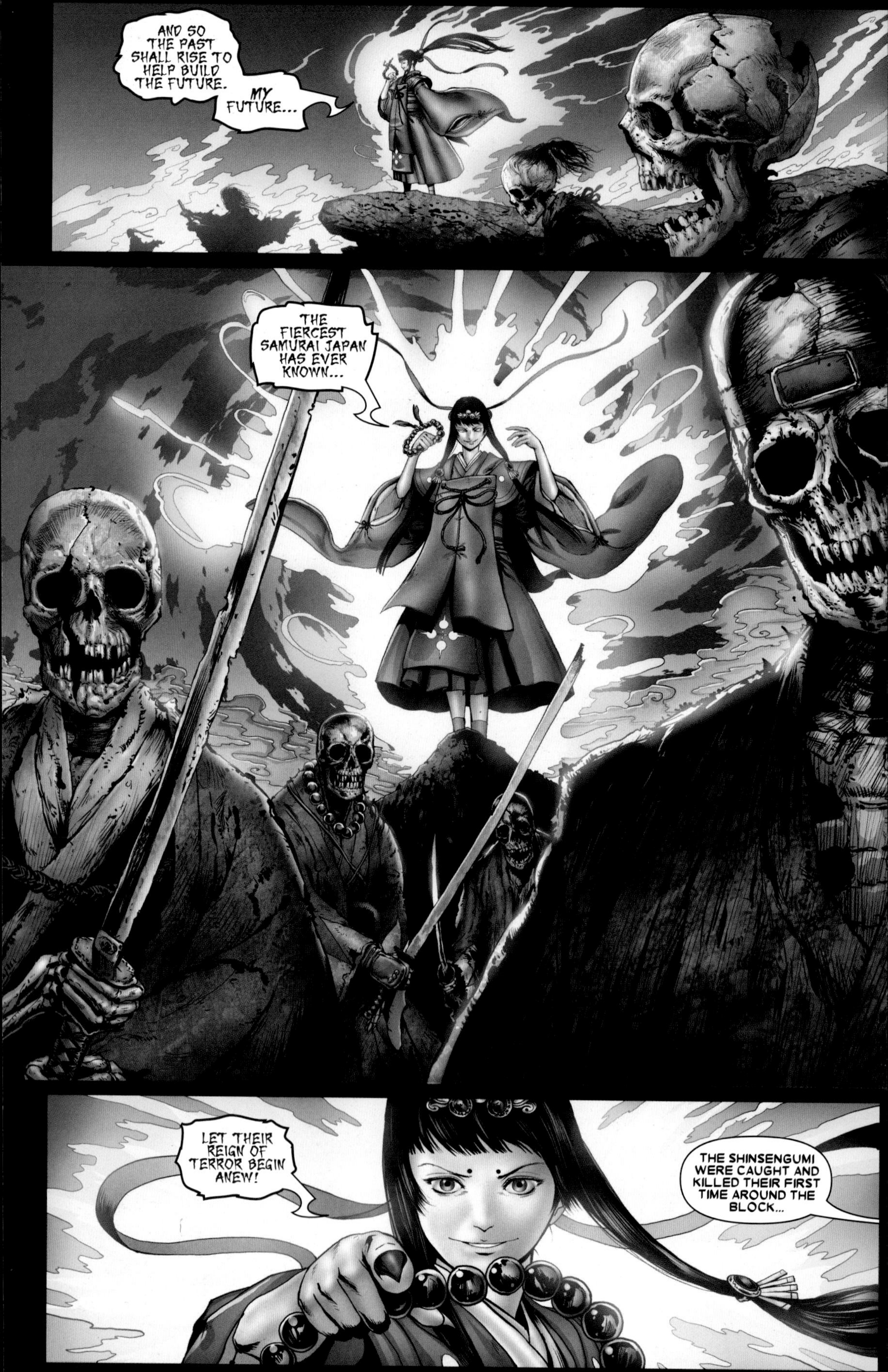
AND SO THE PAST SHALL RISE TO HELP BUILD THE FUTURE.
MY FUTURE...
THE FIERCEST SAMURAI JAPAN HAS EVER KNOWN...
LET THEIR REIGN OF TERROR BEGIN ANEW!
THE SHINSENGUMI WERE CAUGHT AND KILLED THEIR FIRST TIME AROUND THE BLOCK...

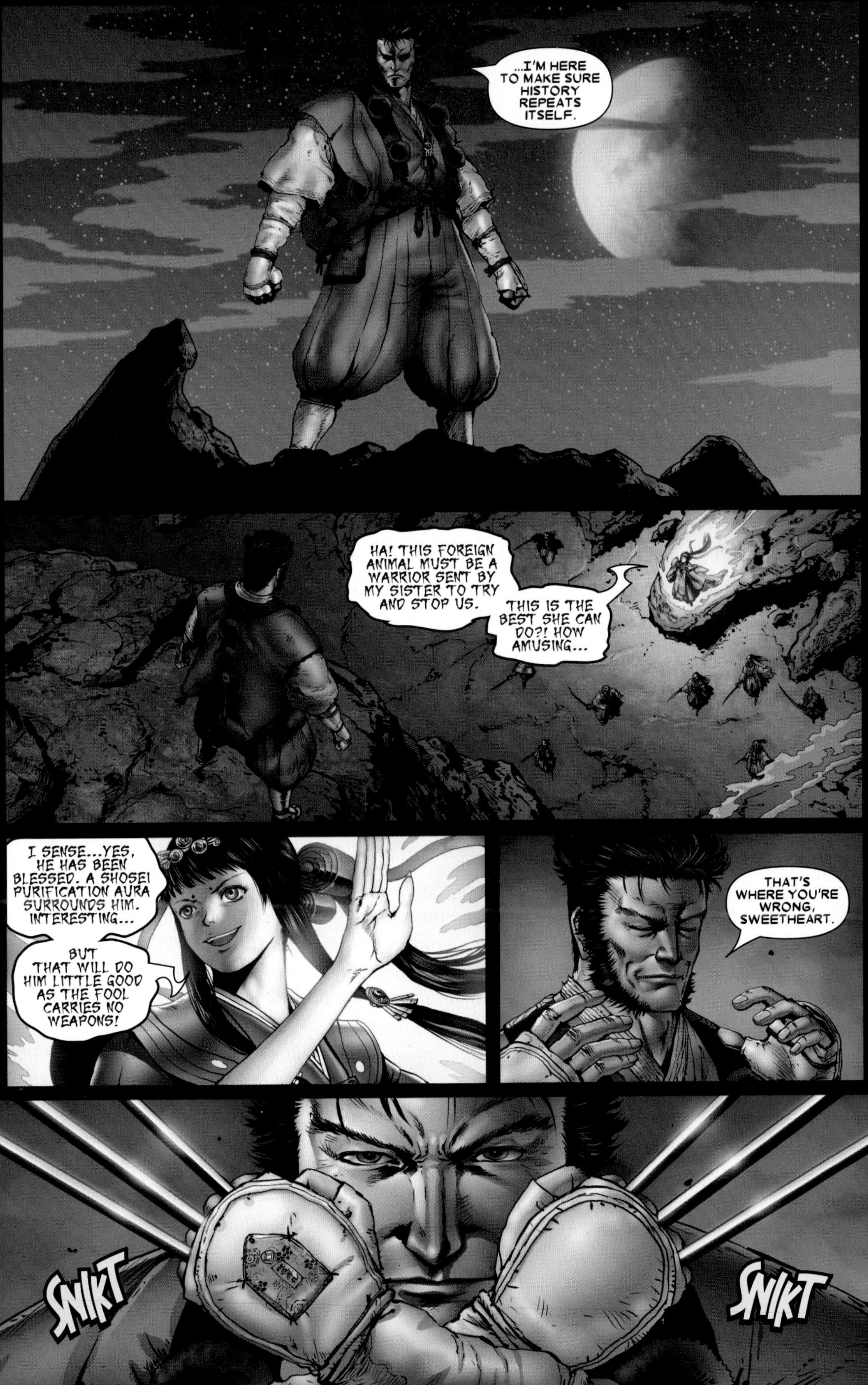
...I'M HERE TO MAKE SURE HISTORY REPEATS ITSELF.
HA! THIS FOREIGN ANIMAL MUST BE A WARRIOR SENT BY MY SISTER TO TRY AND STOP US.
THIS IS THE BEST SHE CAN DO?! HOW AMUSING...
I SENSE...YES, HE HAS BEEN BLESSED. A SHOSEI PURIFICATION AURA SURROUNDS HIM. INTERESTING...
BUT THAT WILL DO HIM LITTLE GOOD AS THE FOOL CARRIES NO WEAPONS!
THAT'S WHERE YOU'RE WRONG, SWEETHEART.
SNIKT
SNIKT

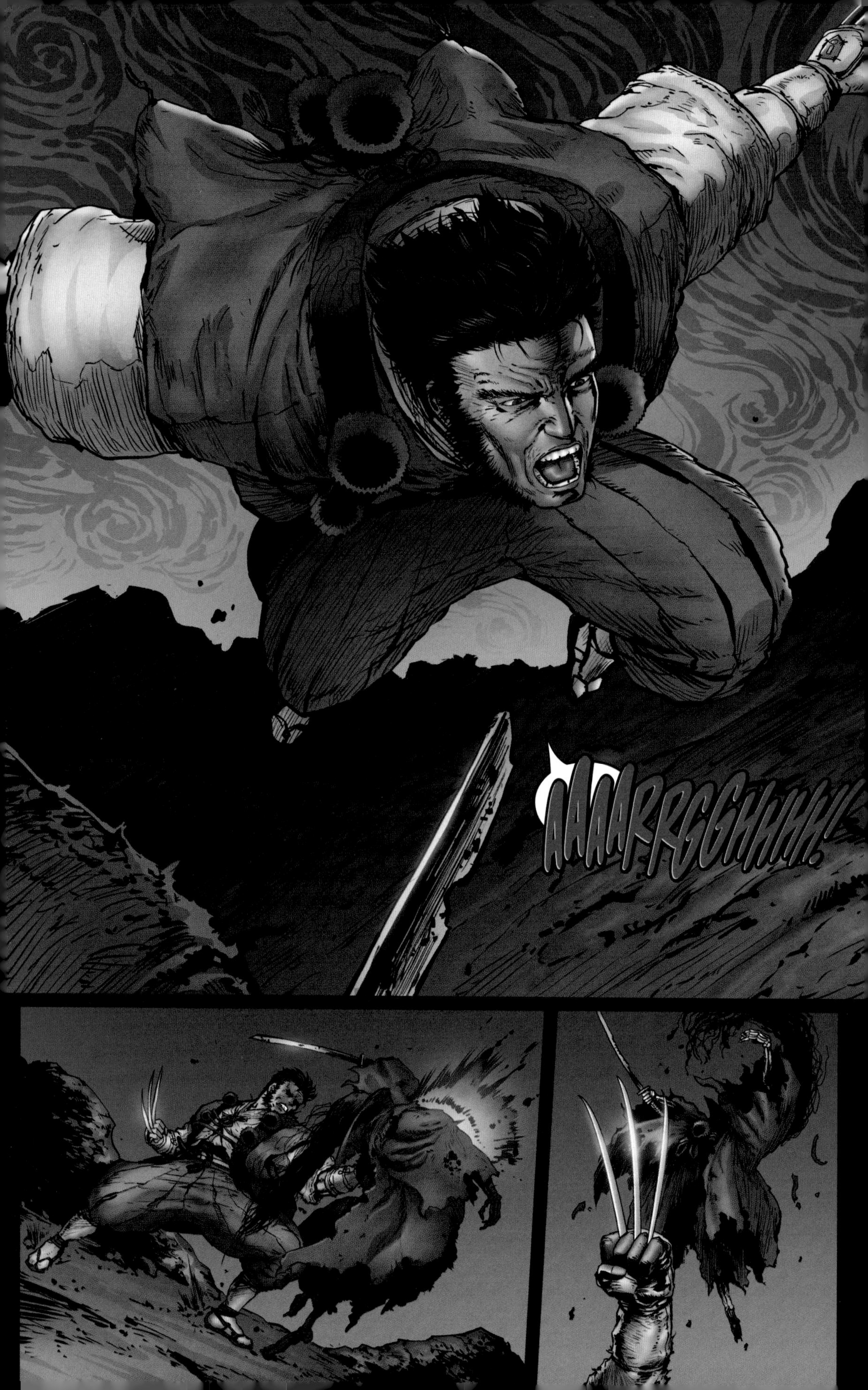
AAAARRGGHHHH!

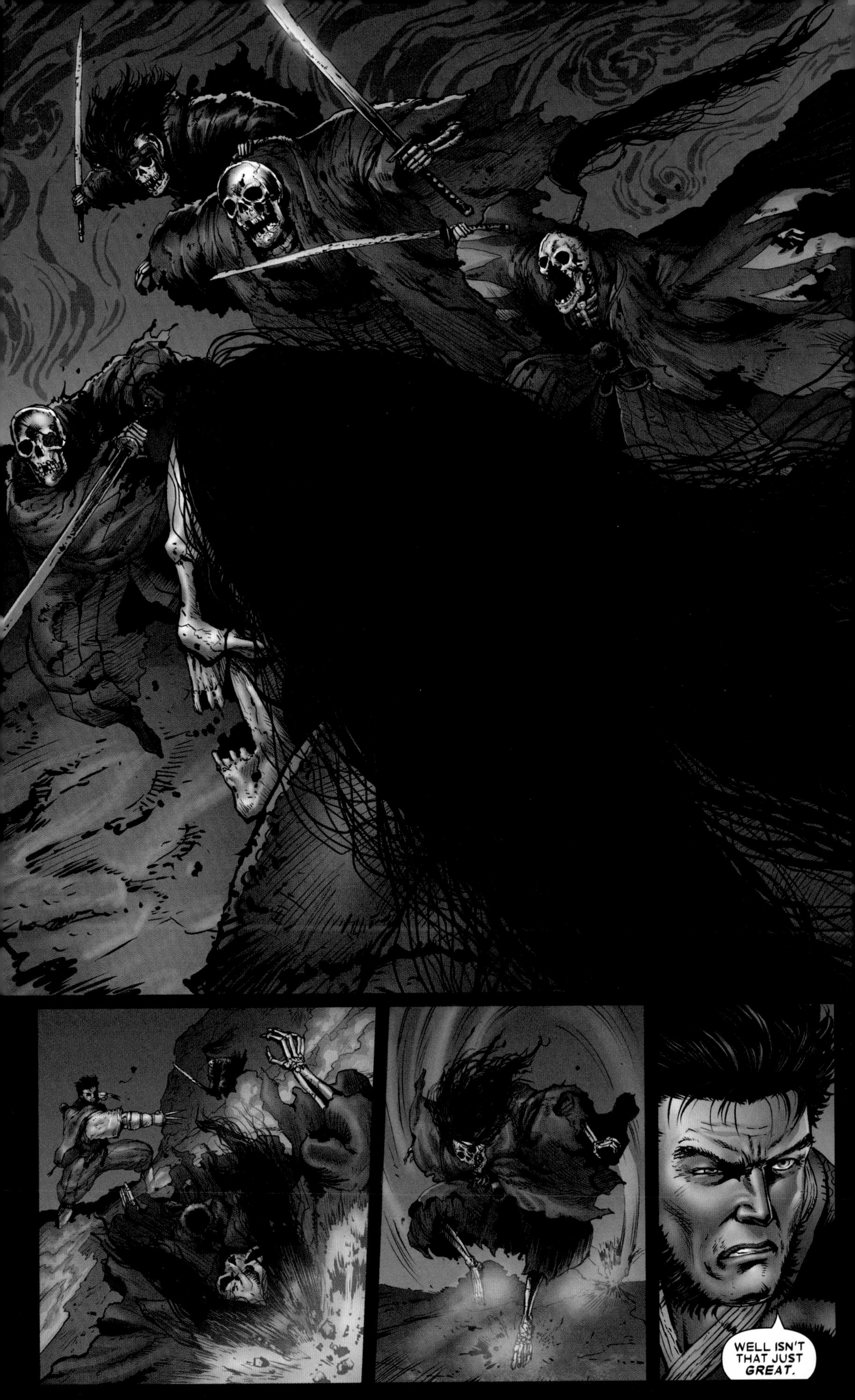
WELL ISN'T THAT JUST GREAT.

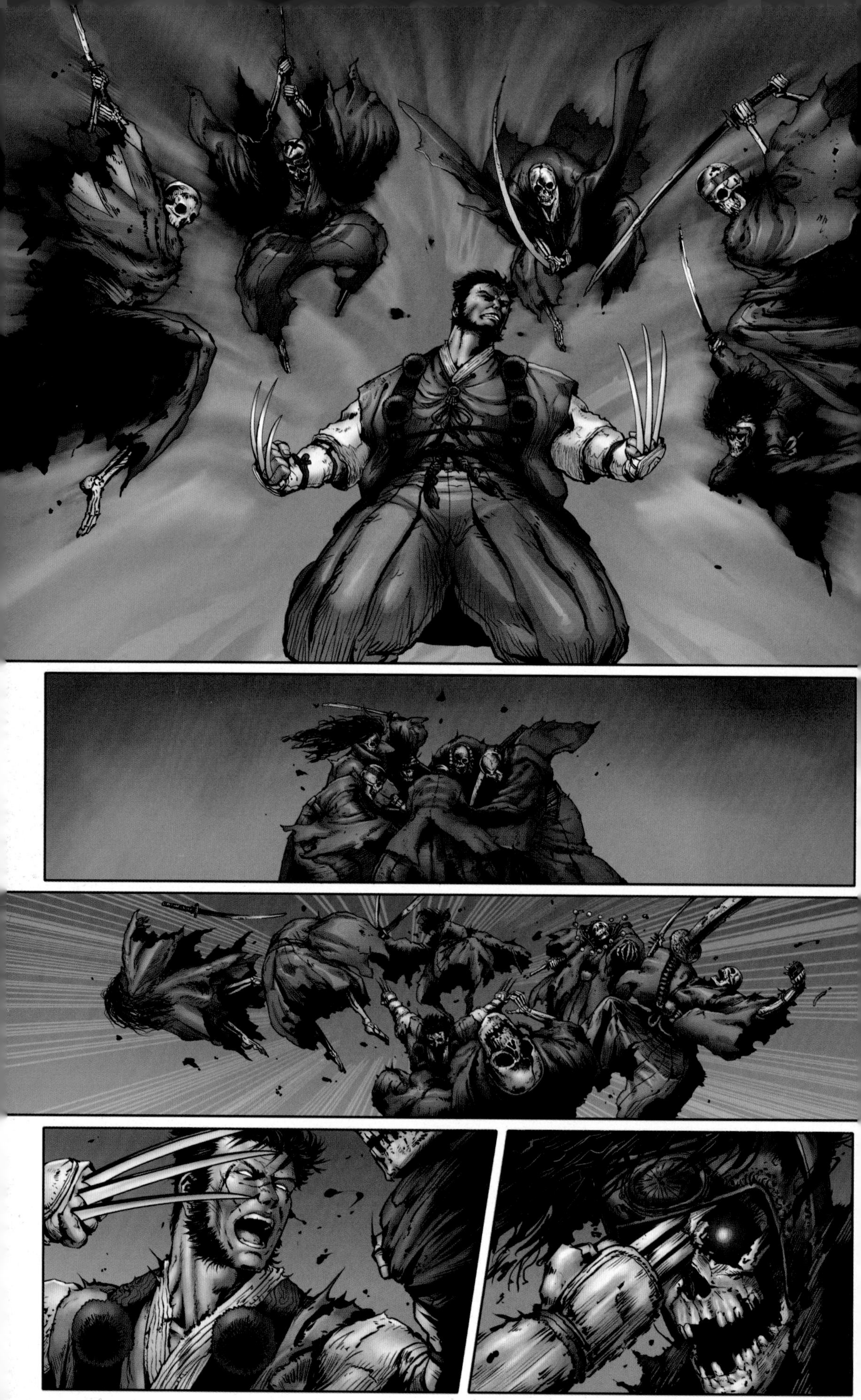

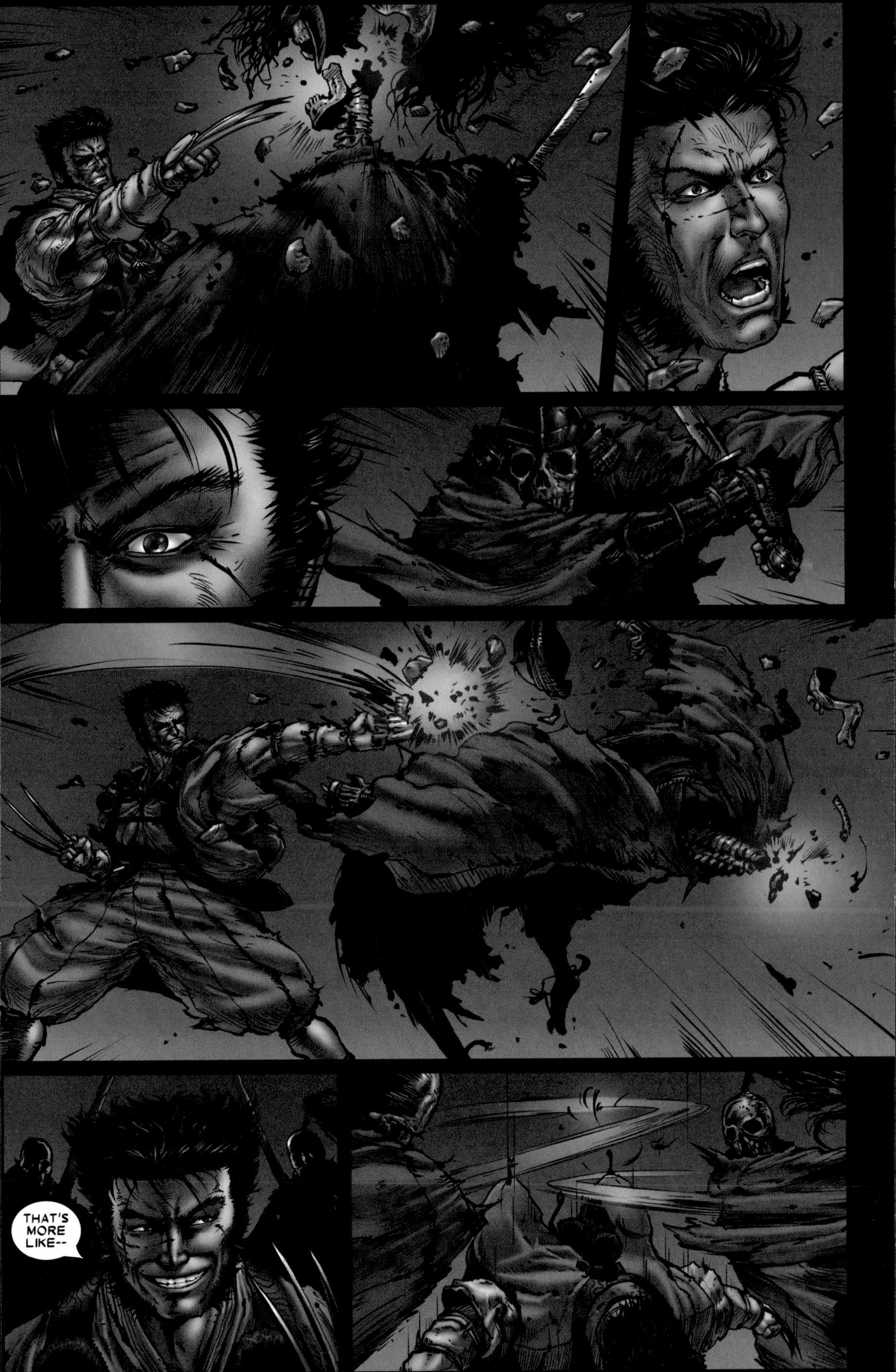
THAT'S MORE LIKE--

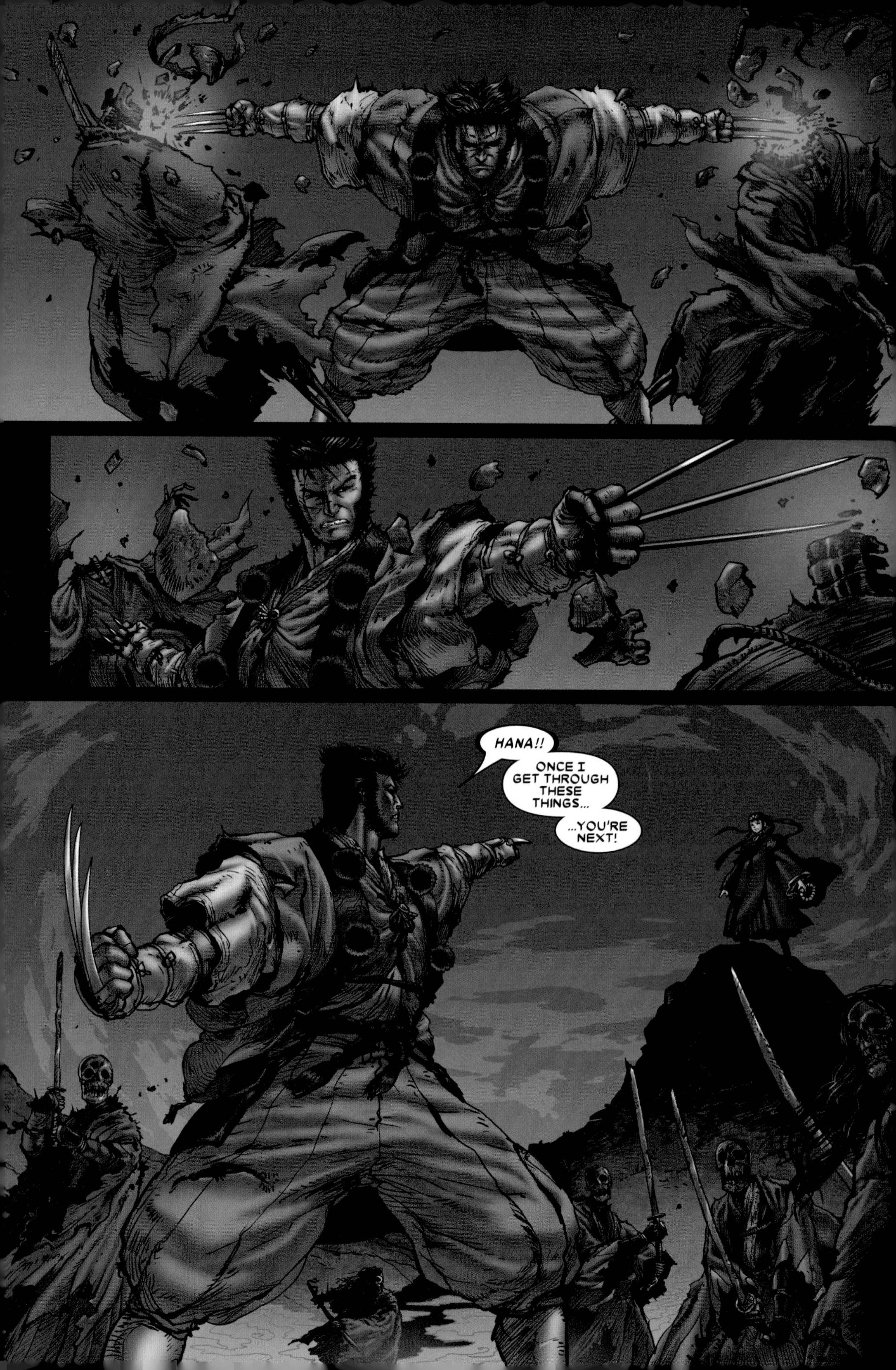
HANA!!
ONCE I GET THROUGH THESE THINGS...
...YOU'RE NEXT!

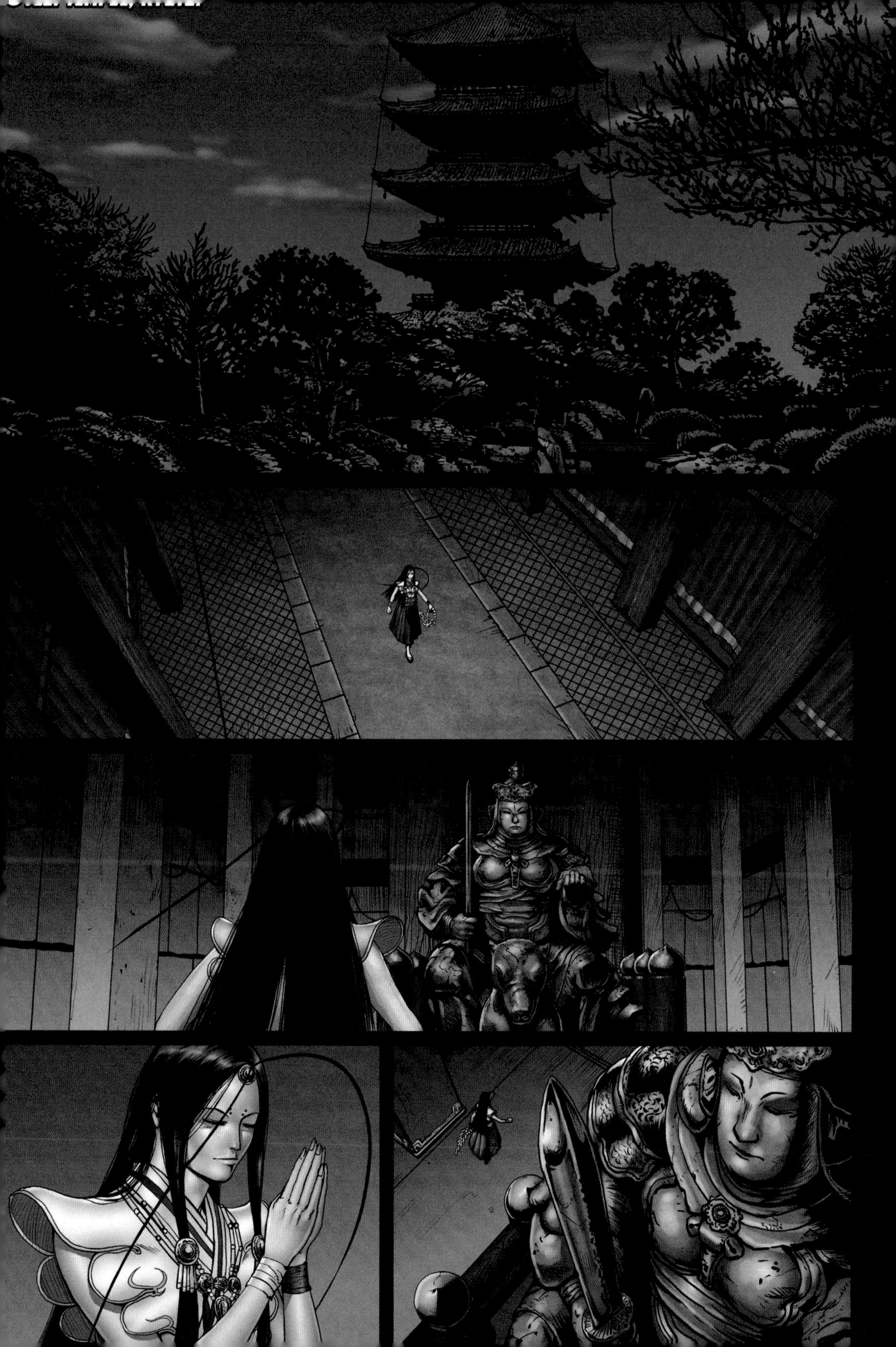

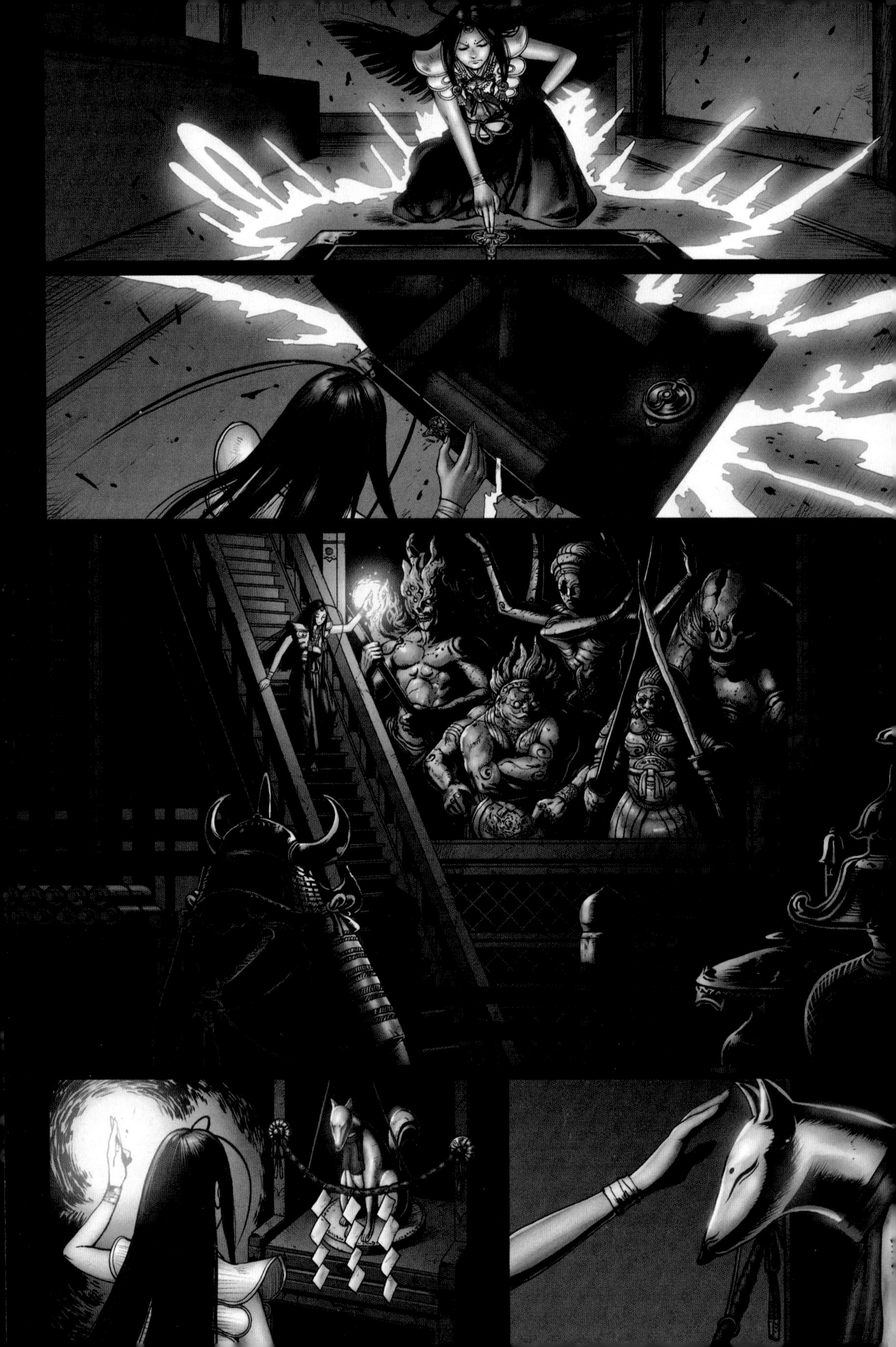

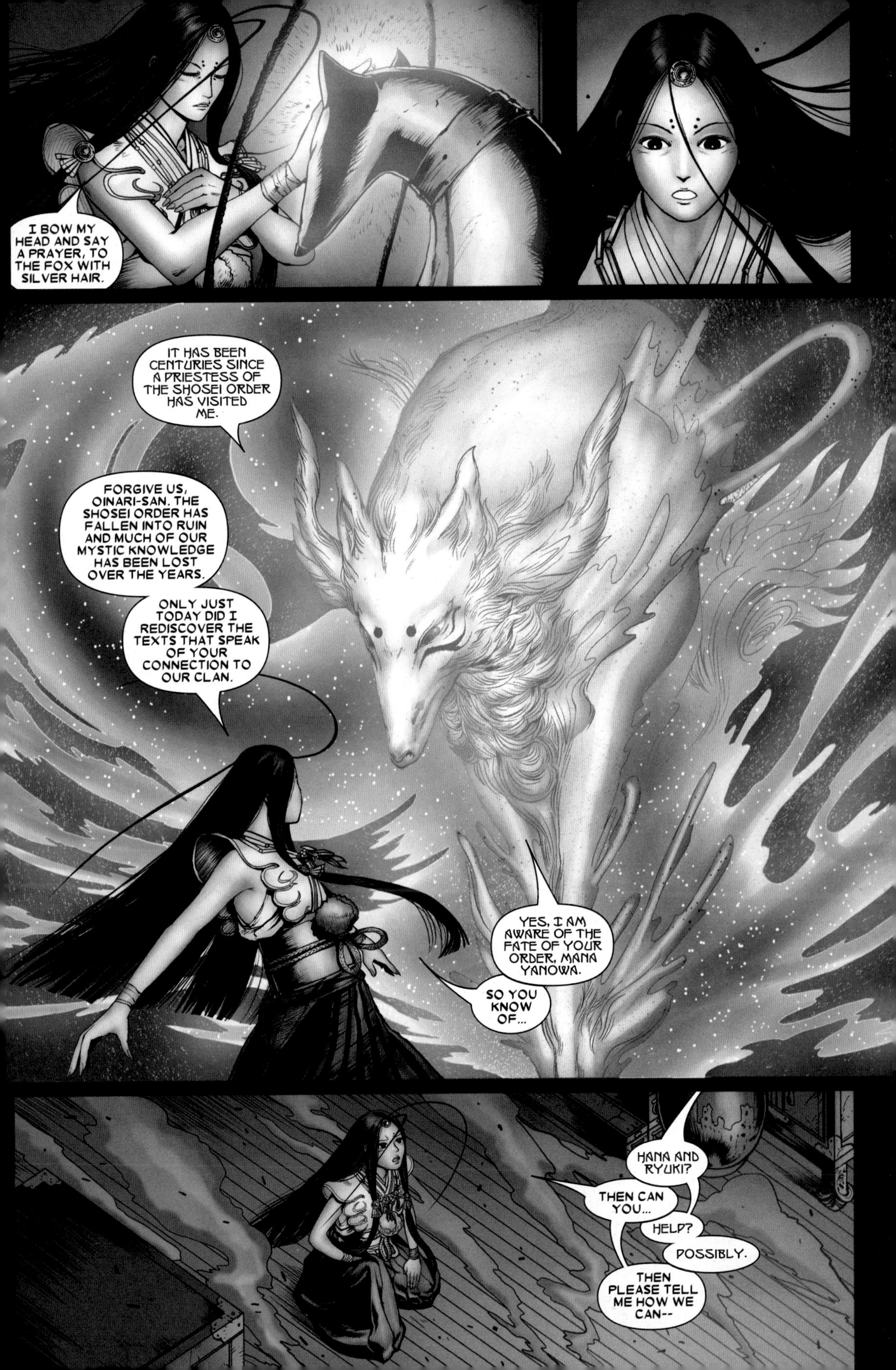
I BOW MY HEAD AND SAY A PRAYER, TO THE FOX WITH SILVER HAIR.
IT HAS BEEN CENTURIES SINCE A PRIESTESS OF THE SHOSEI ORDER HAS VISITED ME.
FORGIVE US, OINARI-SAN. THE SHOSEI ORDER HAS FALLEN INTO RUIN AND MUCH OF OUR MYSTIC KNOWLEDGE HAS BEEN LOST OVER THE YEARS.
ONLY JUST TODAY DID I REDISCOVER THE TEXTS THAT SPEAK OF YOUR CONNECTION TO OUR CLAN.
YES, I AM AWARE OF THE FATE OF YOUR ORDER, MANA YANOWA.
SO YOU KNOW OF...
HANA AND RYUKI?
THEN CAN YOU...
HELP?
POSSIBLY.
THEN PLEASE TELL ME HOW WE CAN--

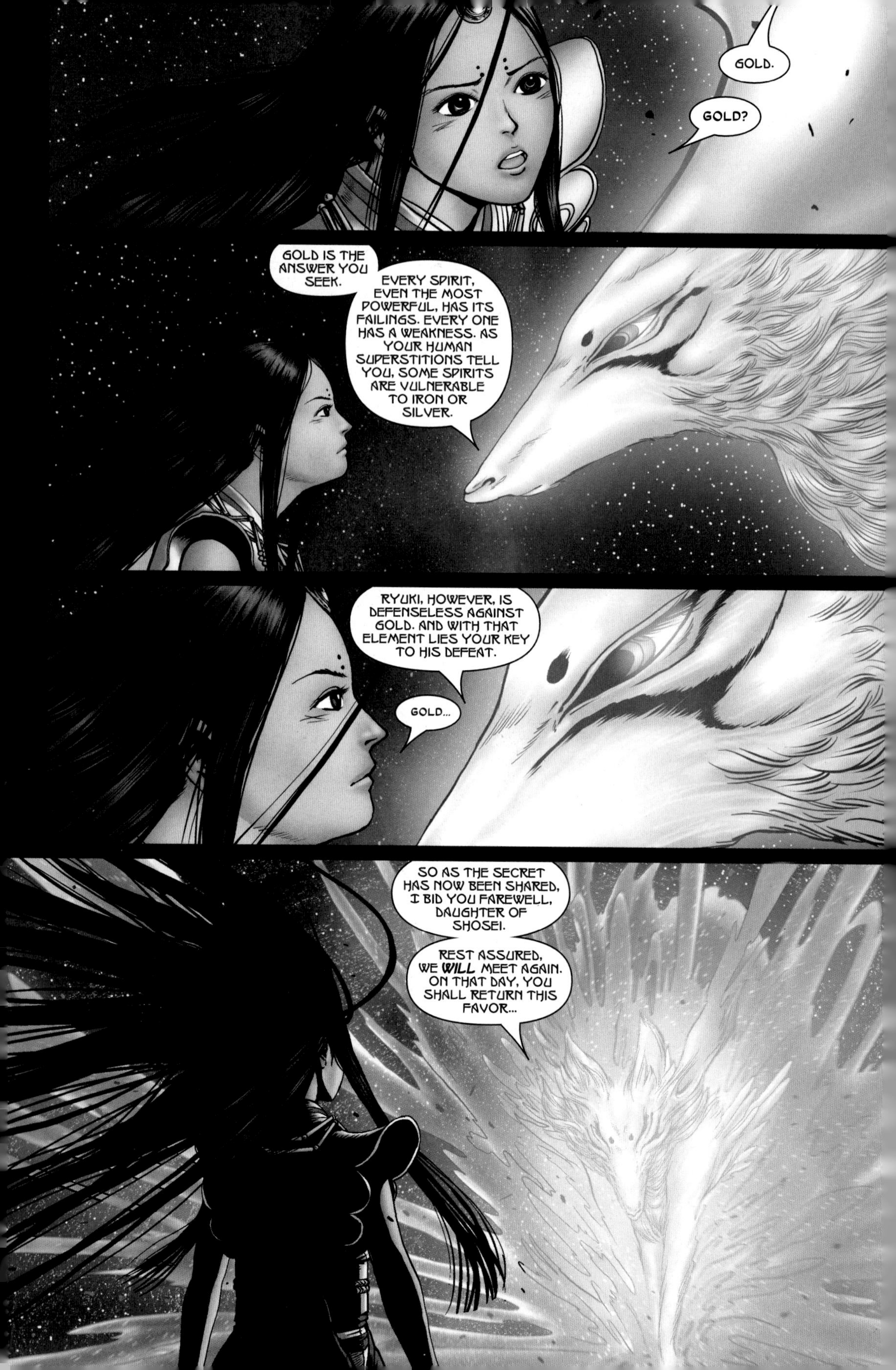
GOLD.
GOLD?
GOLD IS THE ANSWER YOU SEEK.
EVERY SPIRIT, EVEN THE MOST POWERFUL, HAS ITS FAILINGS. EVERY ONE HAS A WEAKNESS. AS YOUR HUMAN SUPERSTITIONS TELL YOU, SOME SPIRITS ARE VULNERABLE TO IRON OR SILVER.
RYUKI, HOWEVER, IS DEFENSELESS AGAINST GOLD. AND WITH THAT ELEMENT LIES YOUR KEY TO HIS DEFEAT.
GOLD...
SO AS THE SECRET HAS NOW BEEN SHARED, I BID YOU FAREWELL, DAUGHTER OF SHOSEI.
REST ASSURED, WE **WILL** MEET AGAIN. ON THAT DAY, YOU SHALL RETURN THIS FAVOR...

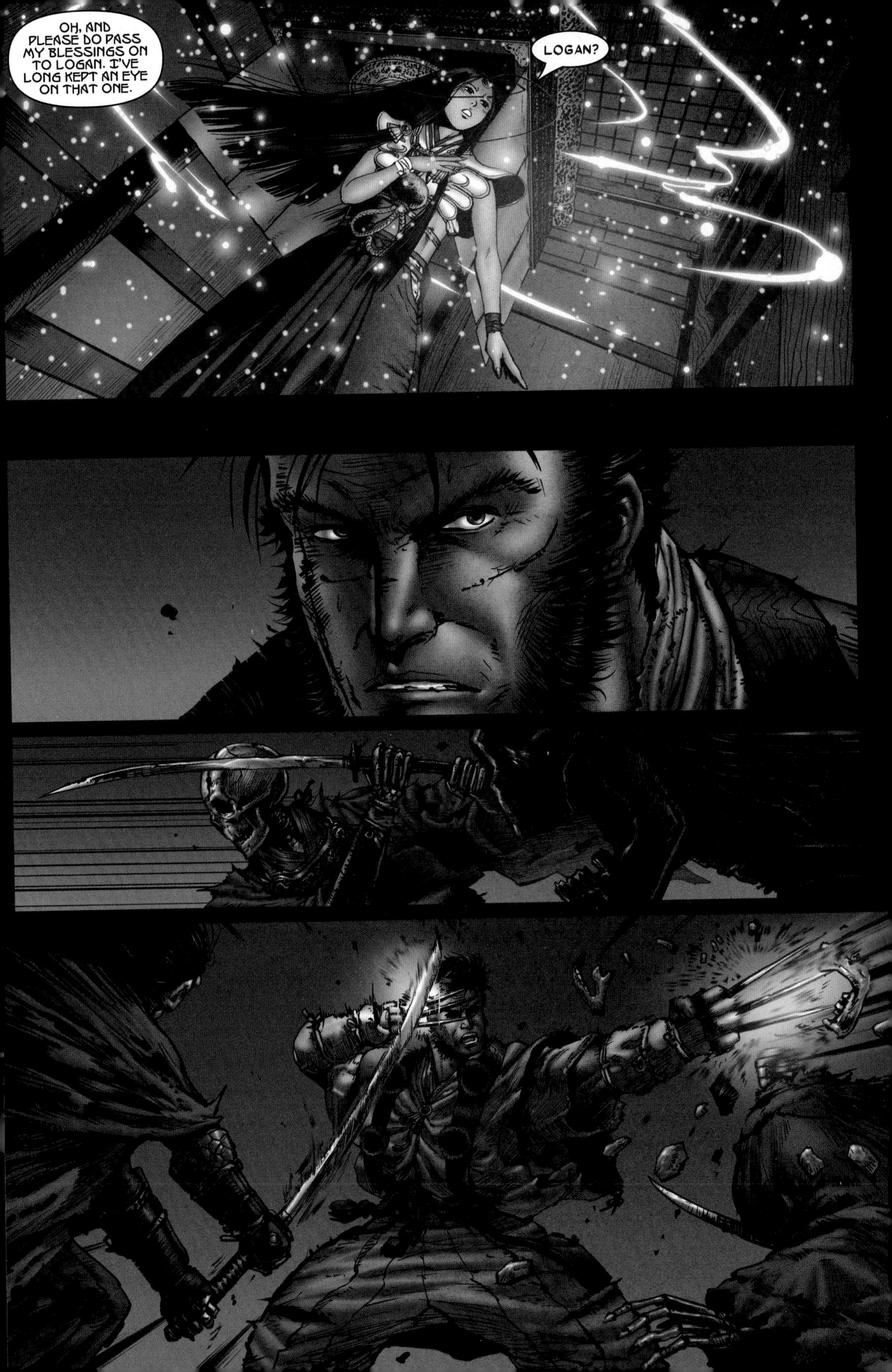
OH, AND PLEASE DO PASS MY BLESSINGS ON TO LOGAN. I'VE LONG KEPT AN EYE ON THAT ONE.
LOGAN?

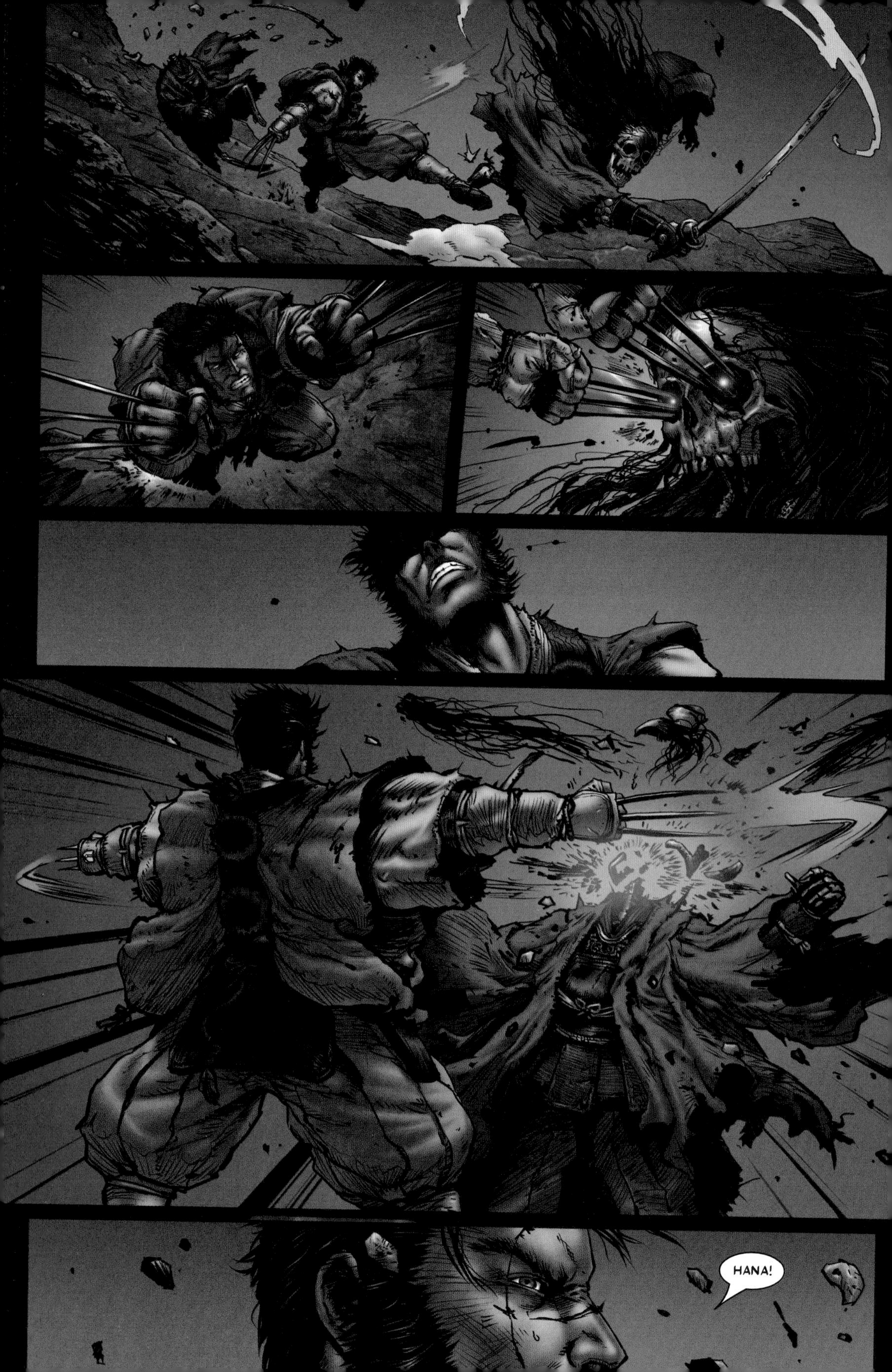
HANA!

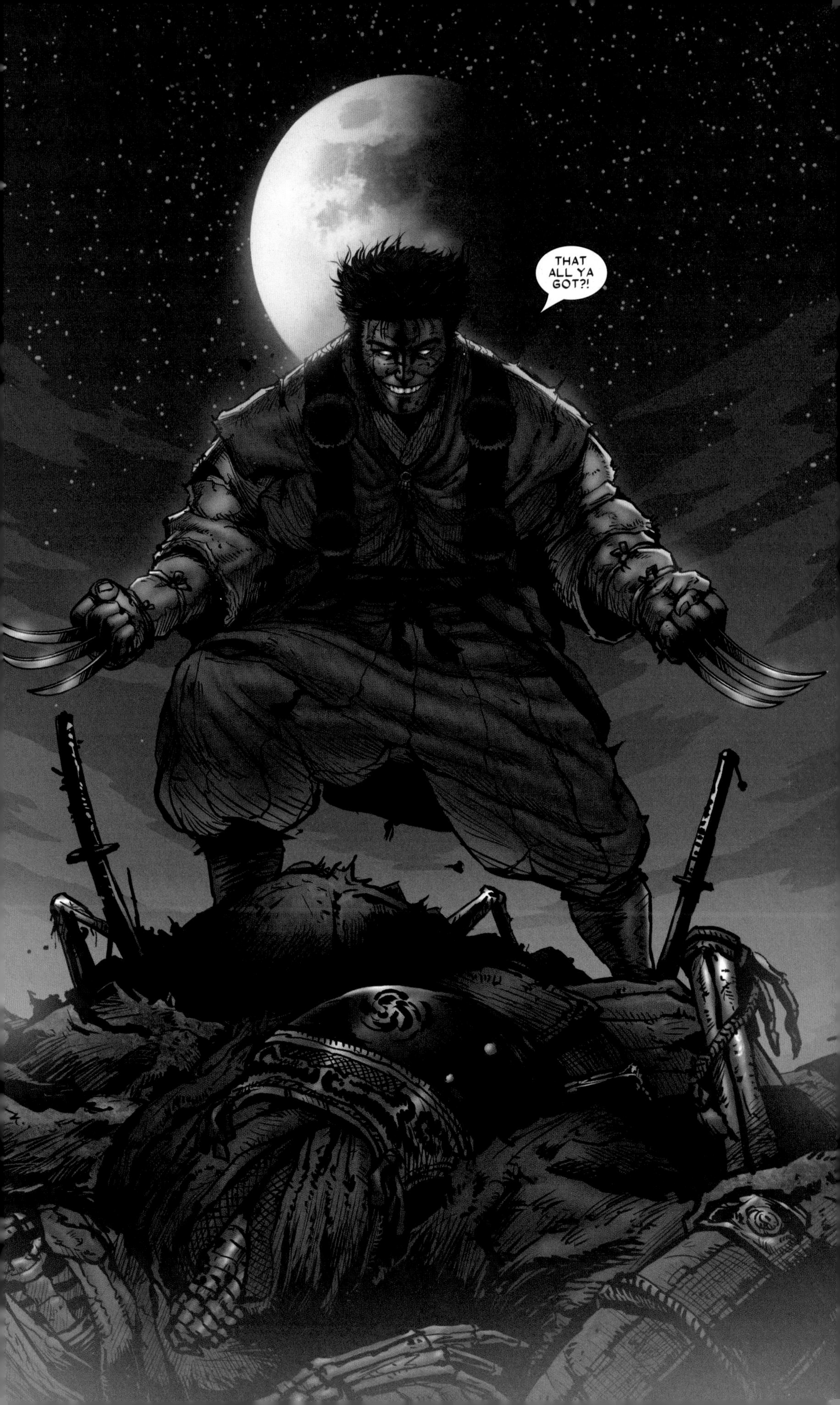
THAT ALL YA GOT?!

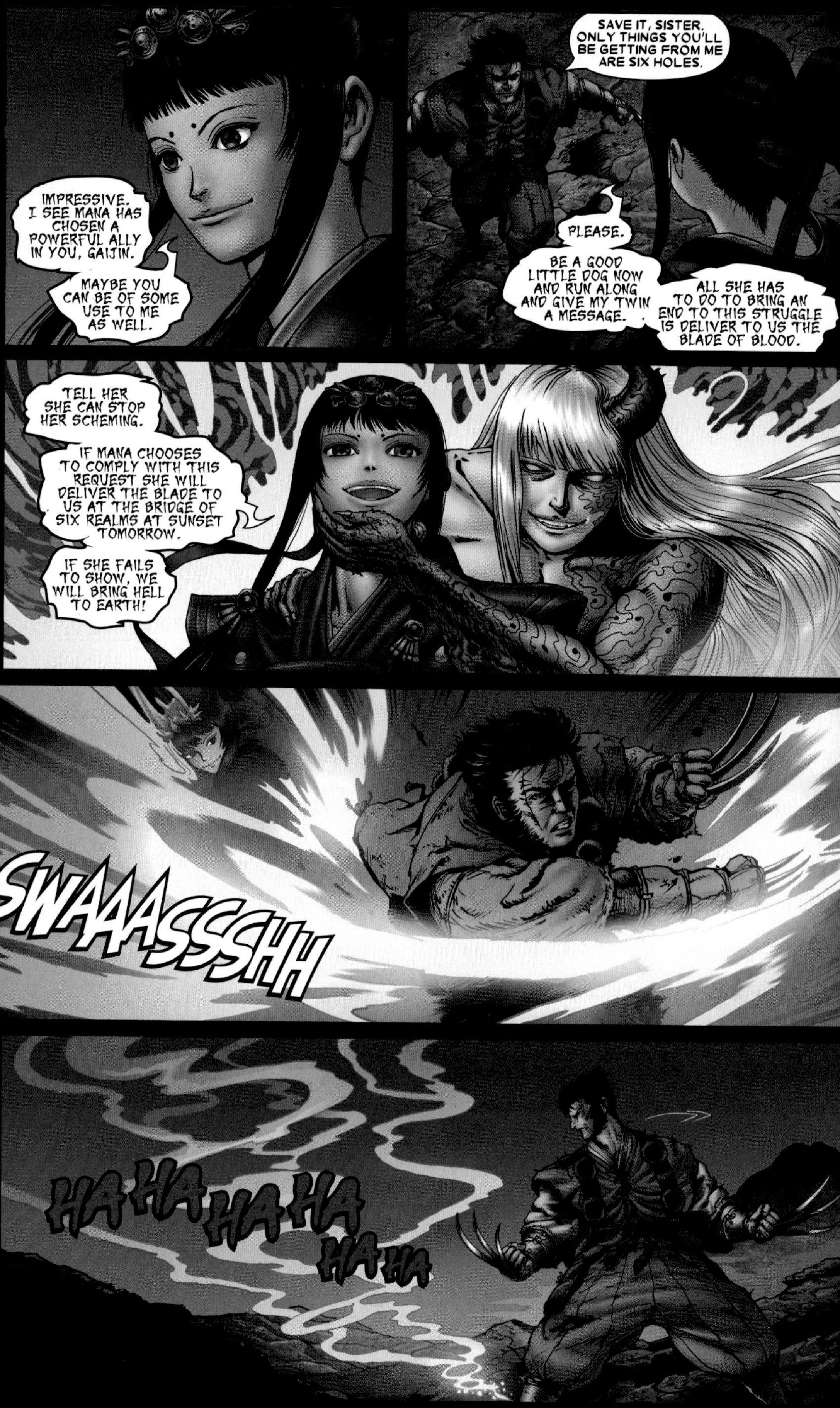

IMPRESSIVE. I SEE MANA HAS CHOSEN A POWERFUL ALLY IN YOU, GAIJIN.
MAYBE YOU CAN BE OF SOME USE TO ME AS WELL.
SAVE IT, SISTER. ONLY THINGS YOU'LL BE GETTING FROM ME ARE SIX HOLES.
PLEASE.
BE A GOOD LITTLE DOG NOW AND RUN ALONG AND GIVE MY TWIN A MESSAGE.
ALL SHE HAS TO DO TO BRING AN END TO THIS STRUGGLE IS DELIVER TO US THE BLADE OF BLOOD.
TELL HER SHE CAN STOP HER SCHEMING.
IF MANA CHOOSES TO COMPLY WITH THIS REQUEST SHE WILL DELIVER THE BLADE TO US AT THE BRIDGE OF SIX REALMS AT SUNSET TOMORROW.
IF SHE FAILS TO SHOW, WE WILL BRING HELL TO EARTH!
SWAAASSSHH
HA HA HA HA HA HA HA

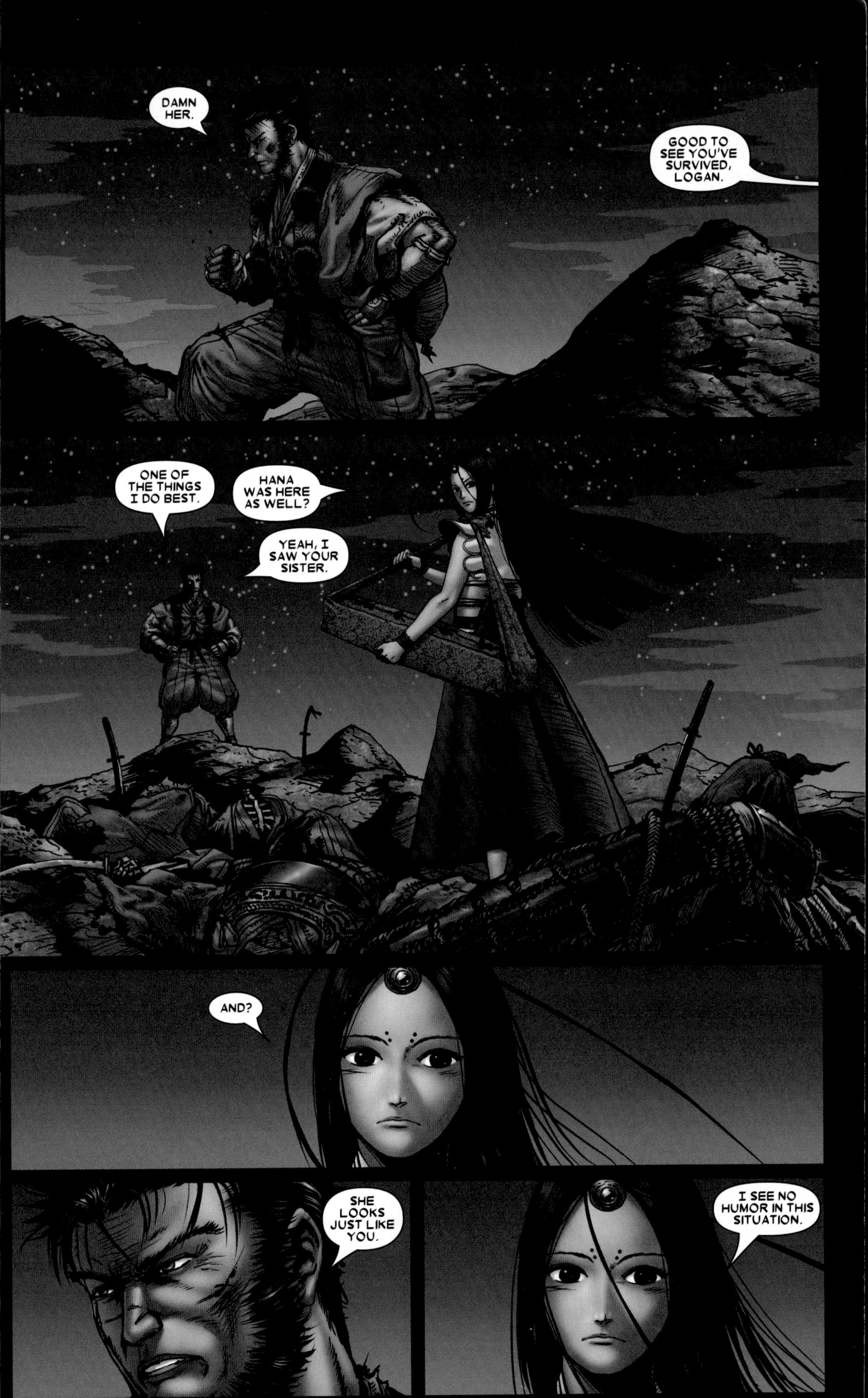
DAMN HER.
GOOD TO SEE YOU'VE SURVIVED, LOGAN.
ONE OF THE THINGS I DO BEST.
HANA WAS HERE AS WELL?
YEAH, I SAW YOUR SISTER.
AND?
SHE LOOKS JUST LIKE YOU.
I SEE NO HUMOR IN THIS SITUATION.

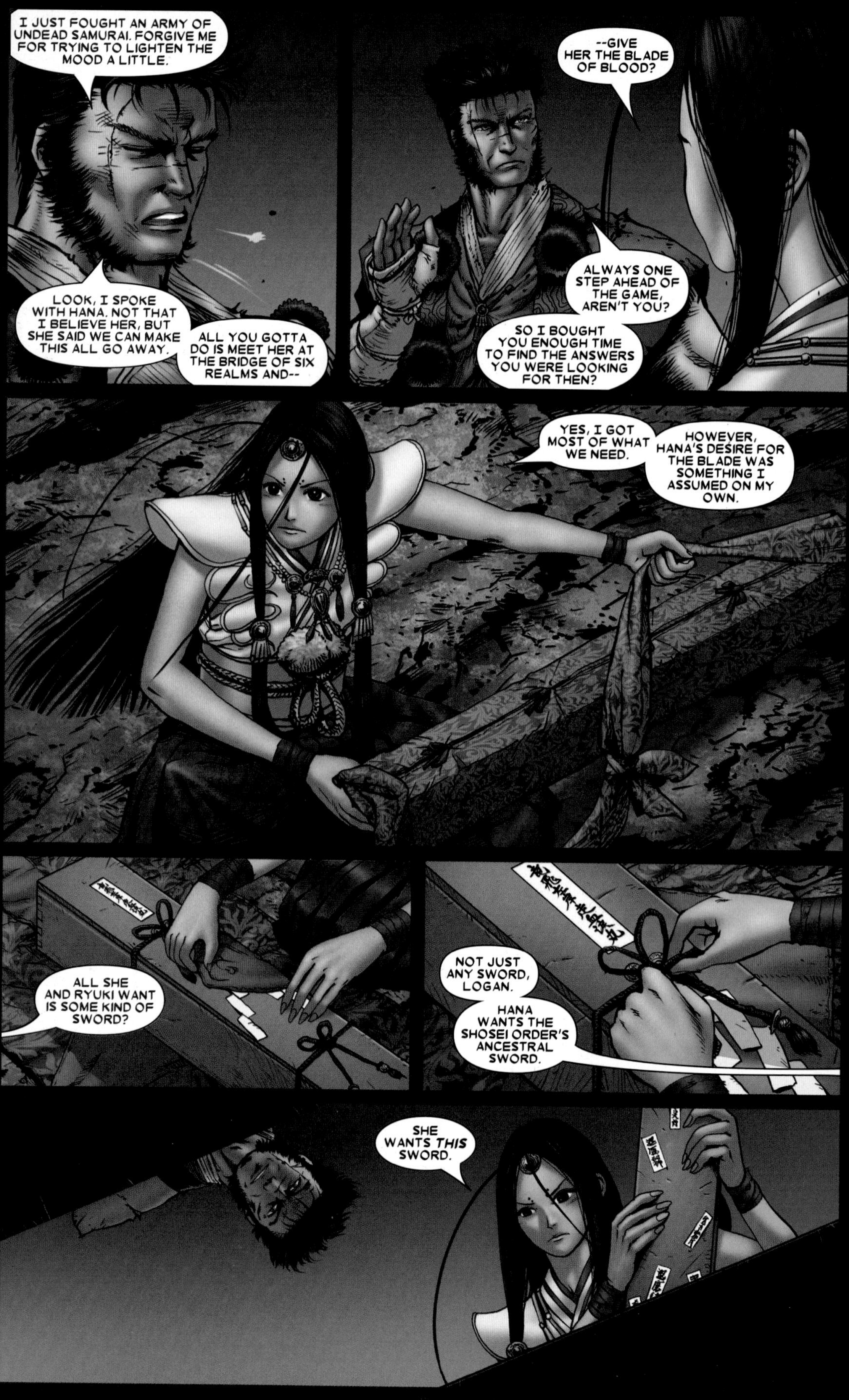

I JUST FOUGHT AN ARMY OF UNDEAD SAMURAI. FORGIVE ME FOR TRYING TO LIGHTEN THE MOOD A LITTLE.
LOOK, I SPOKE WITH HANA. NOT THAT I BELIEVE HER, BUT SHE SAID WE CAN MAKE THIS ALL GO AWAY.
ALL YOU GOTTA DO IS MEET HER AT THE BRIDGE OF SIX REALMS AND--
--GIVE HER THE BLADE OF BLOOD?
ALWAYS ONE STEP AHEAD OF THE GAME, AREN'T YOU?
SO I BOUGHT YOU ENOUGH TIME TO FIND THE ANSWERS YOU WERE LOOKING FOR THEN?
YES, I GOT MOST OF WHAT WE NEED.
HOWEVER, HANA'S DESIRE FOR THE BLADE WAS SOMETHING I ASSUMED ON MY OWN.
ALL SHE AND RYUKI WANT IS SOME KIND OF SWORD?
NOT JUST ANY SWORD, LOGAN.
HANA WANTS THE SHOSEI ORDER'S ANCESTRAL SWORD.
SHE WANTS *THIS* SWORD.

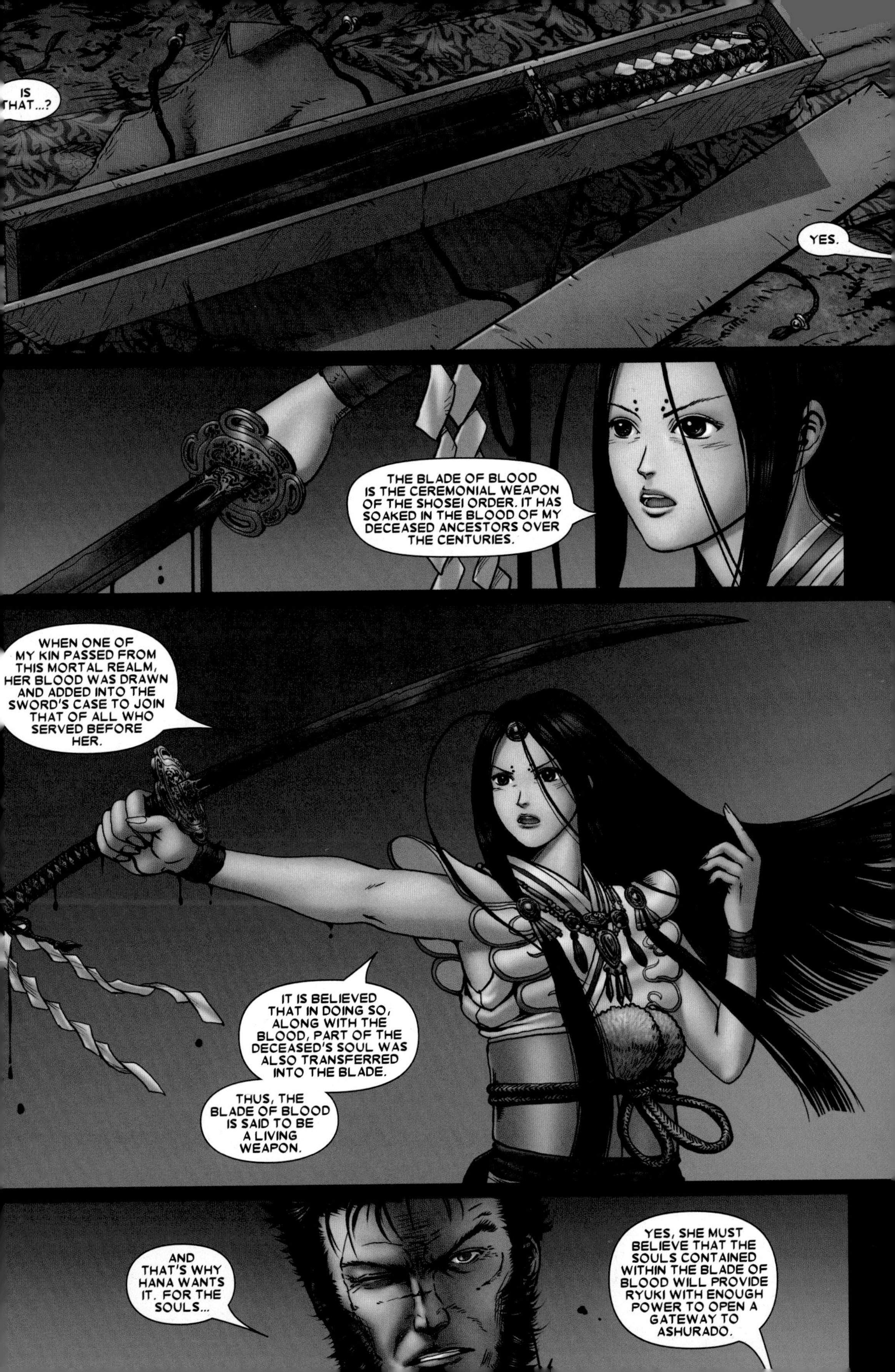
IS THAT...?
YES.
THE BLADE OF BLOOD IS THE CEREMONIAL WEAPON OF THE SHOSEI ORDER. IT HAS SOAKED IN THE BLOOD OF MY DECEASED ANCESTORS OVER THE CENTURIES.
WHEN ONE OF MY KIN PASSED FROM THIS MORTAL REALM, HER BLOOD WAS DRAWN AND ADDED INTO THE SWORD'S CASE TO JOIN THAT OF ALL WHO SERVED BEFORE HER.
IT IS BELIEVED THAT IN DOING SO, ALONG WITH THE BLOOD, PART OF THE DECEASED'S SOUL WAS ALSO TRANSFERRED INTO THE BLADE.
THUS, THE BLADE OF BLOOD IS SAID TO BE A LIVING WEAPON.
AND THAT'S WHY HANA WANTS IT. FOR THE SOULS...
YES, SHE MUST BELIEVE THAT THE SOULS CONTAINED WITHIN THE BLADE OF BLOOD WILL PROVIDE RYUKI WITH ENOUGH POWER TO OPEN A GATEWAY TO ASHURADO.

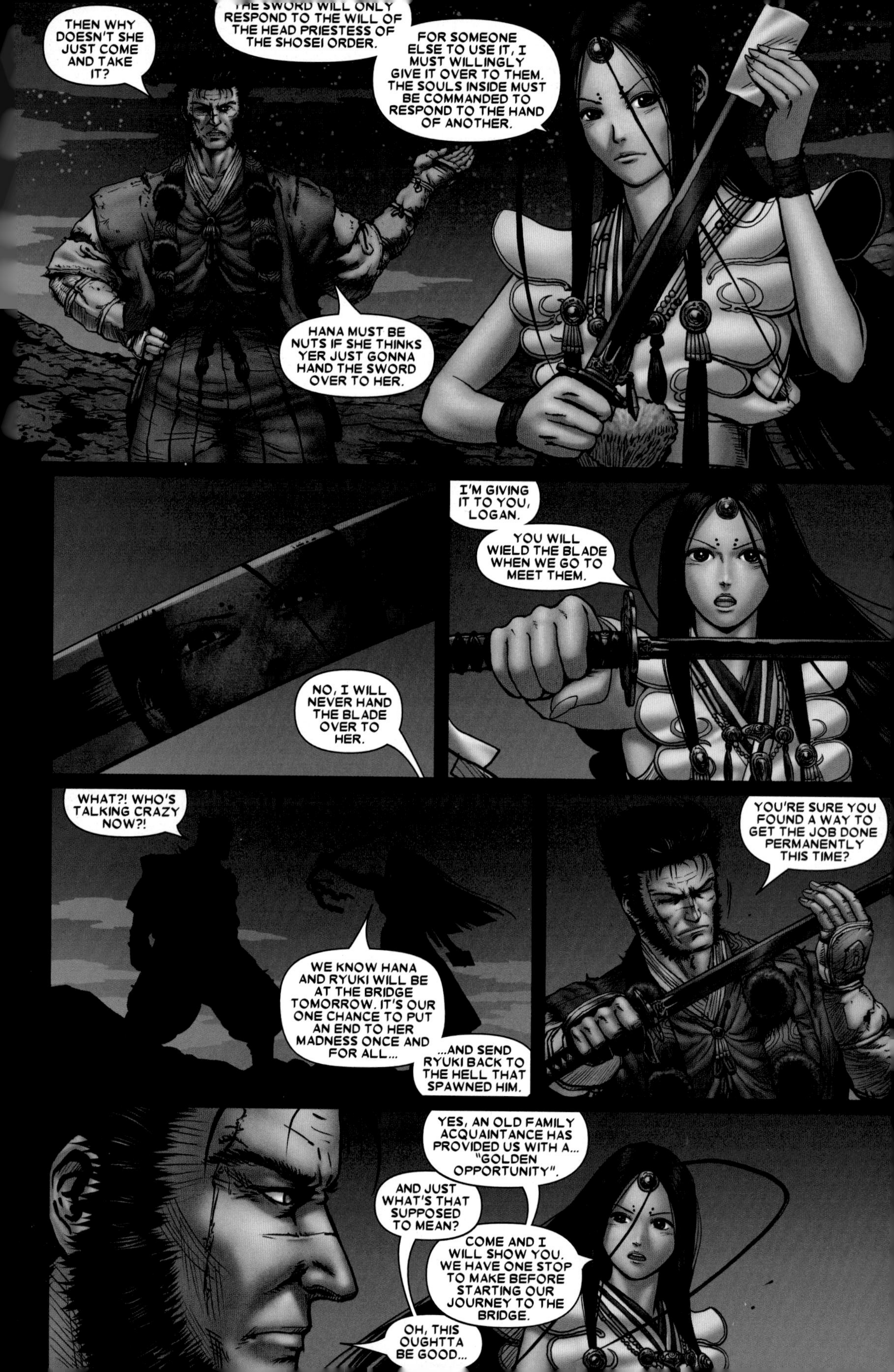
THEN WHY DOESN'T SHE JUST COME AND TAKE IT?
THE SWORD WILL ONLY RESPOND TO THE WILL OF THE HEAD PRIESTESS OF THE SHOSEI ORDER.
FOR SOMEONE ELSE TO USE IT, I MUST WILLINGLY GIVE IT OVER TO THEM. THE SOULS INSIDE MUST BE COMMANDED TO RESPOND TO THE HAND OF ANOTHER.
HANA MUST BE NUTS IF SHE THINKS YER JUST GONNA HAND THE SWORD OVER TO HER.
NO, I WILL NEVER HAND THE BLADE OVER TO HER.
I'M GIVING IT TO YOU, LOGAN.
YOU WILL WIELD THE BLADE WHEN WE GO TO MEET THEM.
WHAT?! WHO'S TALKING CRAZY NOW?!
WE KNOW HANA AND RYUKI WILL BE AT THE BRIDGE TOMORROW. IT'S OUR ONE CHANCE TO PUT AN END TO HER MADNESS ONCE AND FOR ALL...
...AND SEND RYUKI BACK TO THE HELL THAT SPAWNED HIM.
YOU'RE SURE YOU FOUND A WAY TO GET THE JOB DONE PERMANENTLY THIS TIME?
YES, AN OLD FAMILY ACQUAINTANCE HAS PROVIDED US WITH A... "GOLDEN OPPORTUNITY".
AND JUST WHAT'S THAT SUPPOSED TO MEAN?
COME AND I WILL SHOW YOU. WE HAVE ONE STOP TO MAKE BEFORE STARTING OUR JOURNEY TO THE BRIDGE.
OH, THIS OUGHTTA BE GOOD...

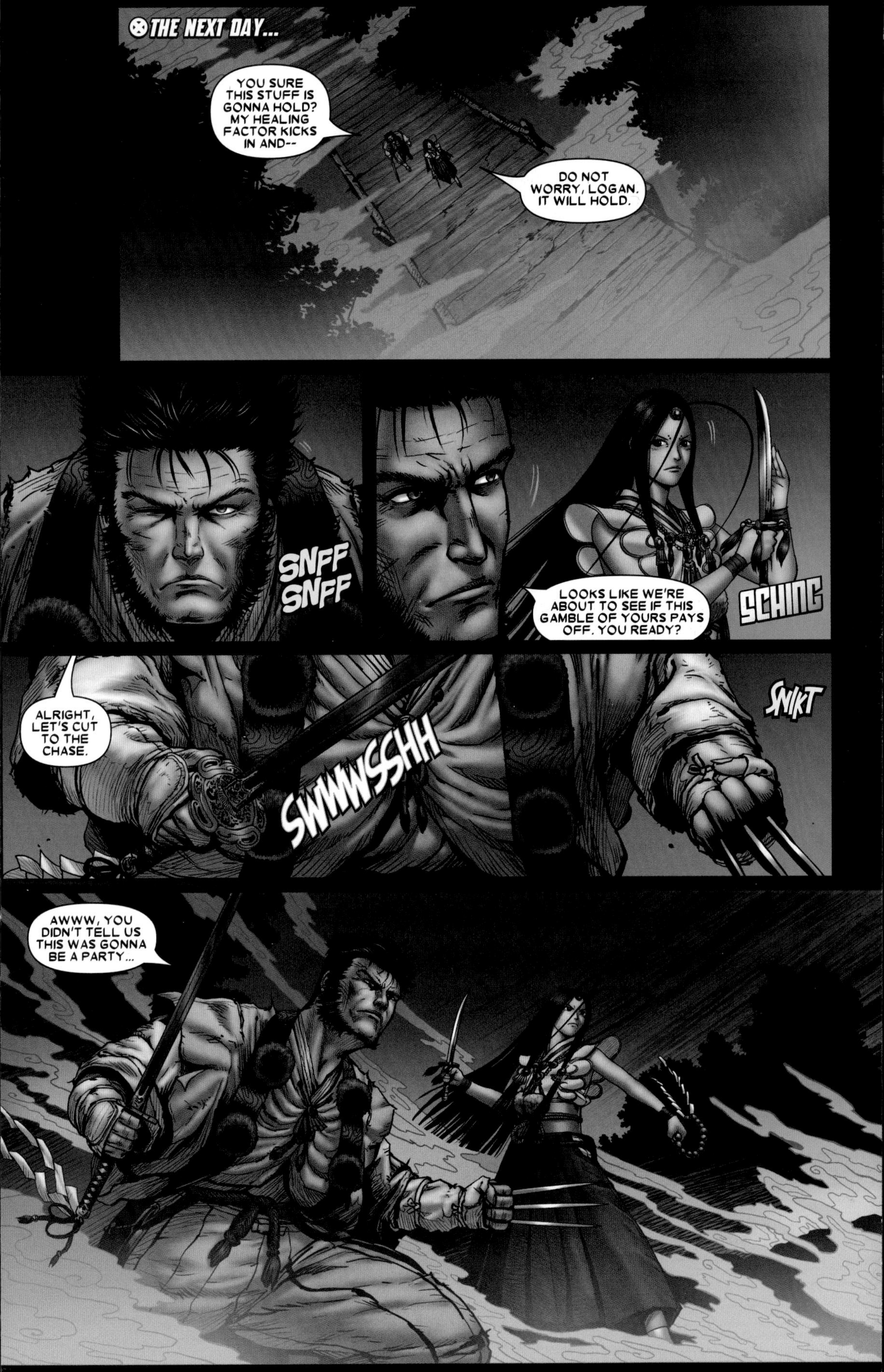
THE NEXT DAY...
YOU SURE THIS STUFF IS GONNA HOLD? MY HEALING FACTOR KICKS IN AND--
DO NOT WORRY, LOGAN. IT WILL HOLD.
SNFF SNFF
LOOKS LIKE WE'RE ABOUT TO SEE IF THIS GAMBLE OF YOURS PAYS OFF. YOU READY?
SCHING
ALRIGHT, LET'S CUT TO THE CHASE.
SWWWSSHH
SNIKT
AWWW, YOU DIDN'T TELL US THIS WAS GONNA BE A PARTY...

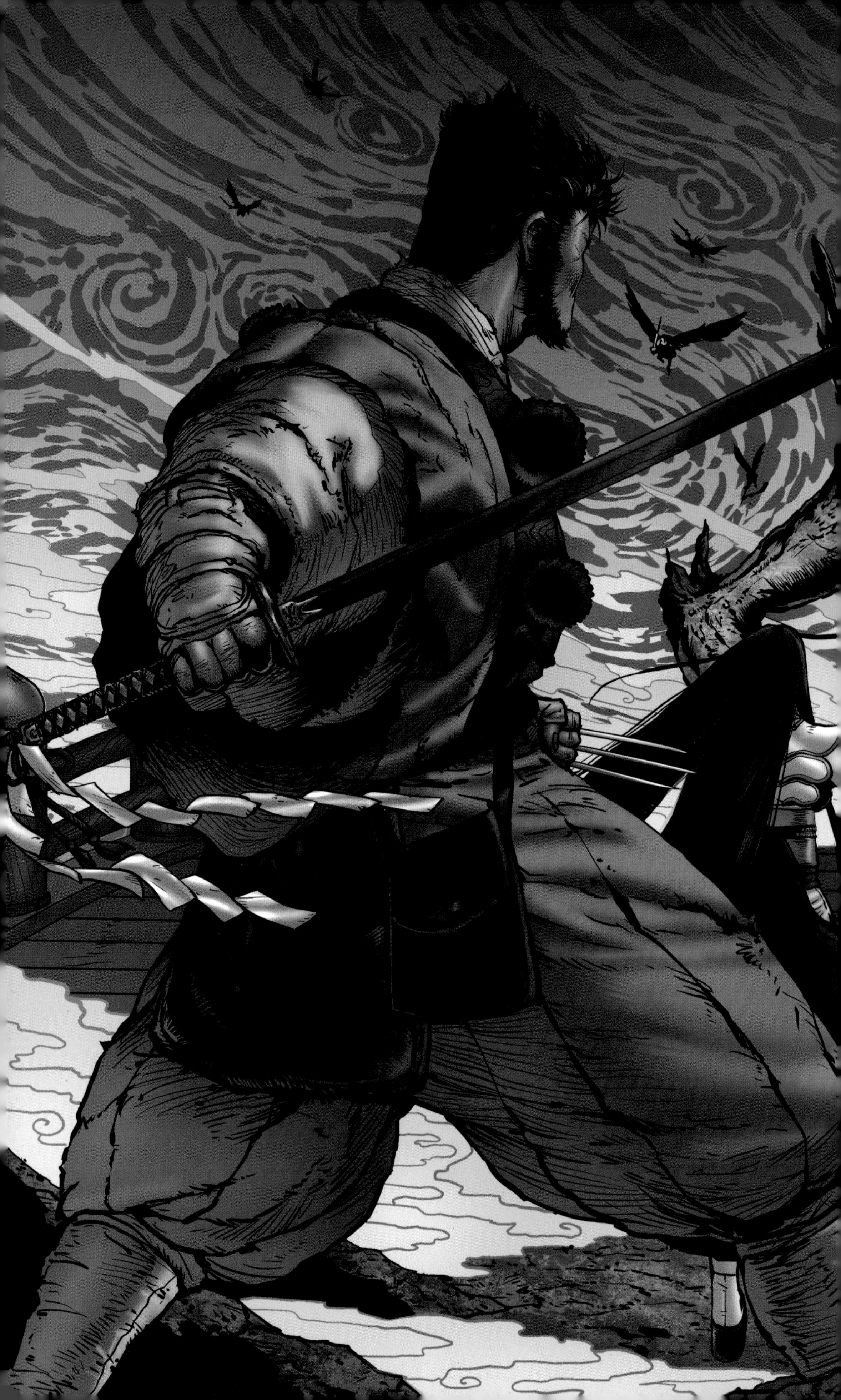

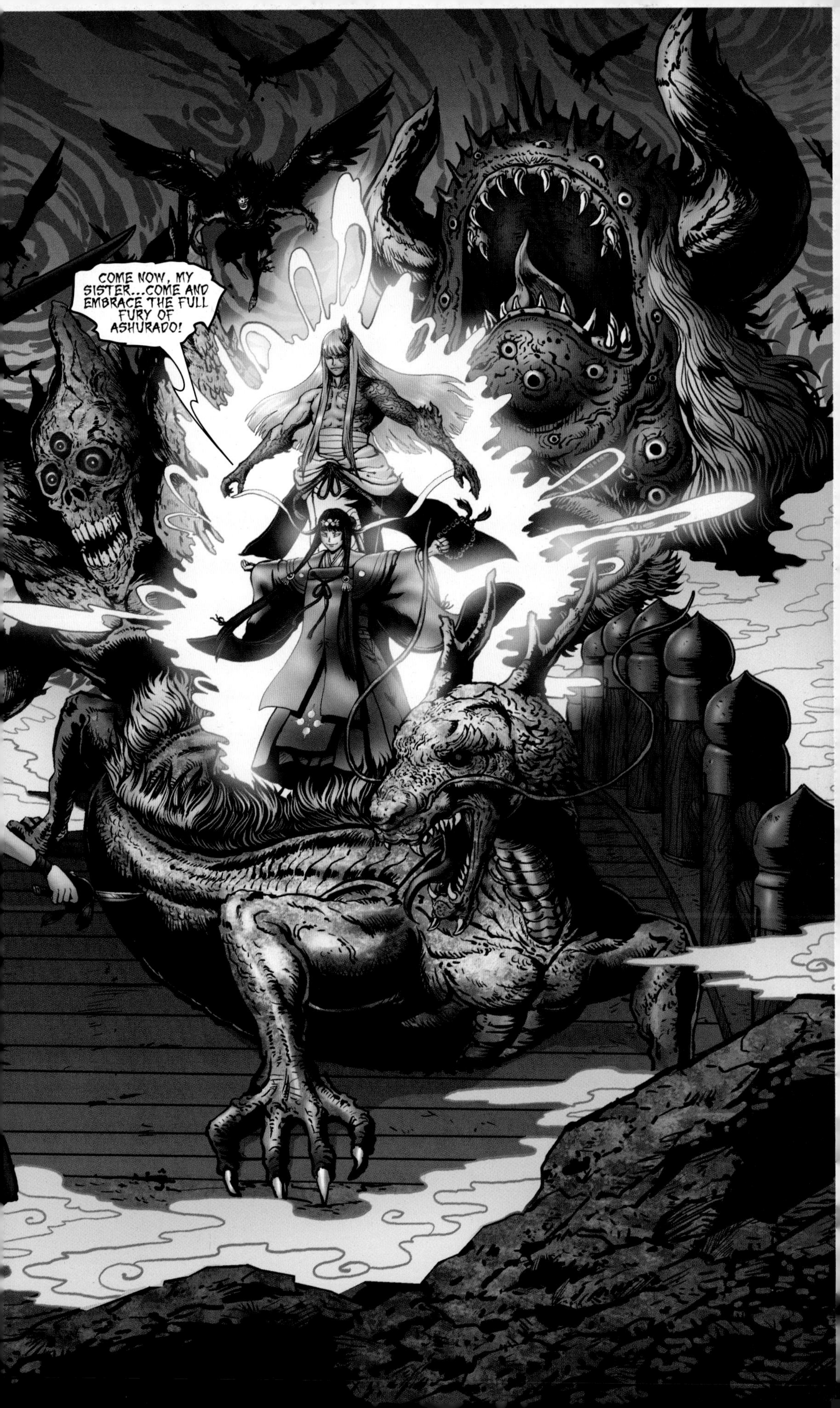
COME NOW, MY SISTER...COME AND EMBRACE THE FULL FURY OF ASHURADO!

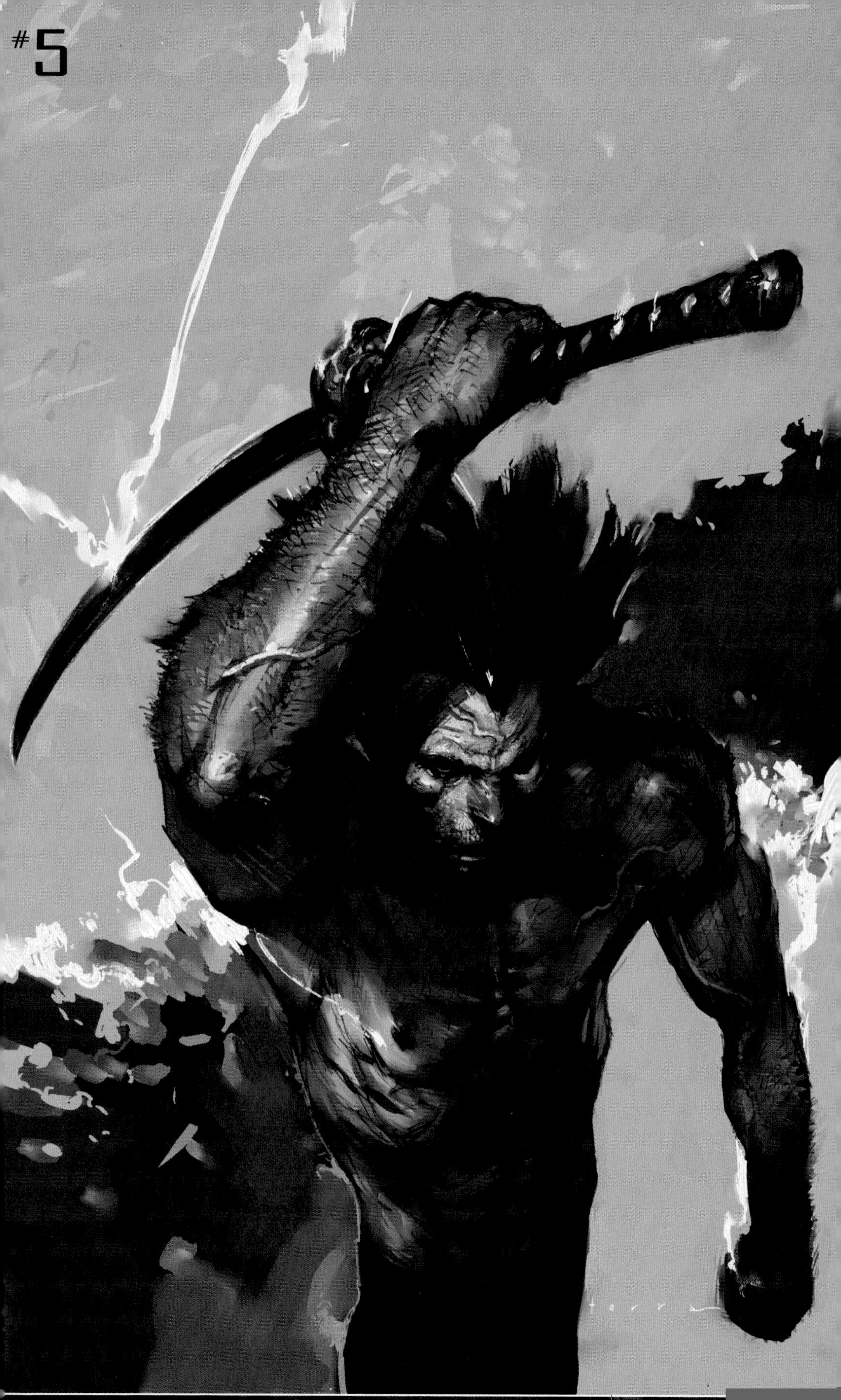
#5
terra

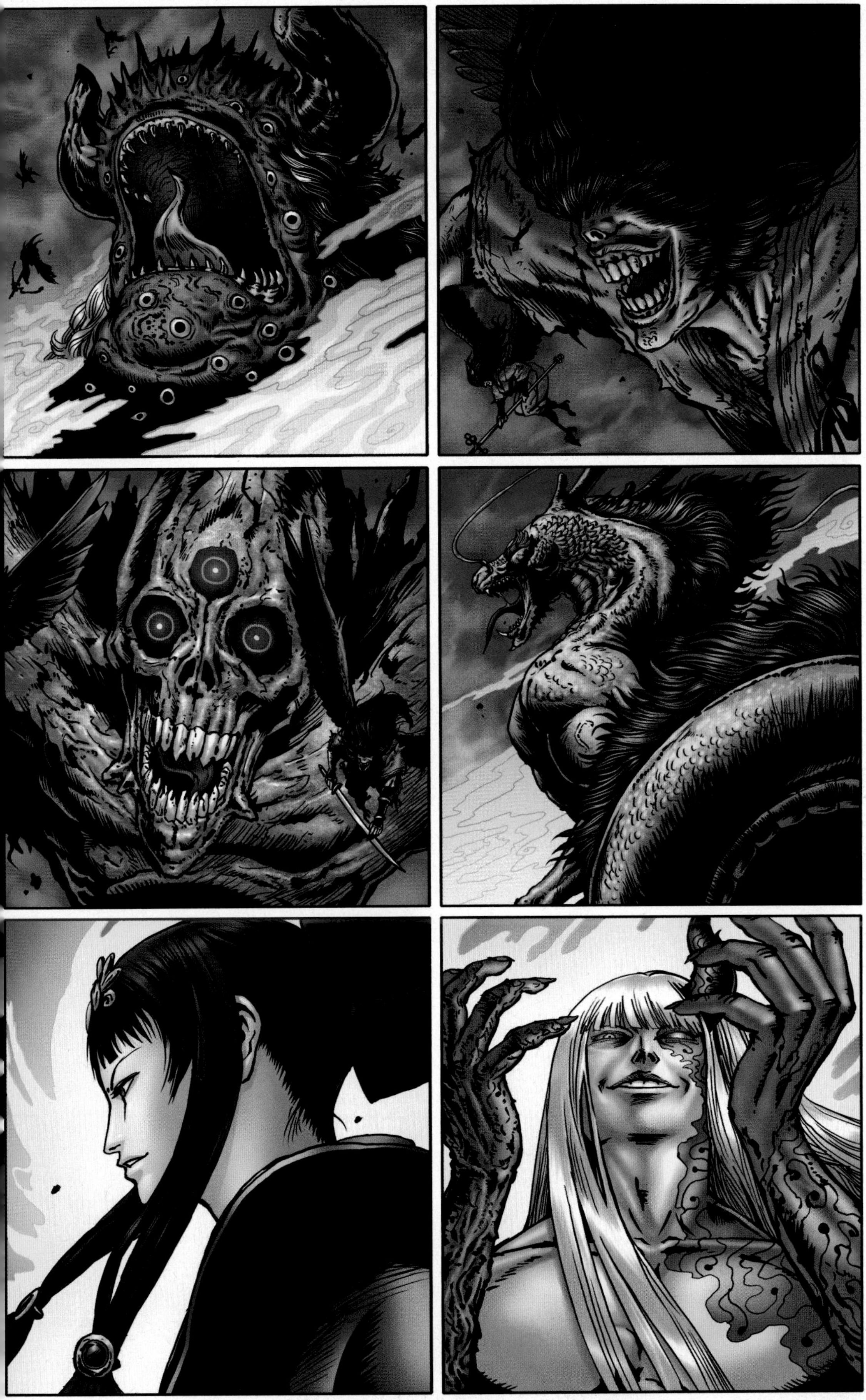

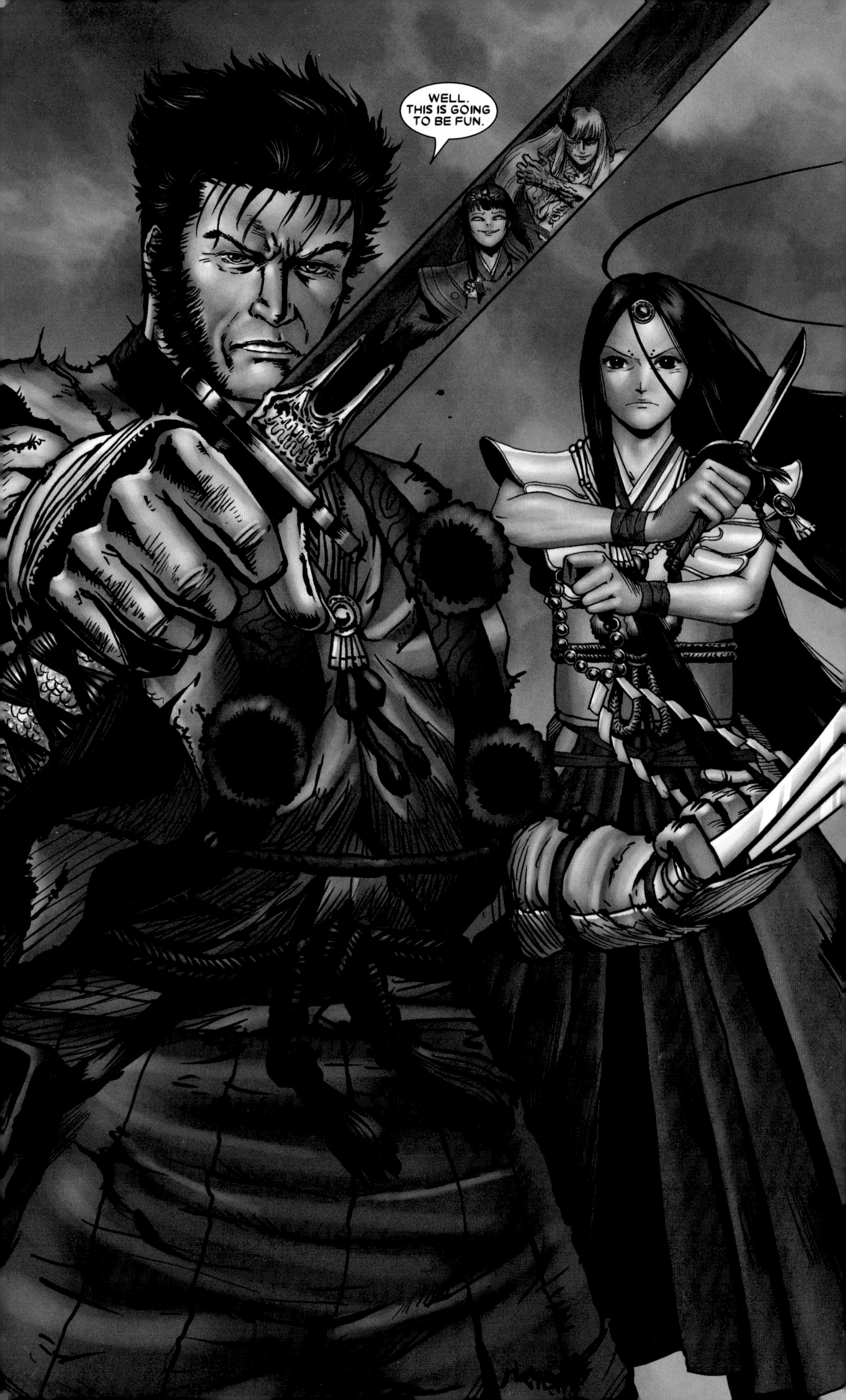
WELL. THIS IS GOING TO BE FUN.

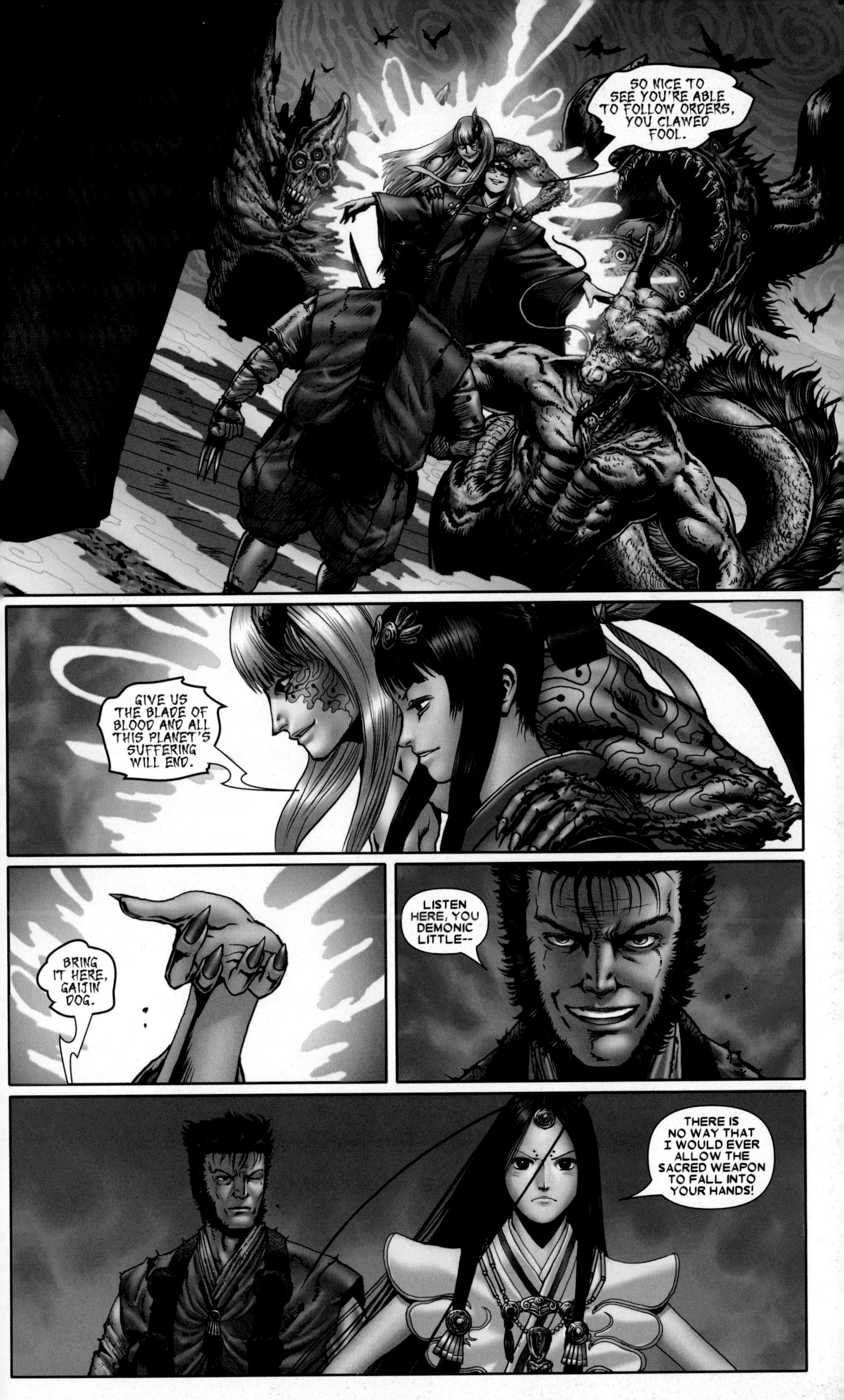
SO NICE TO SEE YOU'RE ABLE TO FOLLOW ORDERS, YOU CLAWED FOOL.
GIVE US THE BLADE OF BLOOD AND ALL THIS PLANET'S SUFFERING WILL END.
BRING IT HERE, GAIJIN DOG.
LISTEN HERE, YOU DEMONIC LITTLE--
THERE IS NO WAY THAT I WOULD EVER ALLOW THE SACRED WEAPON TO FALL INTO YOUR HANDS!

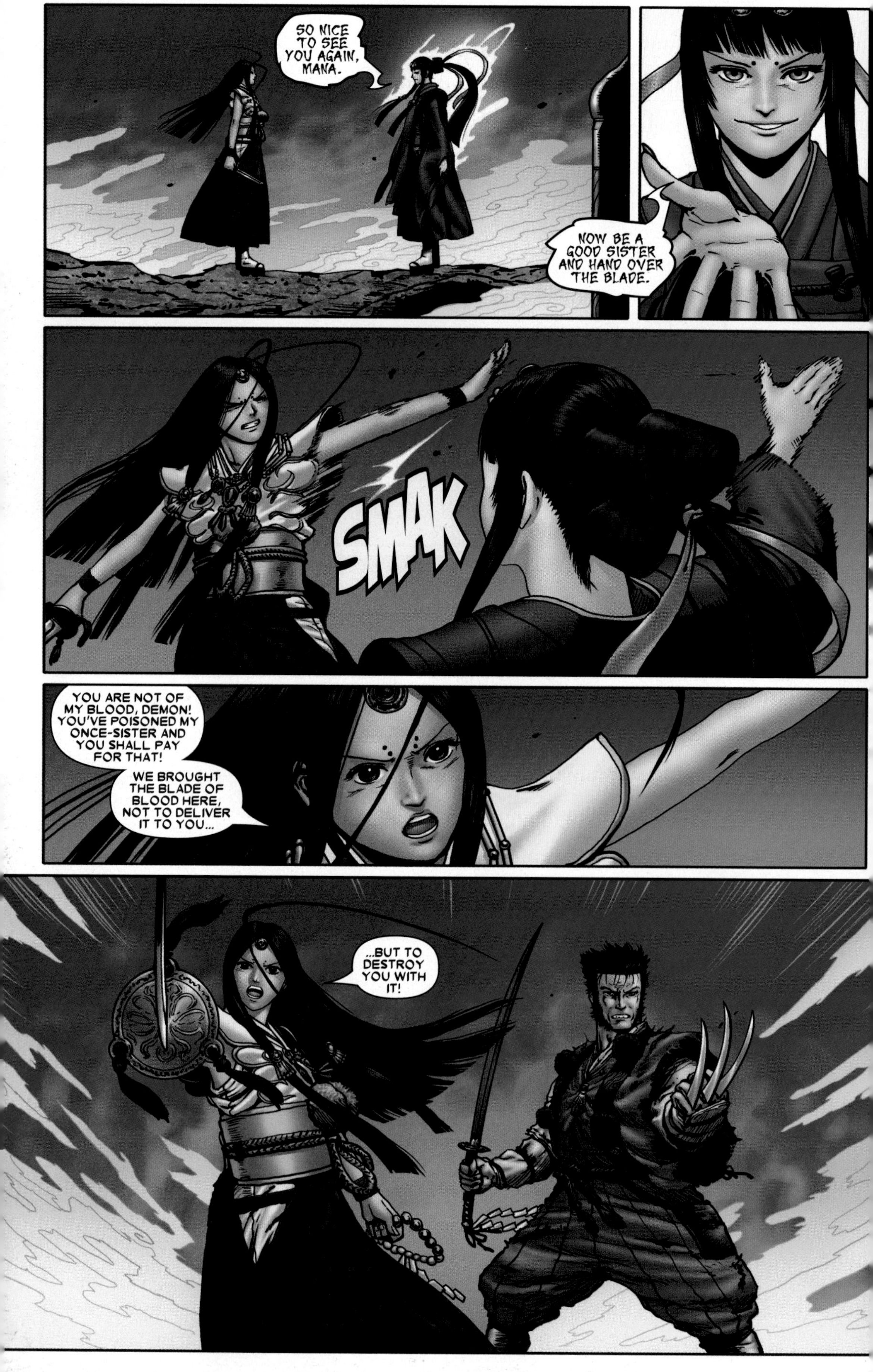
SO NICE TO SEE YOU AGAIN, MANA.
NOW BE A GOOD SISTER AND HAND OVER THE BLADE.
SMAK
YOU ARE NOT OF MY BLOOD, DEMON! YOU'VE POISONED MY ONCE-SISTER AND YOU SHALL PAY FOR THAT!
WE BROUGHT THE BLADE OF BLOOD HERE, NOT TO DELIVER IT TO YOU...
...BUT TO DESTROY YOU WITH IT!

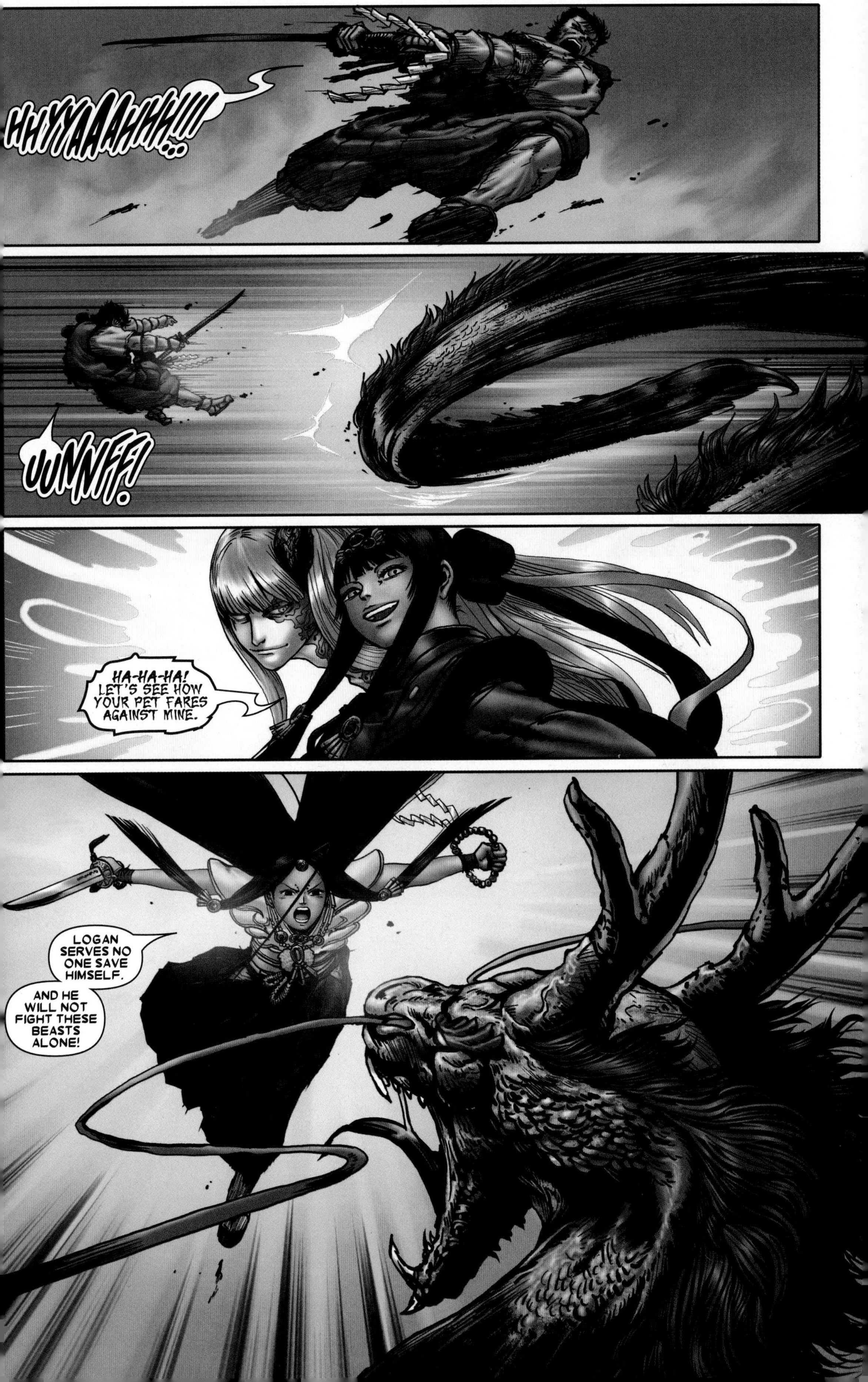
HHYYAAAHHH!!!..
UUNNFF!
HA-HA-HA! LET'S SEE HOW YOUR PET FARES AGAINST MINE.
LOGAN SERVES NO ONE SAVE HIMSELF.
AND HE WILL NOT FIGHT THESE BEASTS ALONE!

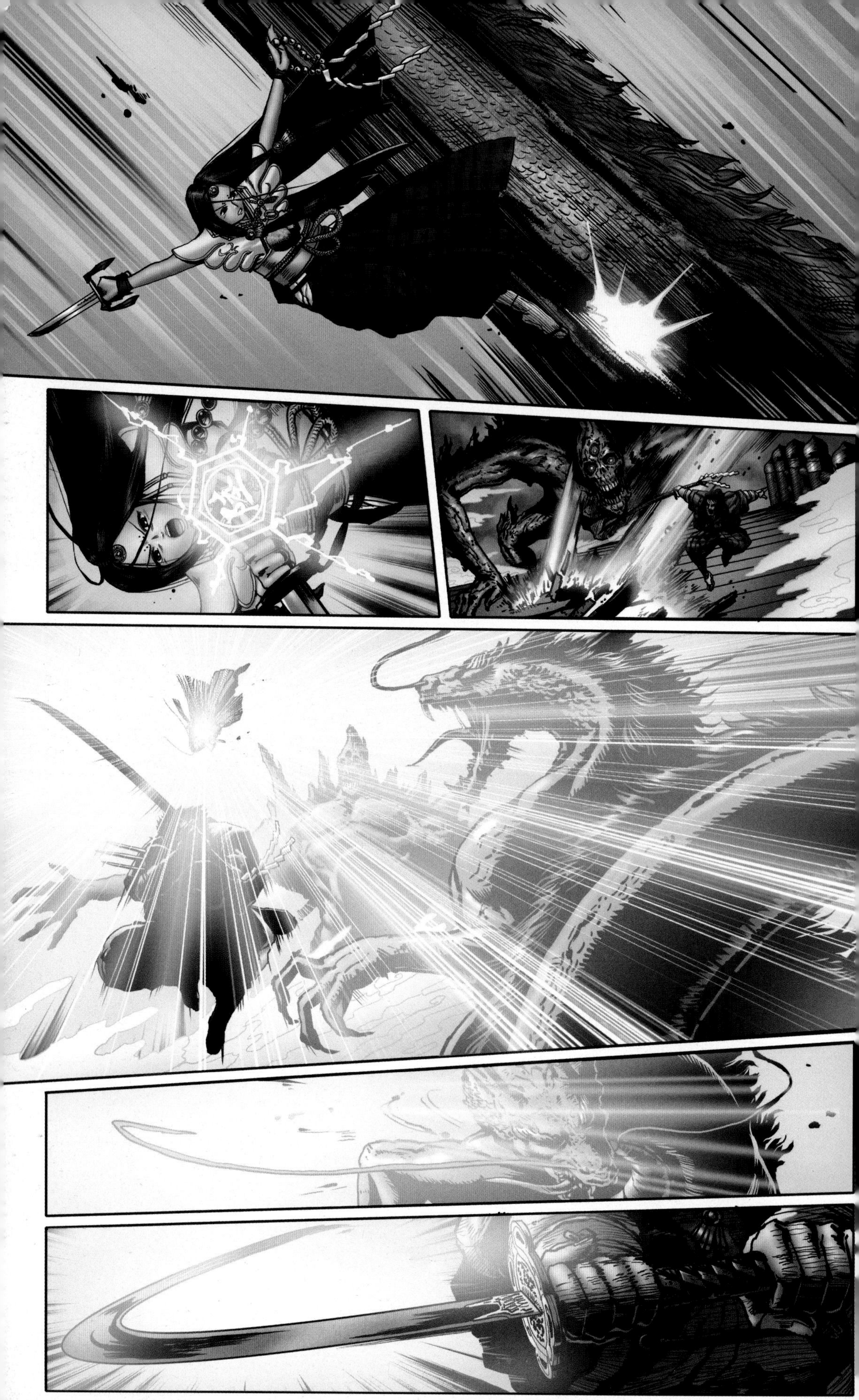

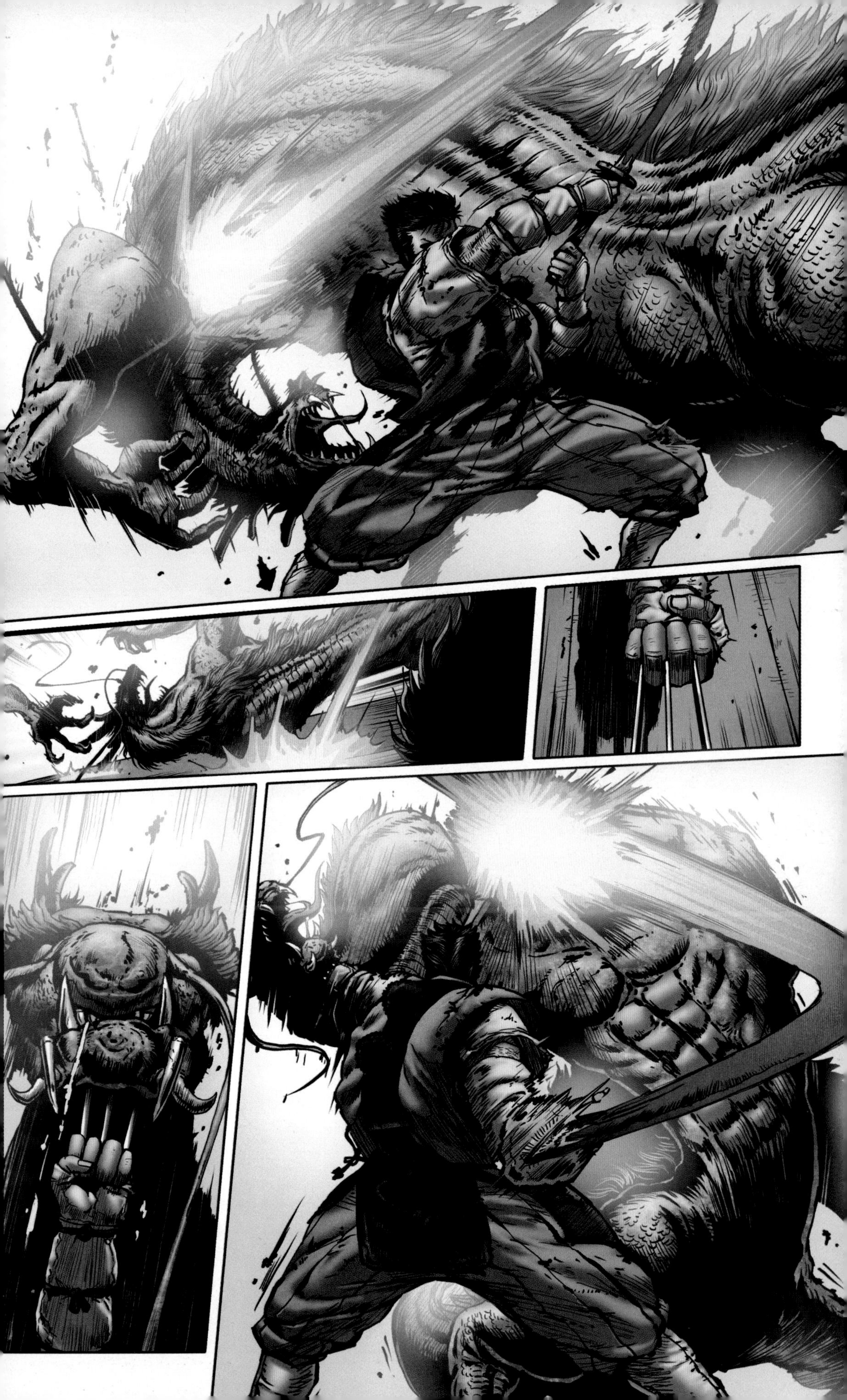

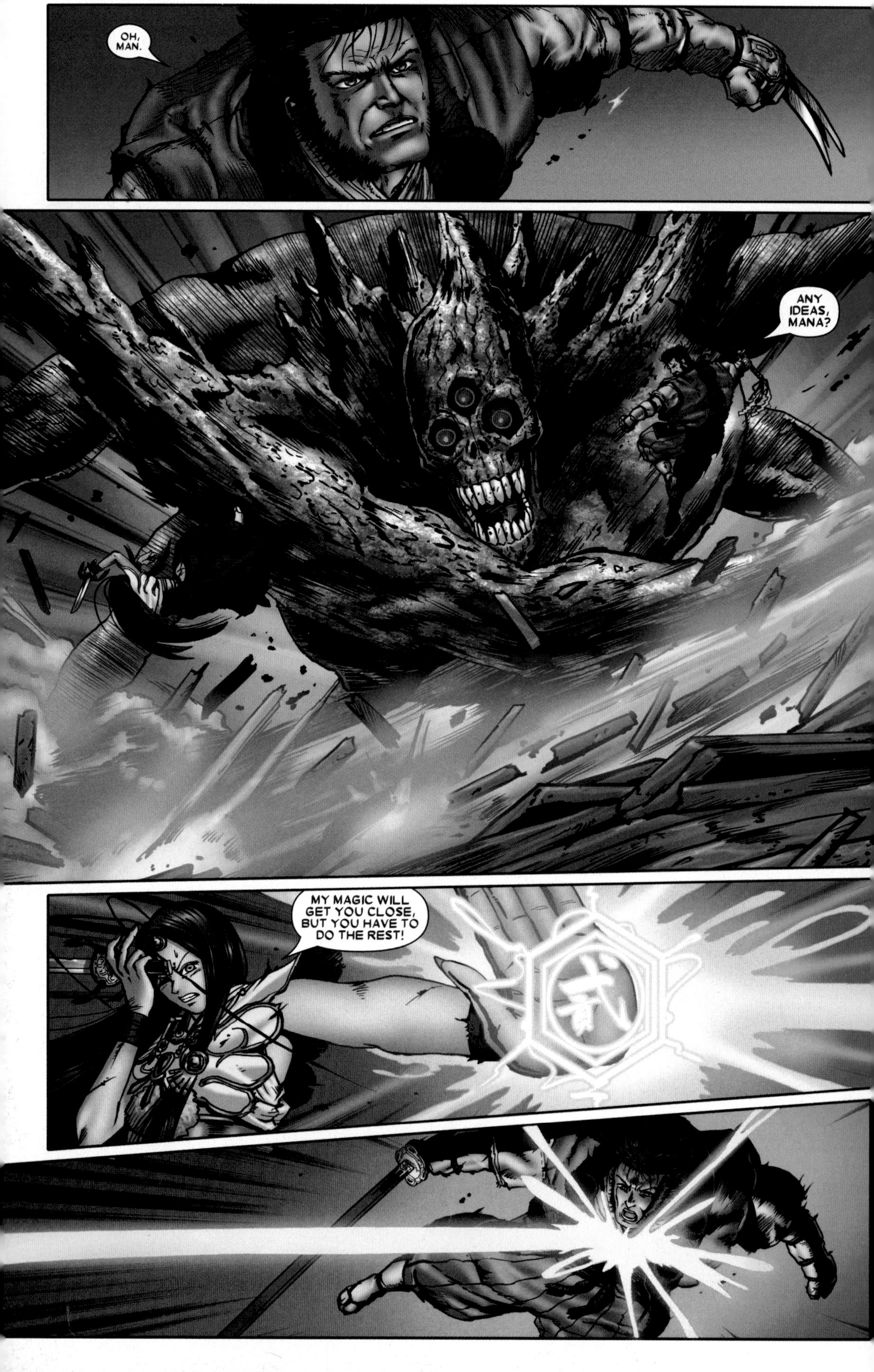
OH, MAN.
ANY IDEAS, MANA?
MY MAGIC WILL GET YOU CLOSE, BUT YOU HAVE TO DO THE REST!

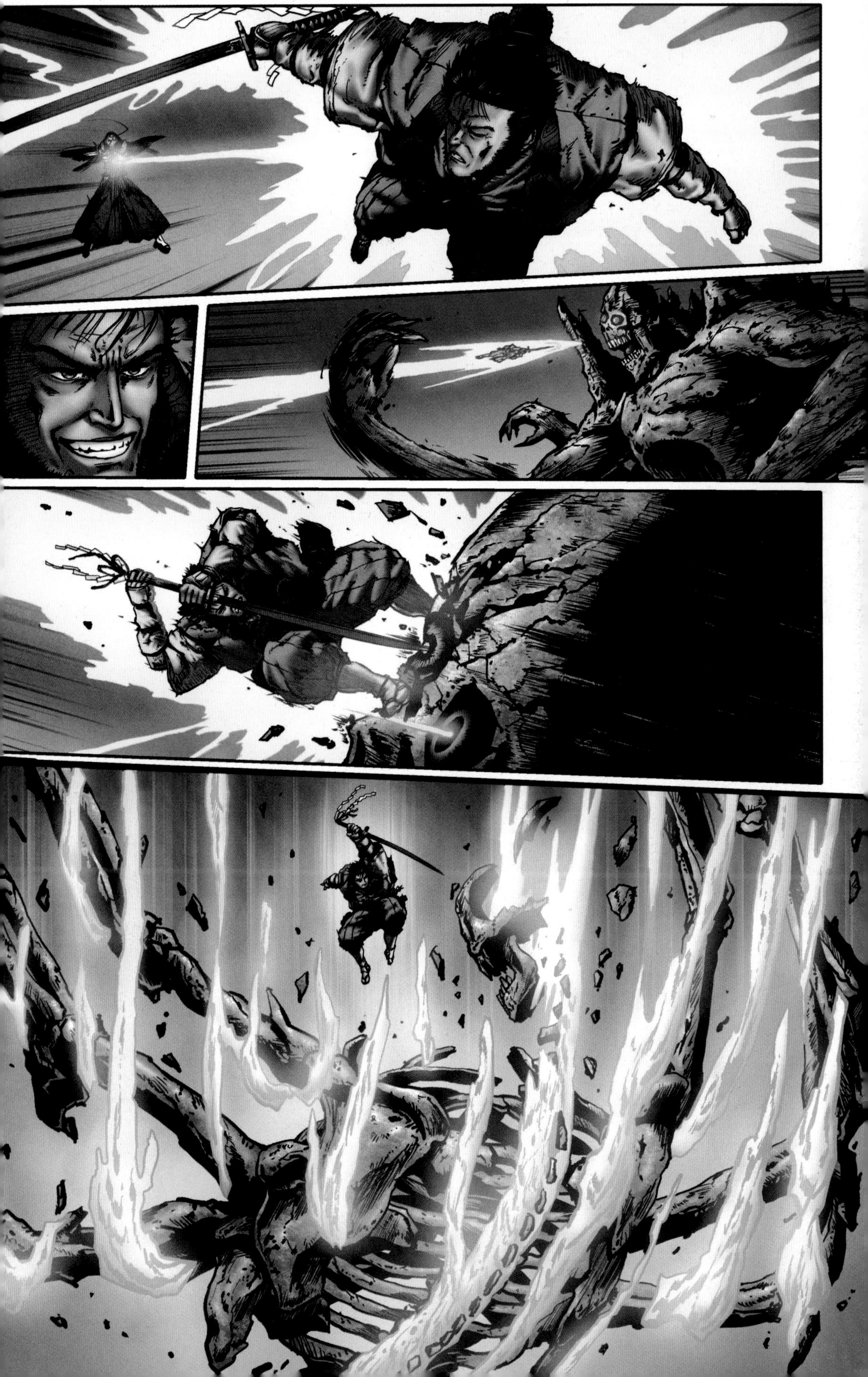

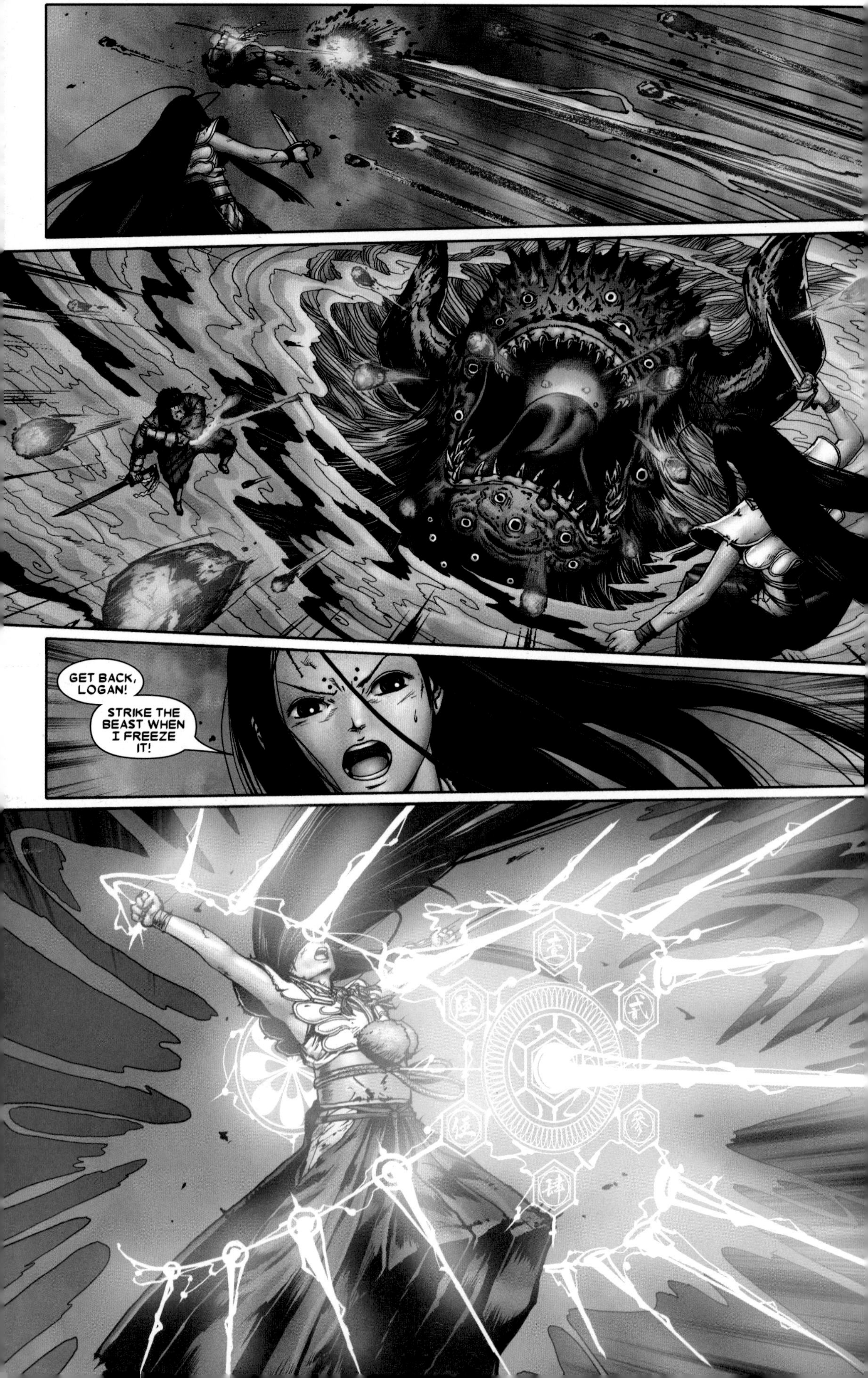
GET BACK, LOGAN!
STRIKE THE BEAST WHEN I FREEZE IT!

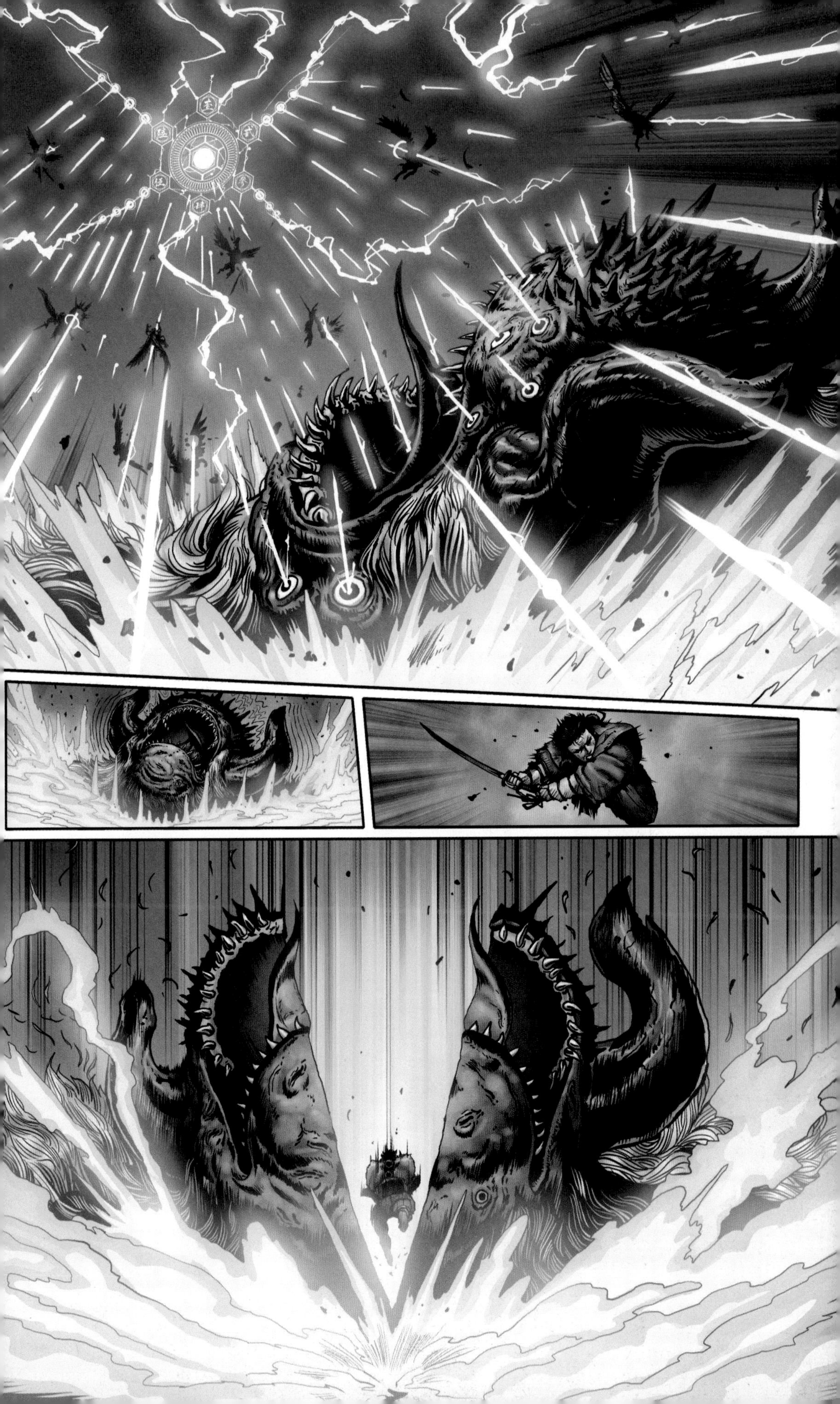

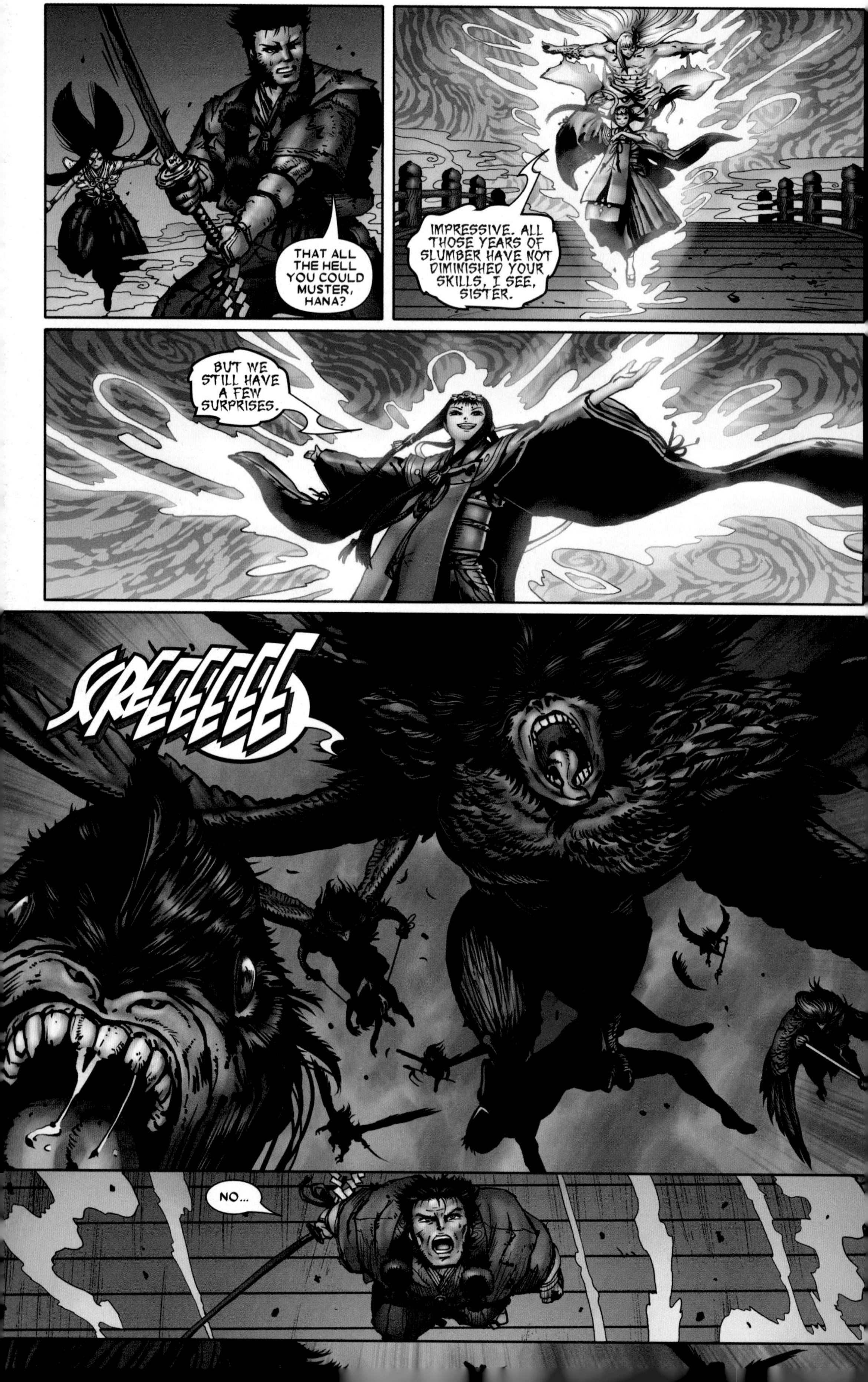
THAT ALL THE HELL YOU COULD MUSTER, HANA?
IMPRESSIVE. ALL THOSE YEARS OF SLUMBER HAVE NOT DIMINISHED YOUR SKILLS, I SEE, SISTER.
BUT WE STILL HAVE A FEW SURPRISES.
SCREEEEEE
NO...

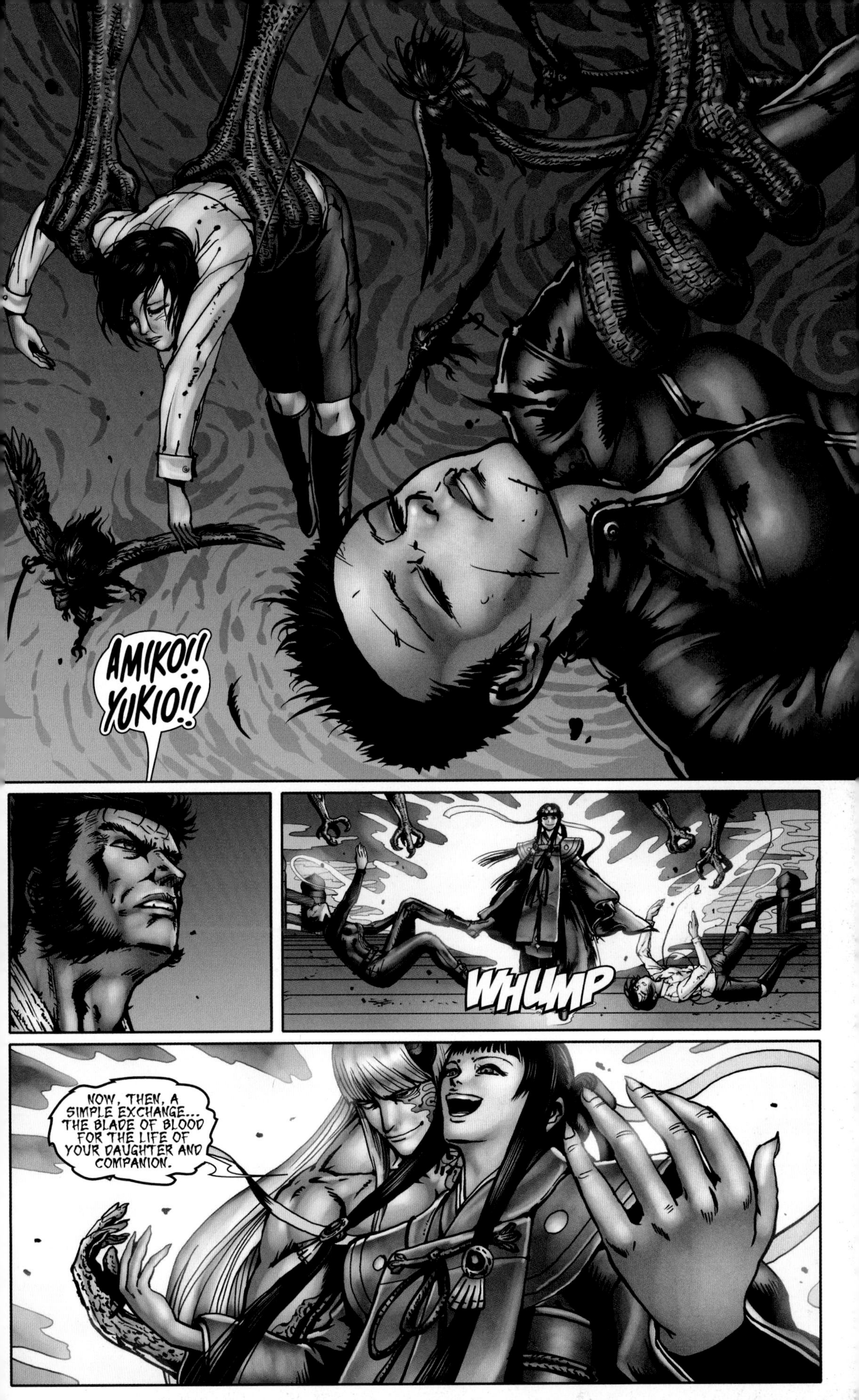
AMIKO!!
YUKIO!!
WHUMP
NOW, THEN, A SIMPLE EXCHANGE... THE BLADE OF BLOOD FOR THE LIFE OF YOUR DAUGHTER AND COMPANION.

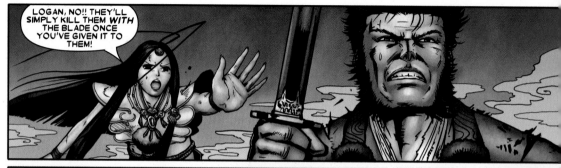

LOGAN, NO!! THEY'LL SIMPLY KILL THEM *WITH* THE BLADE ONCE YOU'VE GIVEN IT TO THEM!

SNAKT!

I'M SORRY, MANA, BUT THAT'S A CHANCE I'M JUST GONNA HAVE TO TAKE.

I'LL SEE YOU SENT BACK TO THE ABYSS THAT SPAWNED YOU IF IT'S THE LAST THING I DO, YOU MONSTER.

HERE. TAKE IT.

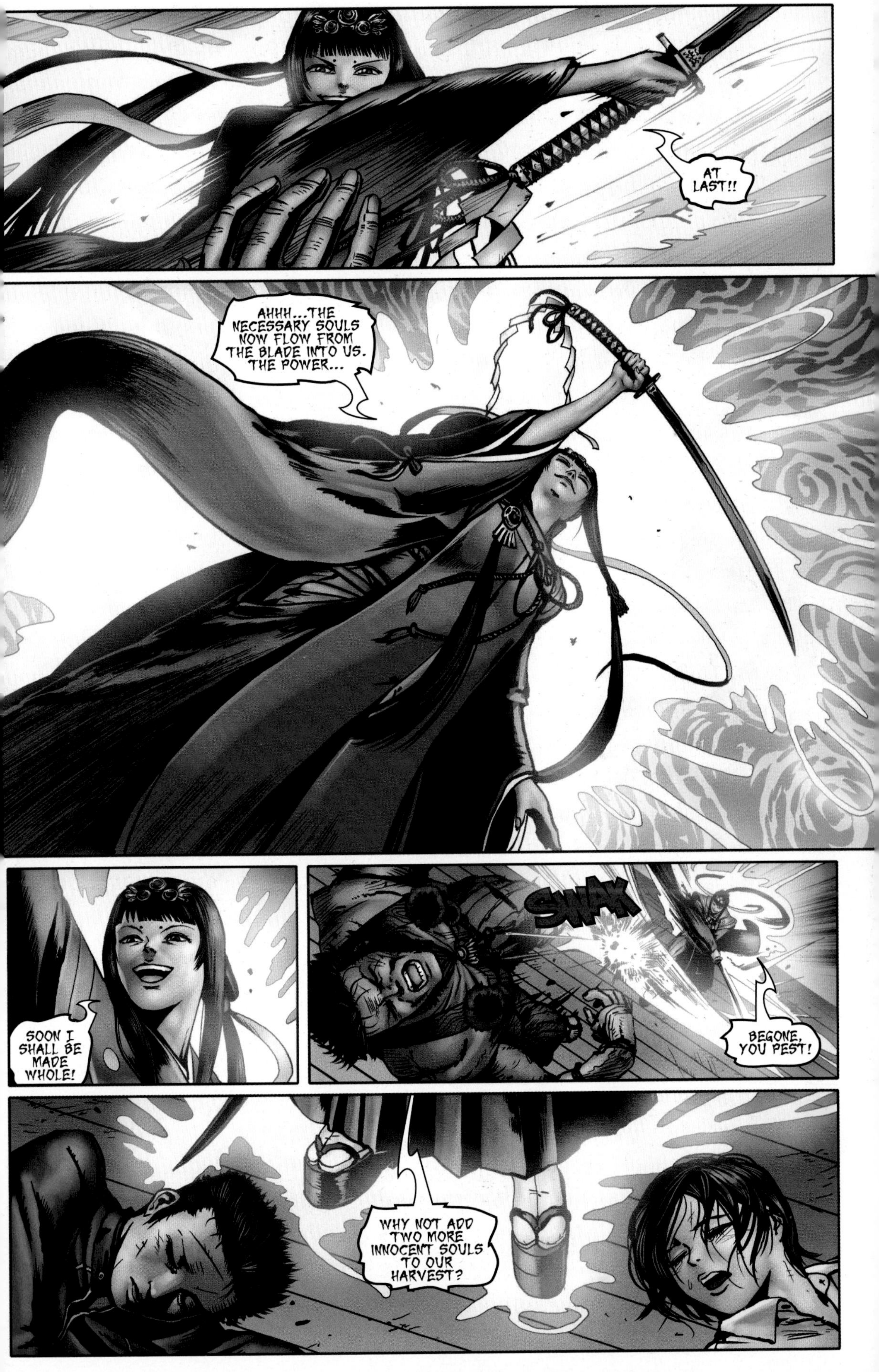
AT LAST!!
AHHH...THE NECESSARY SOULS NOW FLOW FROM THE BLADE INTO US. THE POWER...
SOON I SHALL BE MADE WHOLE!
SWAK
BEGONE, YOU PEST!
WHY NOT ADD TWO MORE INNOCENT SOULS TO OUR HARVEST?

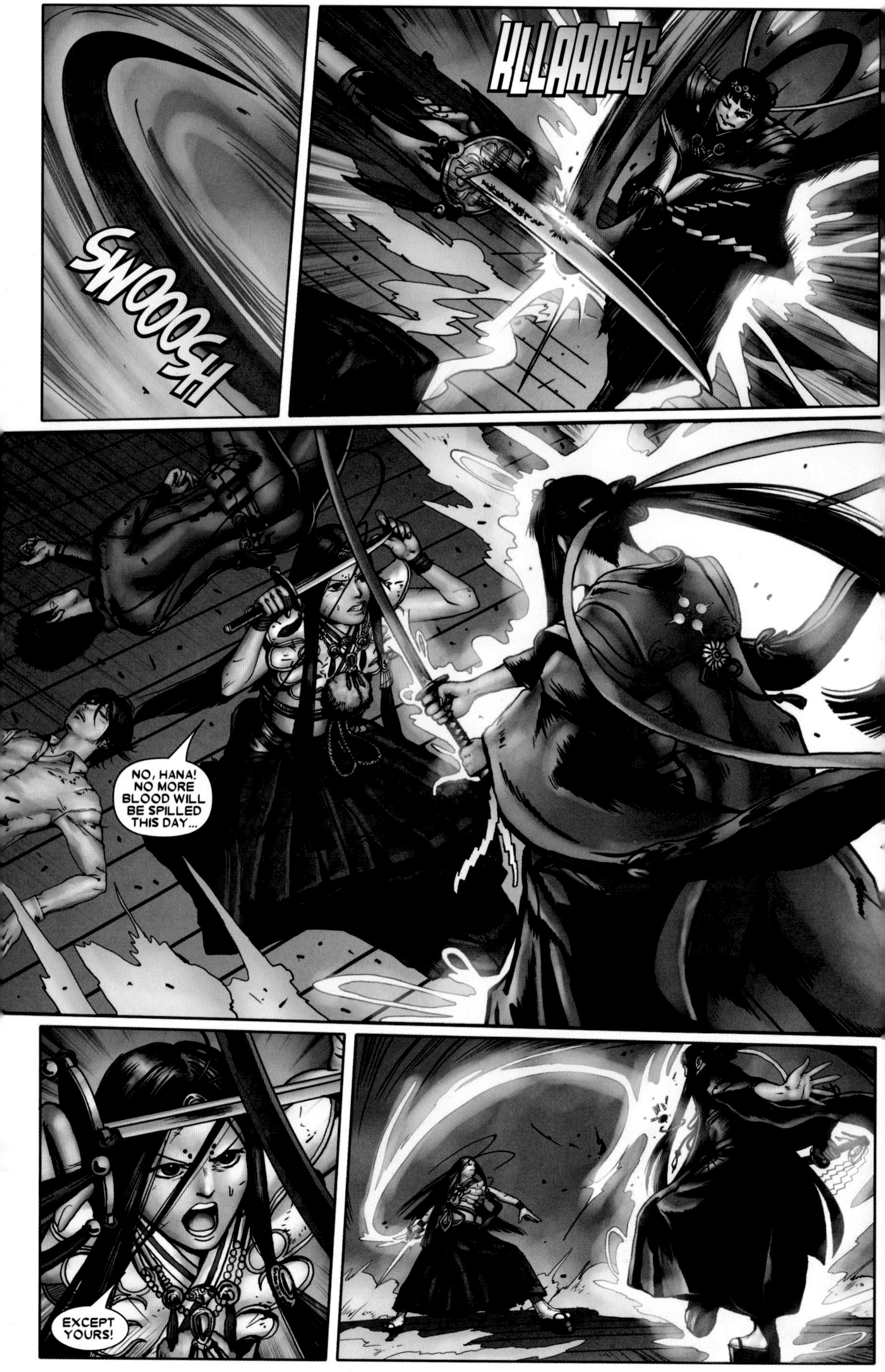
SWOOOSH
KLLAANGG
NO, HANA! NO MORE BLOOD WILL BE SPILLED THIS DAY...
EXCEPT YOURS!

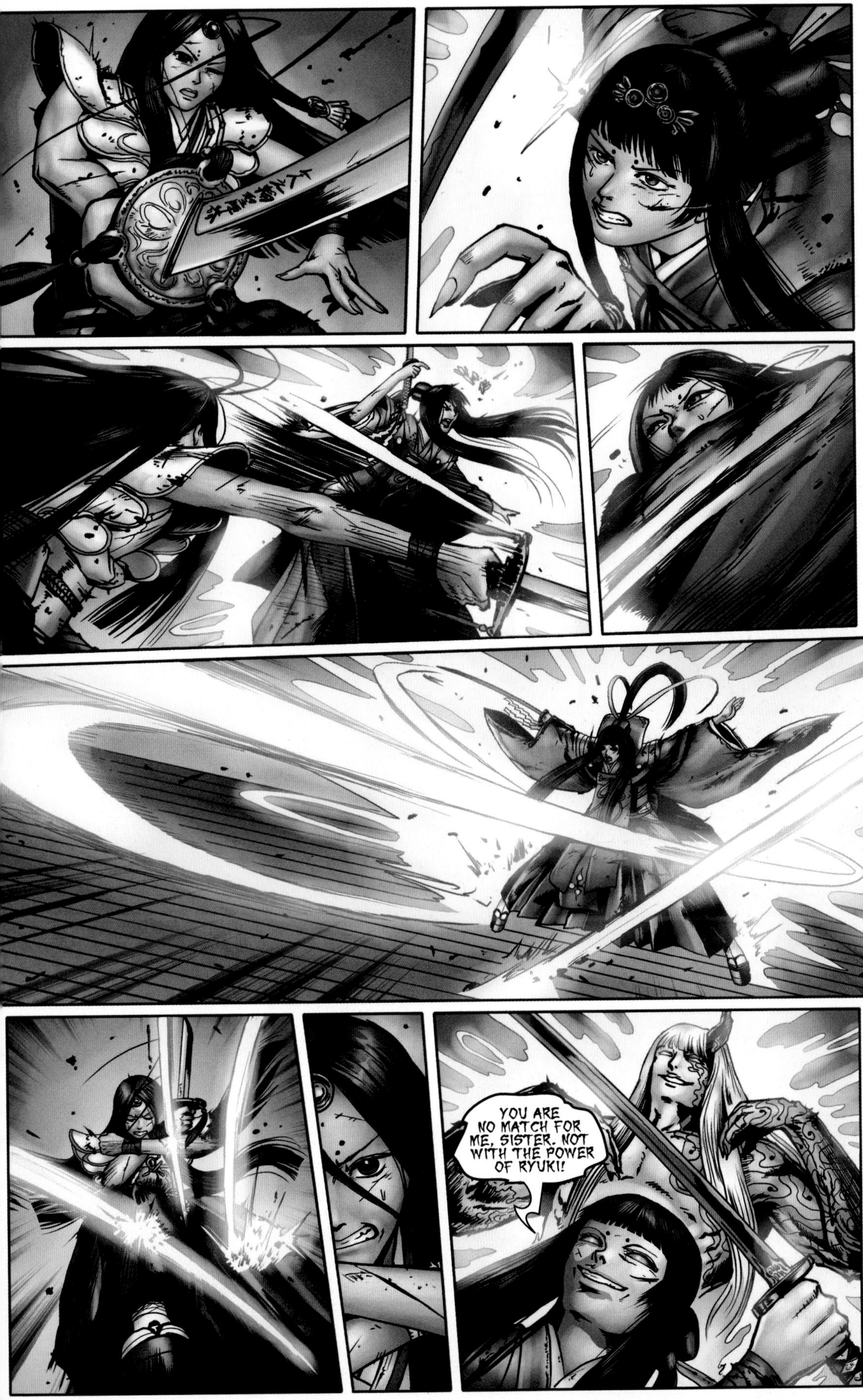
YOU ARE NO MATCH FOR ME, SISTER. NOT WITH THE POWER OF RYUKI!

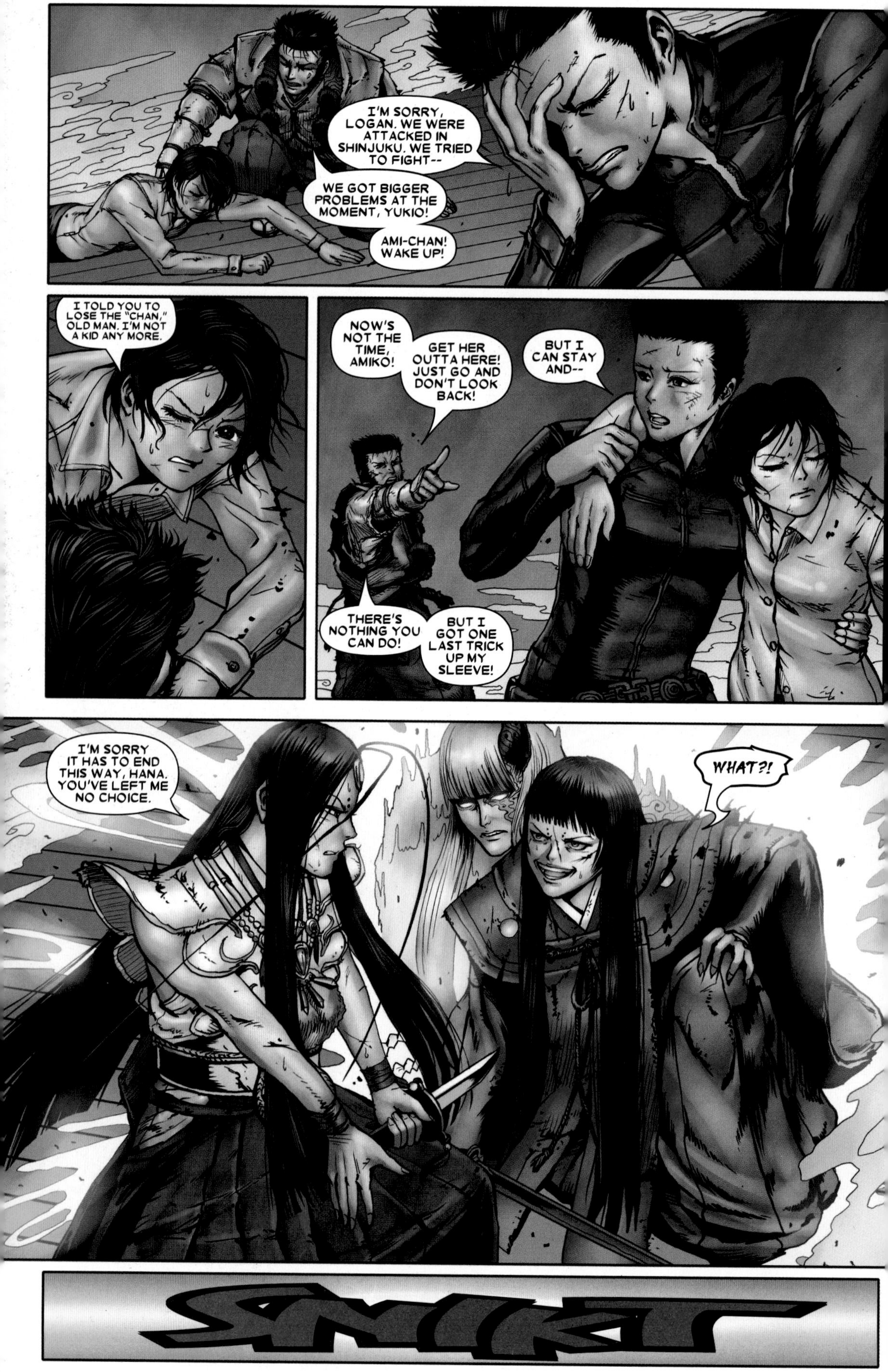
I'M SORRY, LOGAN. WE WERE ATTACKED IN SHINJUKU. WE TRIED TO FIGHT--
WE GOT BIGGER PROBLEMS AT THE MOMENT, YUKIO!
AMI-CHAN! WAKE UP!
I TOLD YOU TO LOSE THE "CHAN," OLD MAN. I'M NOT A KID ANY MORE.
NOW'S NOT THE TIME, AMIKO!
GET HER OUTTA HERE! JUST GO AND DON'T LOOK BACK!
BUT I CAN STAY AND--
THERE'S NOTHING YOU CAN DO!
BUT I GOT ONE LAST TRICK UP MY SLEEVE!
I'M SORRY IT HAS TO END THIS WAY, HANA. YOU'VE LEFT ME NO CHOICE.
WHAT?!
SNIKT

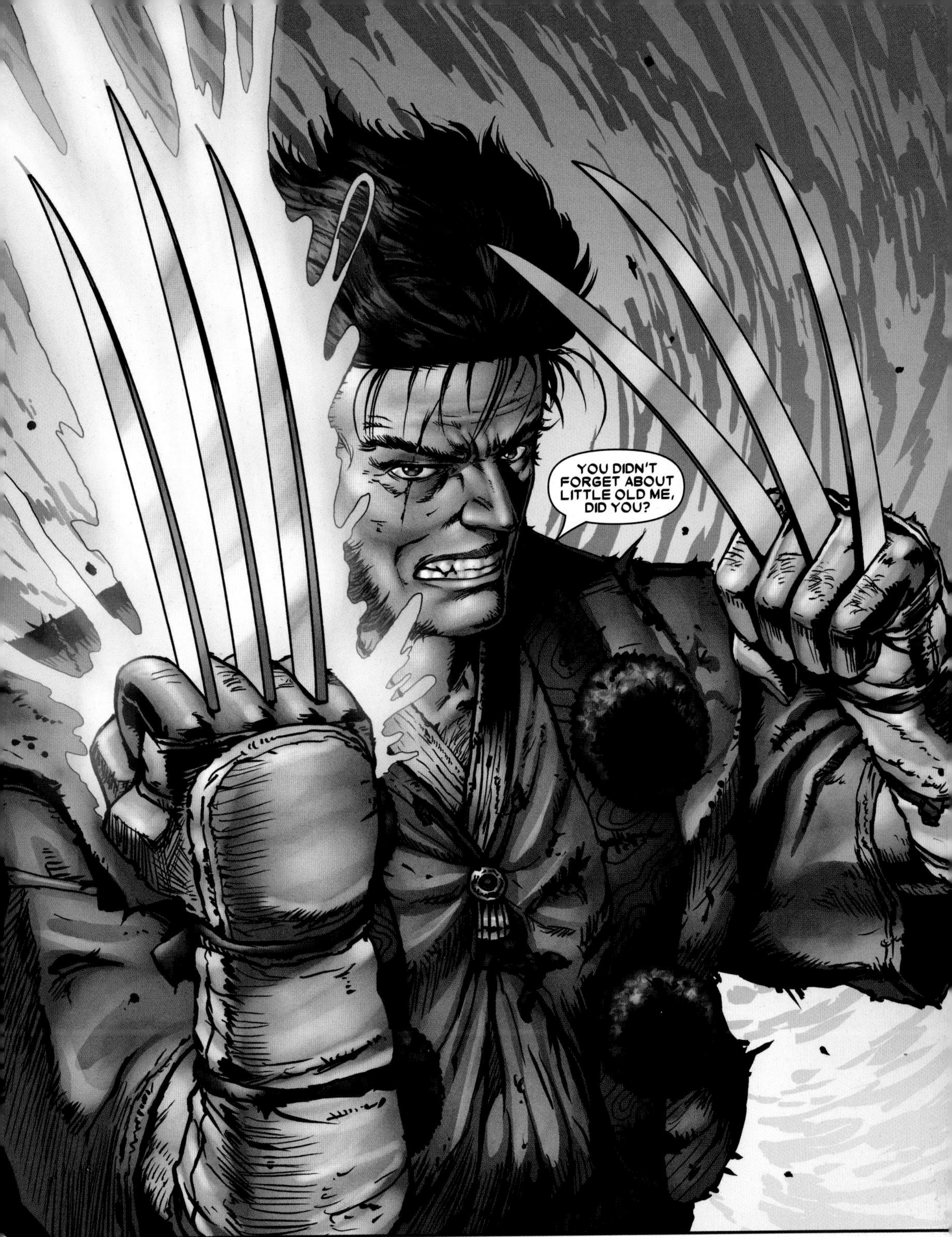
YOU DIDN'T FORGET ABOUT LITTLE OLD ME, DID YOU?

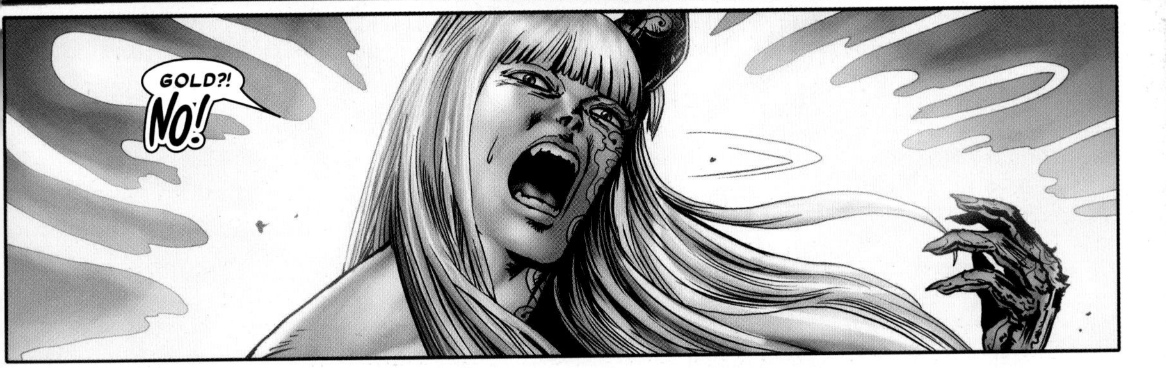
GOLD?! NO!

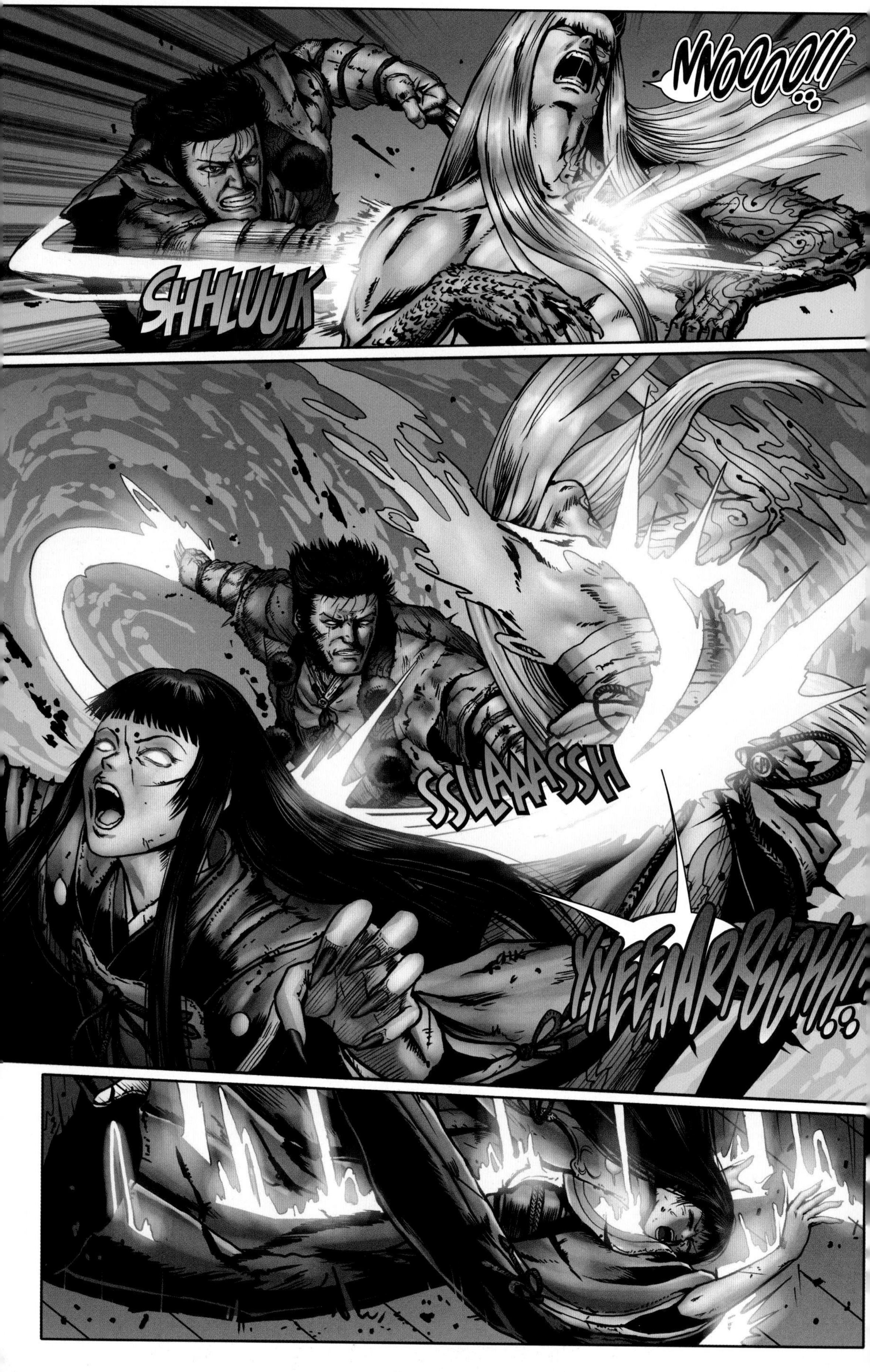
NNOOOOO!!
SHHLUUK
SSLAAASSH
YYEEAARRGGHH!!

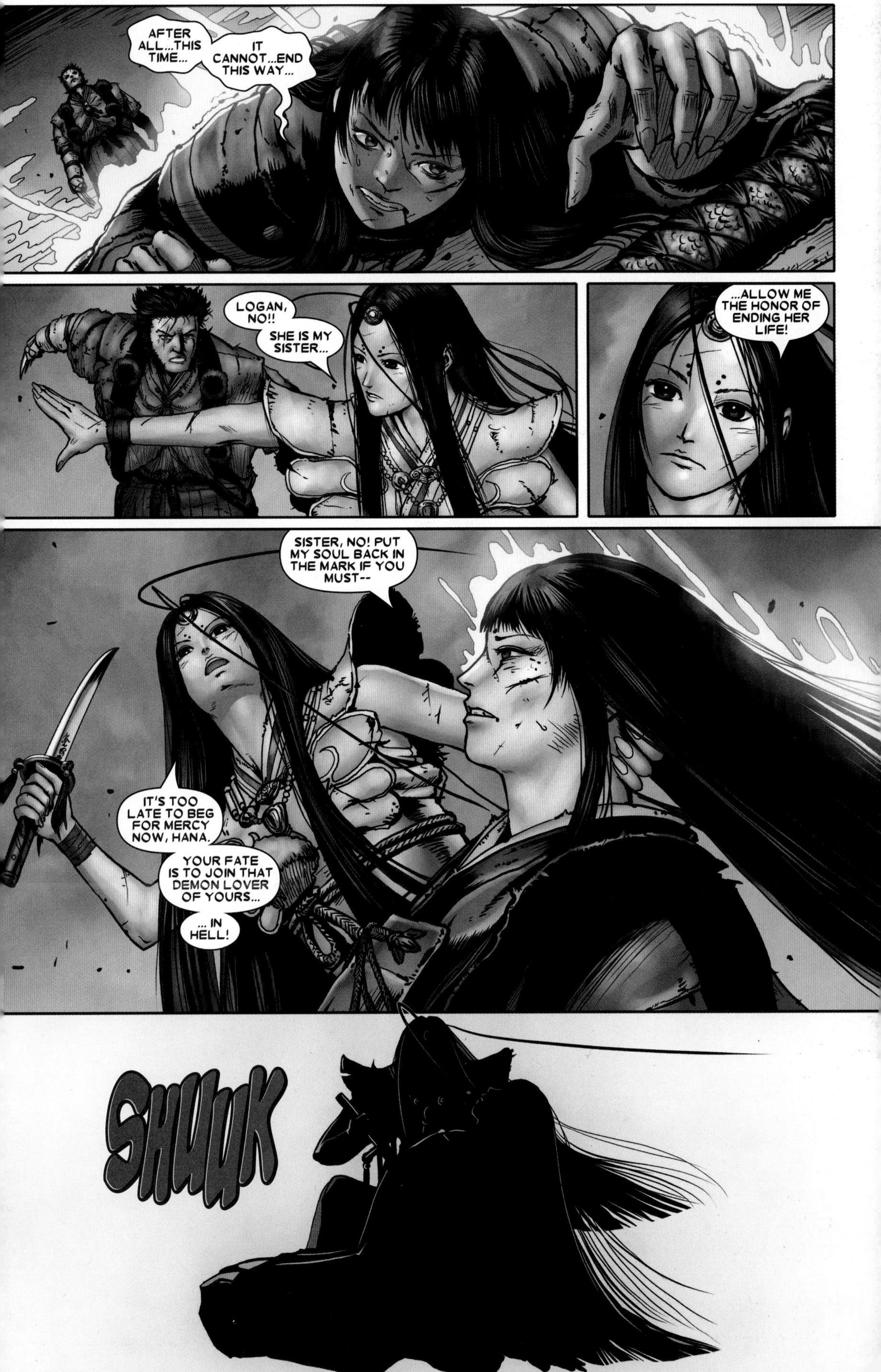
AFTER ALL...THIS TIME...
IT CANNOT...END THIS WAY...
LOGAN, NO!!
SHE IS MY SISTER...
...ALLOW ME THE HONOR OF ENDING HER LIFE!
SISTER, NO! PUT MY SOUL BACK IN THE MARK IF YOU MUST--
IT'S TOO LATE TO BEG FOR MERCY NOW, HANA.
YOUR FATE IS TO JOIN THAT DEMON LOVER OF YOURS...
... IN HELL!
SHUUK

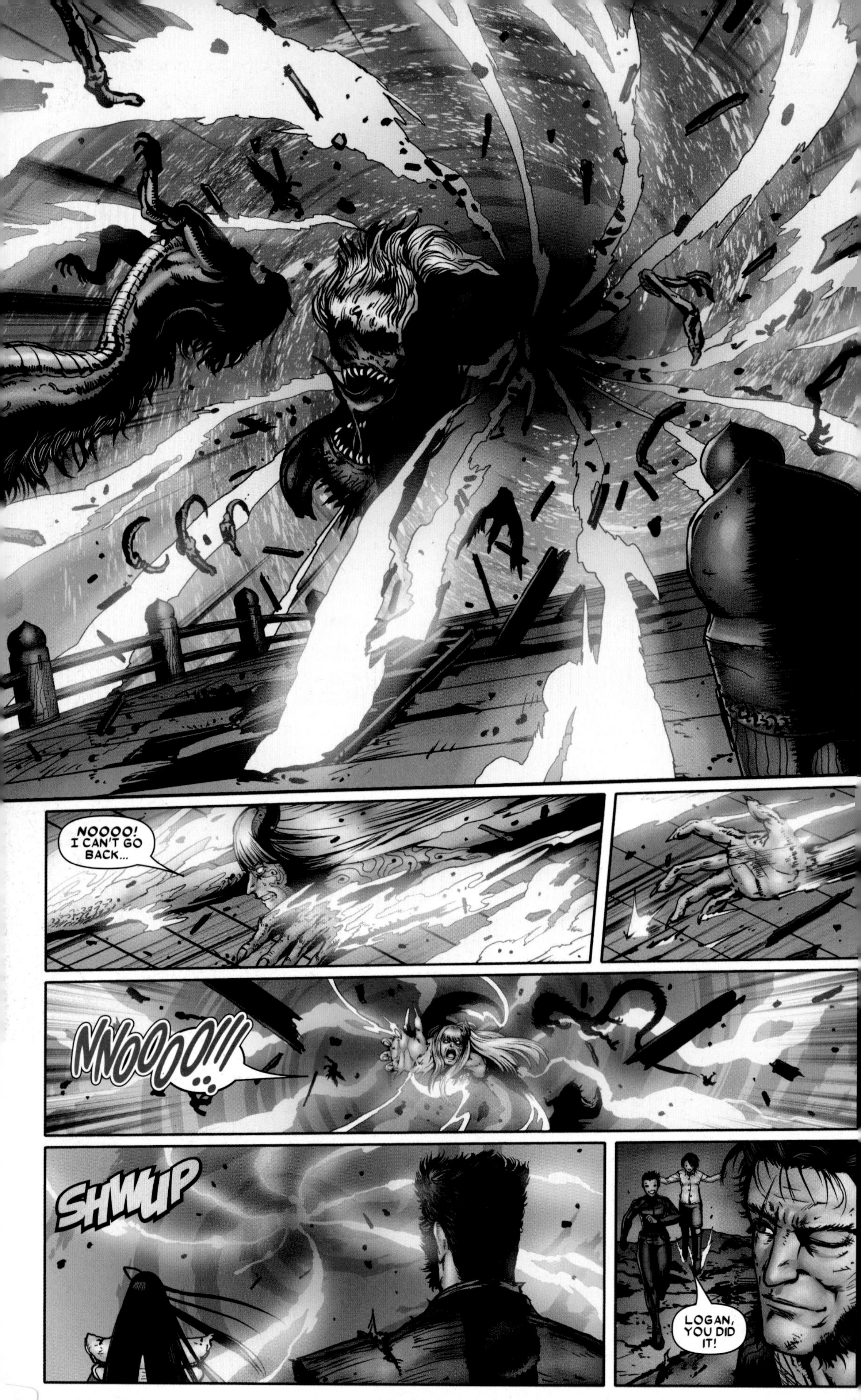
NOOOO! I CAN'T GO BACK...
NNOOOOO!!!
SHWUP
LOGAN, YOU DID IT!

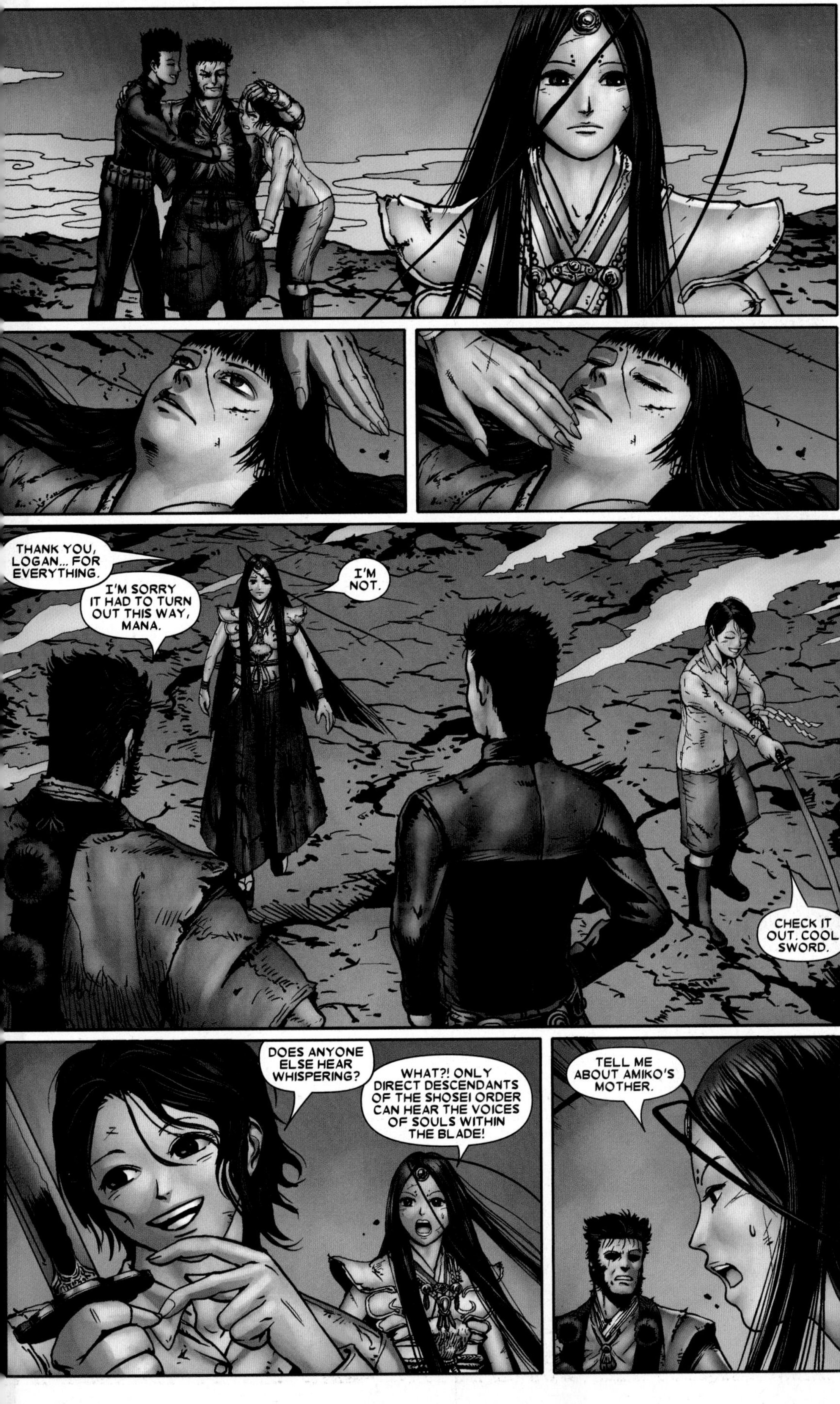
THANK YOU, LOGAN... FOR EVERYTHING.
I'M SORRY IT HAD TO TURN OUT THIS WAY, MANA.
I'M NOT.
CHECK IT OUT. COOL SWORD.
DOES ANYONE ELSE HEAR WHISPERING?
WHAT?! ONLY DIRECT DESCENDANTS OF THE SHOSEI ORDER CAN HEAR THE VOICES OF SOULS WITHIN THE BLADE!
TELL ME ABOUT AMIKO'S MOTHER.

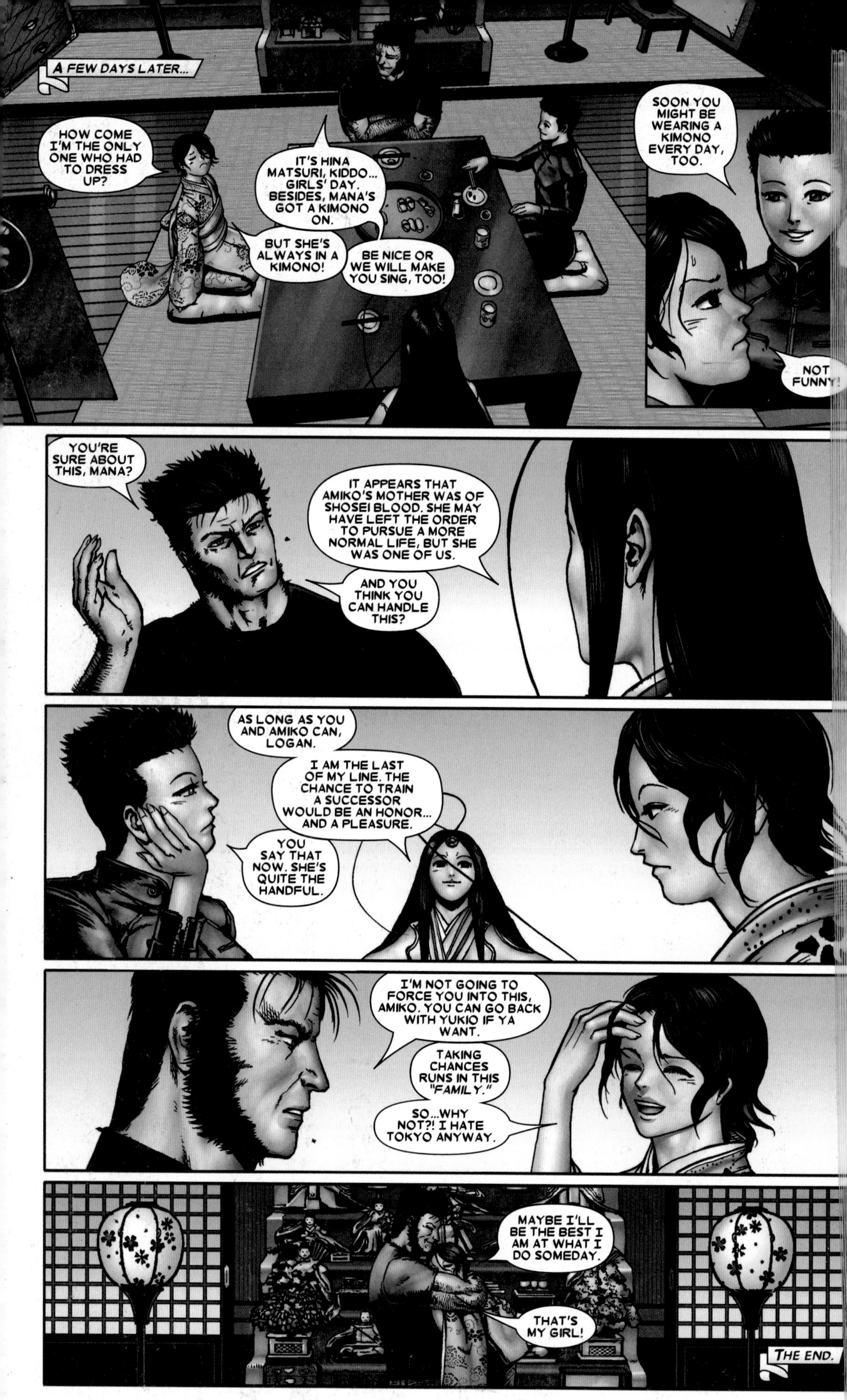
A FEW DAYS LATER...
HOW COME I'M THE ONLY ONE WHO HAD TO DRESS UP?
IT'S HINA MATSURI, KIDDO... GIRLS' DAY. BESIDES, MANA'S GOT A KIMONO ON.
BUT SHE'S ALWAYS IN A KIMONO!
BE NICE OR WE WILL MAKE YOU SING, TOO!
SOON YOU MIGHT BE WEARING A KIMONO EVERY DAY, TOO.
NOT FUNNY!
YOU'RE SURE ABOUT THIS, MANA?
IT APPEARS THAT AMIKO'S MOTHER WAS OF SHOSEI BLOOD. SHE MAY HAVE LEFT THE ORDER TO PURSUE A MORE NORMAL LIFE, BUT SHE WAS ONE OF US.
AND YOU THINK YOU CAN HANDLE THIS?
AS LONG AS YOU AND AMIKO CAN, LOGAN.
I AM THE LAST OF MY LINE. THE CHANCE TO TRAIN A SUCCESSOR WOULD BE AN HONOR... AND A PLEASURE.
YOU SAY THAT NOW. SHE'S QUITE THE HANDFUL.
I'M NOT GOING TO FORCE YOU INTO THIS, AMIKO. YOU CAN GO BACK WITH YUKIO IF YA WANT.
TAKING CHANCES RUNS IN THIS "FAMILY."
SO...WHY NOT?! I HATE TOKYO ANYWAY.
MAYBE I'LL BE THE BEST I AM AT WHAT I DO SOMEDAY.
THAT'S MY GIRL!
THE END.

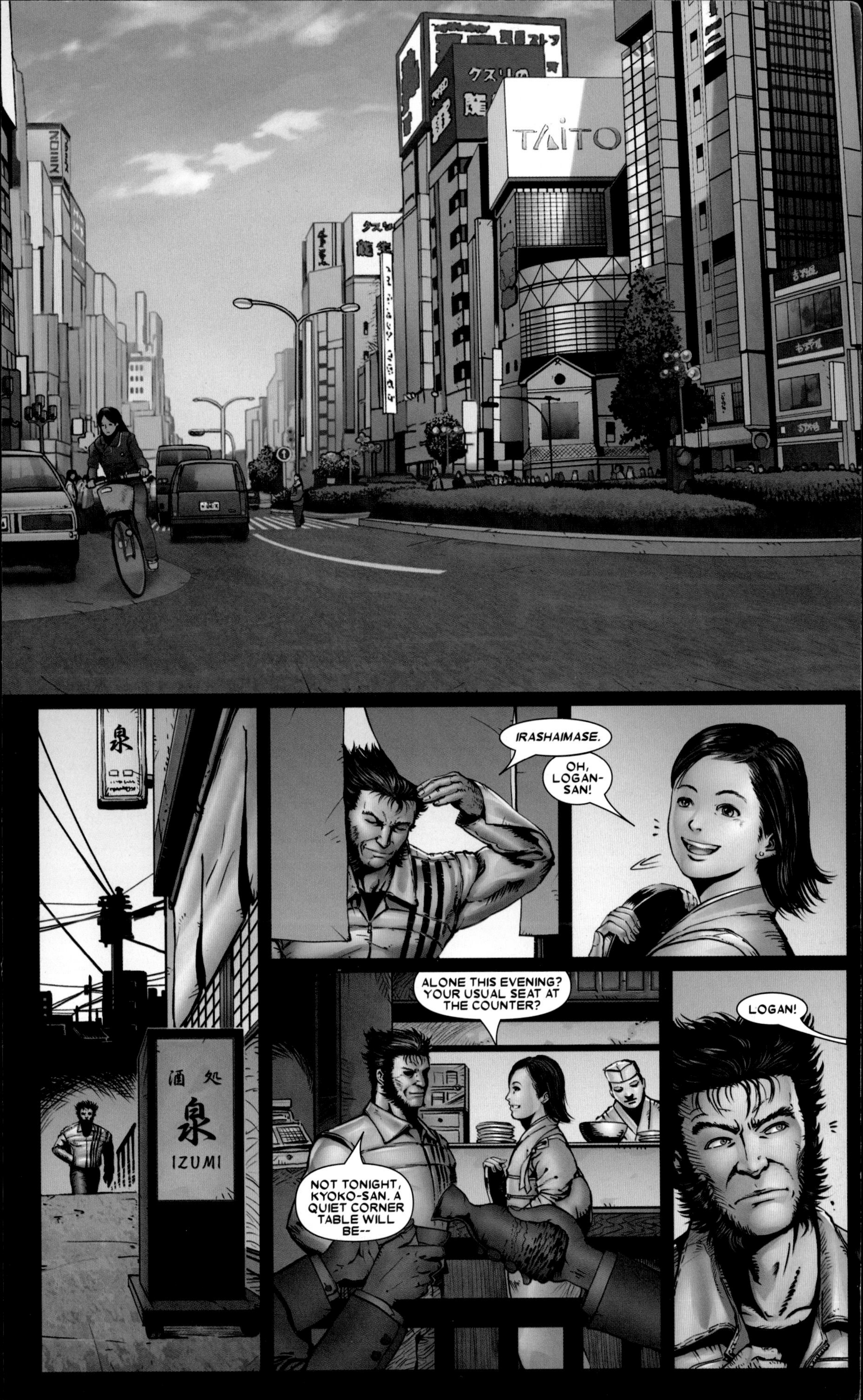
TAITO
酒処
泉
IZUMI
IRASHAIMASE.
OH, LOGAN-SAN!
ALONE THIS EVENING? YOUR USUAL SEAT AT THE COUNTER?
NOT TONIGHT, KYOKO-SAN. A QUIET CORNER TABLE WILL BE--
LOGAN!

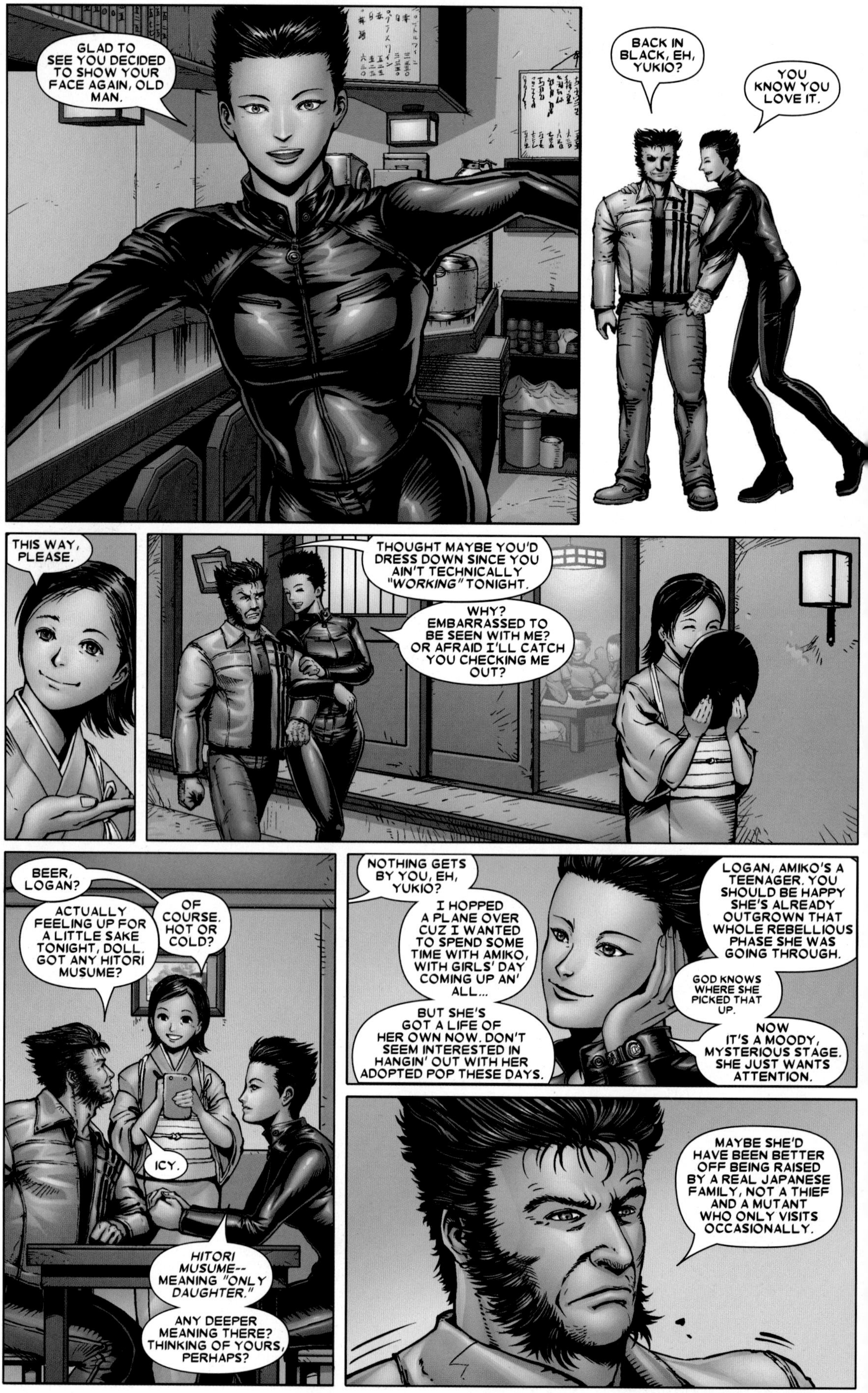
GLAD TO SEE YOU DECIDED TO SHOW YOUR FACE AGAIN, OLD MAN.
BACK IN BLACK, EH, YUKIO?
YOU KNOW YOU LOVE IT.
THIS WAY, PLEASE.
THOUGHT MAYBE YOU'D DRESS DOWN SINCE YOU AIN'T TECHNICALLY "WORKING" TONIGHT.
WHY? EMBARRASSED TO BE SEEN WITH ME? OR AFRAID I'LL CATCH YOU CHECKING ME OUT?
BEER, LOGAN?
ACTUALLY FEELING UP FOR A LITTLE SAKE TONIGHT, DOLL. GOT ANY HITORI MUSUME?
OF COURSE. HOT OR COLD?
ICY.
HITORI MUSUME-- MEANING "ONLY DAUGHTER."
ANY DEEPER MEANING THERE? THINKING OF YOURS, PERHAPS?
NOTHING GETS BY YOU, EH, YUKIO?
I HOPPED A PLANE OVER CUZ I WANTED TO SPEND SOME TIME WITH AMIKO, WITH GIRLS' DAY COMING UP AN' ALL...
BUT SHE'S GOT A LIFE OF HER OWN NOW. DON'T SEEM INTERESTED IN HANGIN' OUT WITH HER ADOPTED POP THESE DAYS.
LOGAN, AMIKO'S A TEENAGER. YOU SHOULD BE HAPPY SHE'S ALREADY OUTGROWN THAT WHOLE REBELLIOUS PHASE SHE WAS GOING THROUGH.
GOD KNOWS WHERE SHE PICKED THAT UP.
NOW IT'S A MOODY, MYSTERIOUS STAGE. SHE JUST WANTS ATTENTION.
MAYBE SHE'D HAVE BEEN BETTER OFF BEING RAISED BY A REAL JAPANESE FAMILY, NOT A THIEF AND A MUTANT WHO ONLY VISITS OCCASIONALLY.

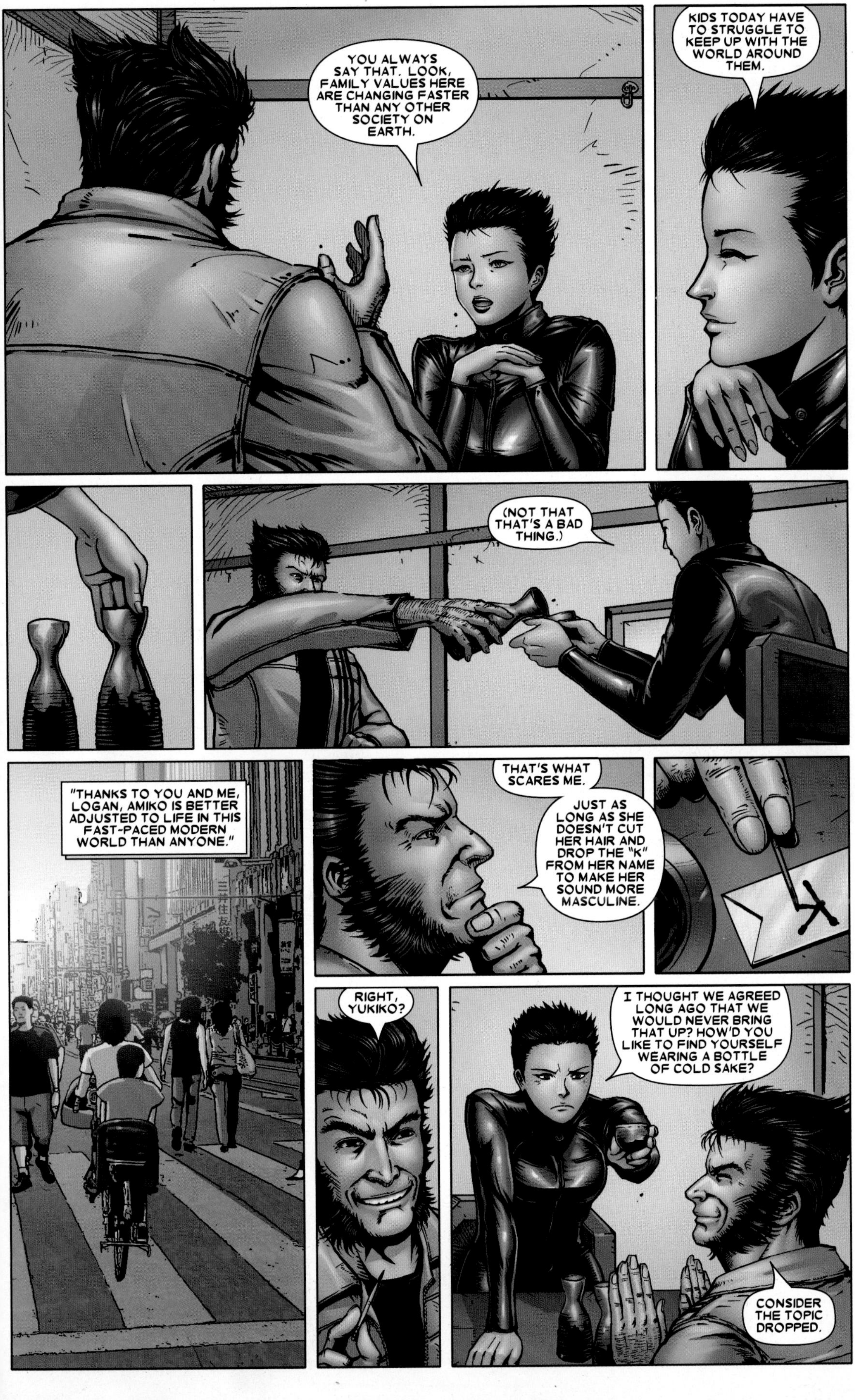

YOU ALWAYS SAY THAT. LOOK, FAMILY VALUES HERE ARE CHANGING FASTER THAN ANY OTHER SOCIETY ON EARTH.
KIDS TODAY HAVE TO STRUGGLE TO KEEP UP WITH THE WORLD AROUND THEM.
(NOT THAT THAT'S A BAD THING.)
"THANKS TO YOU AND ME, LOGAN, AMIKO IS BETTER ADJUSTED TO LIFE IN THIS FAST-PACED MODERN WORLD THAN ANYONE."
THAT'S WHAT SCARES ME.
JUST AS LONG AS SHE DOESN'T CUT HER HAIR AND DROP THE "K" FROM HER NAME TO MAKE HER SOUND MORE MASCULINE.
RIGHT, YUKIKO?
I THOUGHT WE AGREED LONG AGO THAT WE WOULD NEVER BRING THAT UP? HOW'D YOU LIKE TO FIND YOURSELF WEARING A BOTTLE OF COLD SAKE?
CONSIDER THE TOPIC DROPPED.

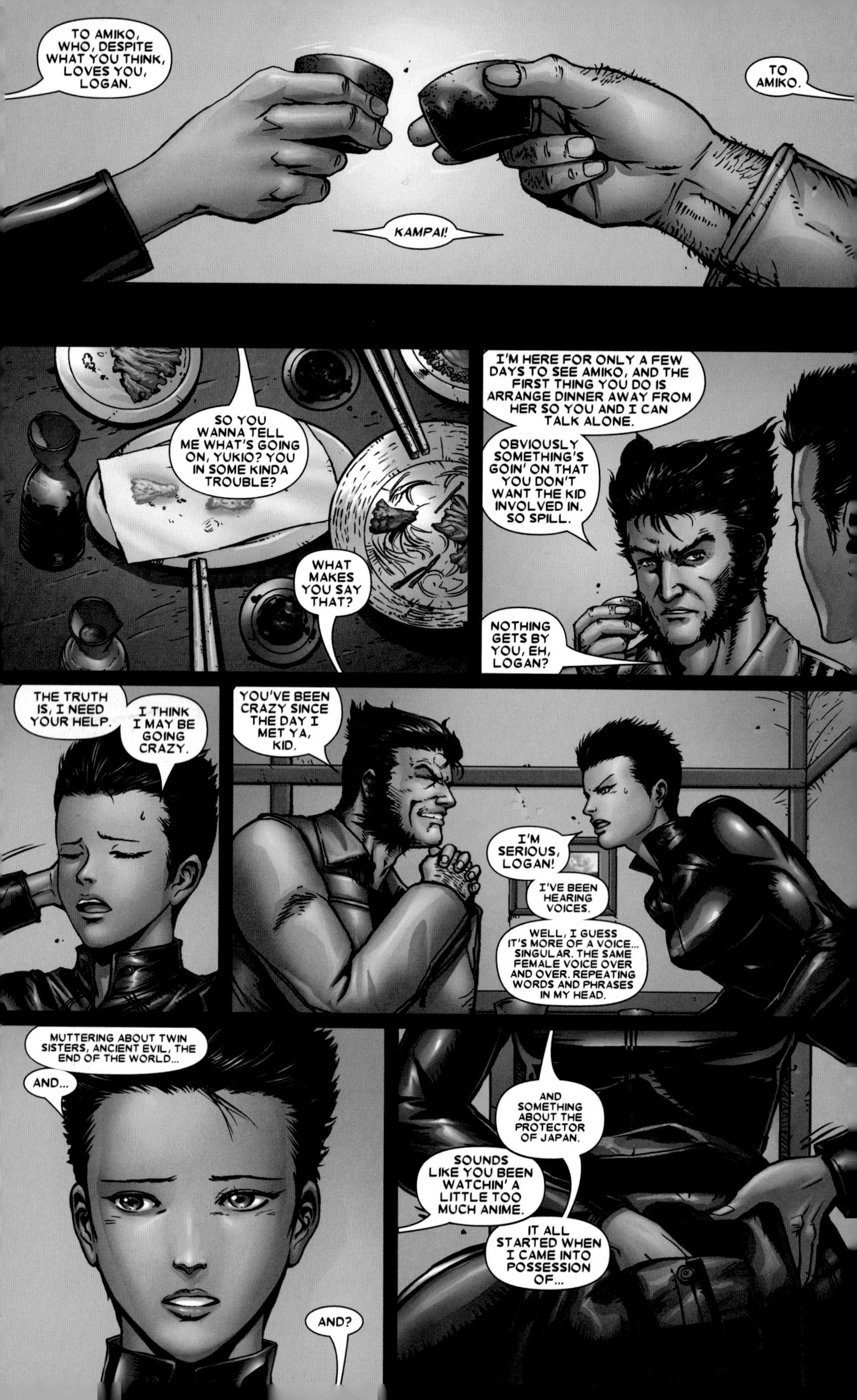
TO AMIKO, WHO, DESPITE WHAT YOU THINK, LOVES YOU, LOGAN.
TO AMIKO.
KAMPAI!
SO YOU WANNA TELL ME WHAT'S GOING ON, YUKIO? YOU IN SOME KINDA TROUBLE?
WHAT MAKES YOU SAY THAT?
I'M HERE FOR ONLY A FEW DAYS TO SEE AMIKO, AND THE FIRST THING YOU DO IS ARRANGE DINNER AWAY FROM HER SO YOU AND I CAN TALK ALONE.
OBVIOUSLY SOMETHING'S GOIN' ON THAT YOU DON'T WANT THE KID INVOLVED IN. SO SPILL.
NOTHING GETS BY YOU, EH, LOGAN?
THE TRUTH IS, I NEED YOUR HELP.
I THINK I MAY BE GOING CRAZY.
YOU'VE BEEN CRAZY SINCE THE DAY I MET YA, KID.
I'M SERIOUS, LOGAN!
I'VE BEEN HEARING VOICES.
WELL, I GUESS IT'S MORE OF A VOICE... SINGULAR. THE SAME FEMALE VOICE OVER AND OVER. REPEATING WORDS AND PHRASES IN MY HEAD.
MUTTERING ABOUT TWIN SISTERS, ANCIENT EVIL, THE END OF THE WORLD...
AND...
AND?
AND SOMETHING ABOUT THE PROTECTOR OF JAPAN.
SOUNDS LIKE YOU BEEN WATCHIN' A LITTLE TOO MUCH ANIME.
IT ALL STARTED WHEN I CAME INTO POSSESSION OF...

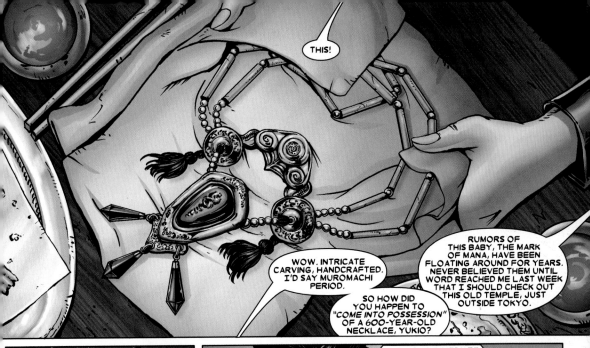

THIS!

WOW. INTRICATE CARVING, HANDCRAFTED. I'D SAY MUROMACHI PERIOD.

RUMORS OF THIS BABY, THE MARK OF MANA, HAVE BEEN FLOATING AROUND FOR YEARS. NEVER BELIEVED THEM UNTIL WORD REACHED ME LAST WEEK THAT I SHOULD CHECK OUT THIS OLD TEMPLE, JUST OUTSIDE TOKYO.

SO HOW DID YOU HAPPEN TO *"COME INTO POSSESSION"* OF A 600-YEAR-OLD NECKLACE, YUKIO?

"I'M NOT A BIG FAN OF VENTURING BEYOND TOKYO CITY LIMITS, BUT THE SOURCE WAS SOLID, SO I TOOK A CHANCE. AND THERE IT WAS."

AND YOUR IMMEDIATE SOLUTION TO THIS PROBLEM IS TO TELL ME BECAUSE...?

C'MON, LOGAN...WHO ELSE AM I GONNA TURN TO? AND YOU KNOW MORE ABOUT THIS MYSTICAL MUMBO-JUMBO THAN ANYONE ELSE I KNOW.

WHAT ABOUT ONE OF THESE JAPANESE HERO TYPES?

MAYBE YOU SHOULD CALL SUNFIRE. OR THE SILVER SAMURAI.

YEAH, RIGHT. I'M SURE THEY'D RUSH TO THE AID OF A THIEF LIKE ME.

"I GRABBED THE NECKLACE AND ESCAPED FROM THESE BUDDHIST WARRIOR MONKS WHO WERE PROTECTING IT...

"AND THAT'S WHEN THE VOICES STARTED."

IF ANYONE CAN HELP ME, IT'S YOU.

PLEASE.

WHY DO I GET THE FEELING I'M GOING TO REGRET THIS?

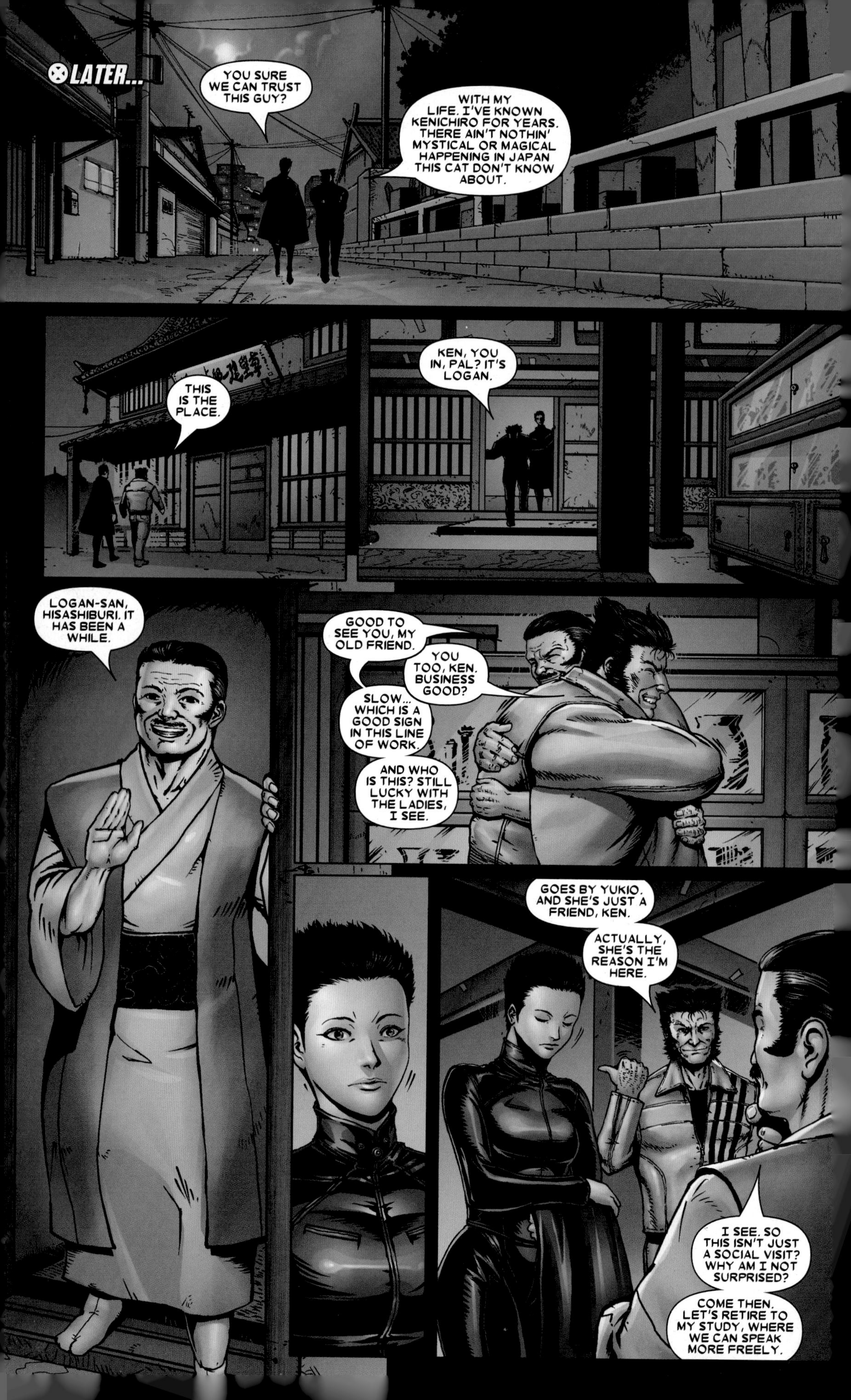
LATER...
YOU SURE WE CAN TRUST THIS GUY?
WITH MY LIFE. I'VE KNOWN KENICHIRO FOR YEARS. THERE AIN'T NOTHIN' MYSTICAL OR MAGICAL HAPPENING IN JAPAN THIS CAT DON'T KNOW ABOUT.
THIS IS THE PLACE.
KEN, YOU IN, PAL? IT'S LOGAN.
LOGAN-SAN, HISASHIBURI. IT HAS BEEN A WHILE.
GOOD TO SEE YOU, MY OLD FRIEND.
YOU TOO, KEN. BUSINESS GOOD?
SLOW... WHICH IS A GOOD SIGN IN THIS LINE OF WORK.
AND WHO IS THIS? STILL LUCKY WITH THE LADIES, I SEE.
GOES BY YUKIO. AND SHE'S JUST A FRIEND, KEN.
ACTUALLY, SHE'S THE REASON I'M HERE.
I SEE. SO THIS ISN'T JUST A SOCIAL VISIT? WHY AM I NOT SURPRISED?
COME THEN. LET'S RETIRE TO MY STUDY, WHERE WE CAN SPEAK MORE FREELY.

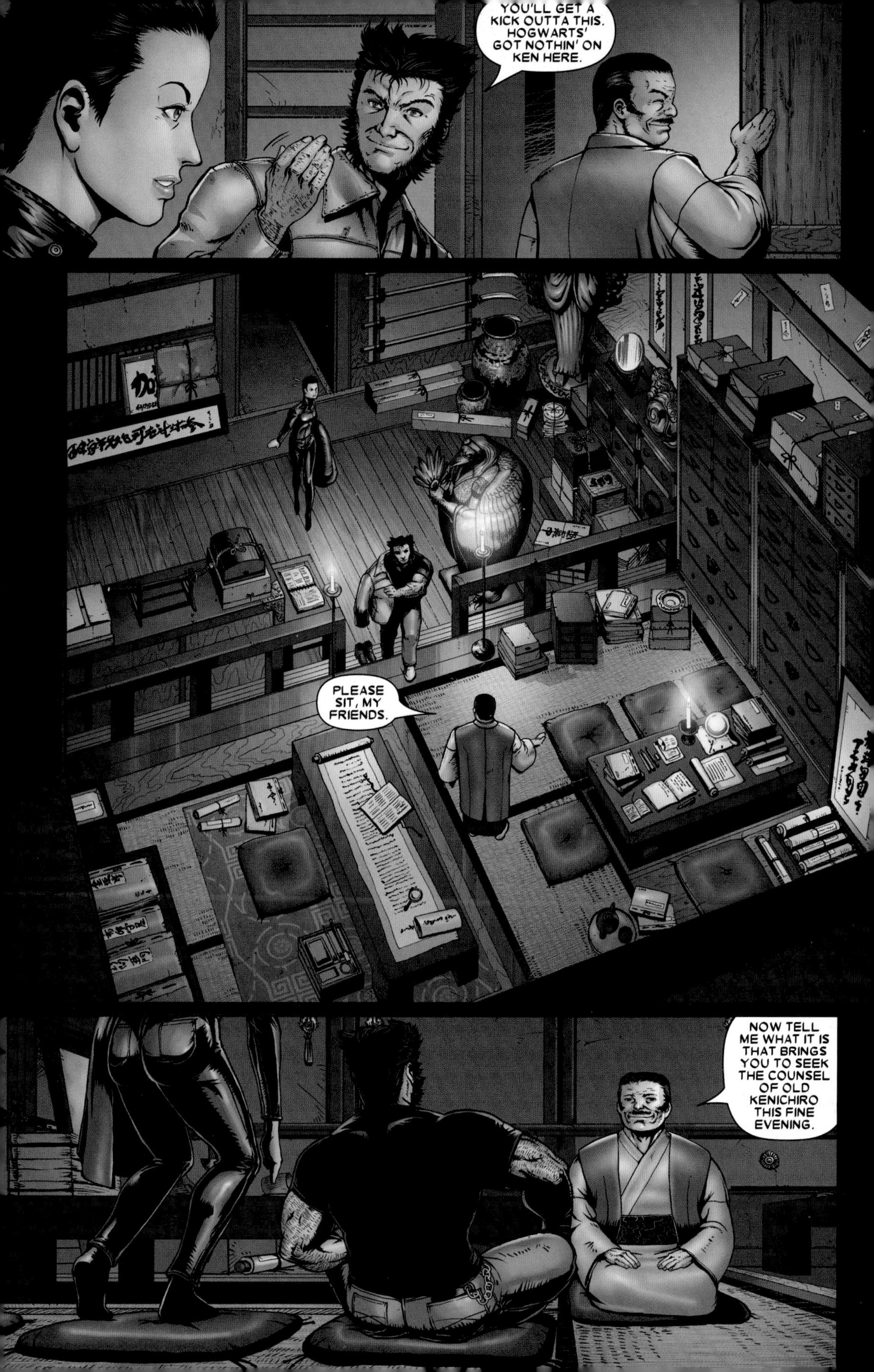

YOU'LL GET A KICK OUTTA THIS. HOGWARTS' GOT NOTHIN' ON KEN HERE.
PLEASE SIT, MY FRIENDS.
NOW TELL ME WHAT IT IS THAT BRINGS YOU TO SEEK THE COUNSEL OF OLD KENICHIRO THIS FINE EVENING.

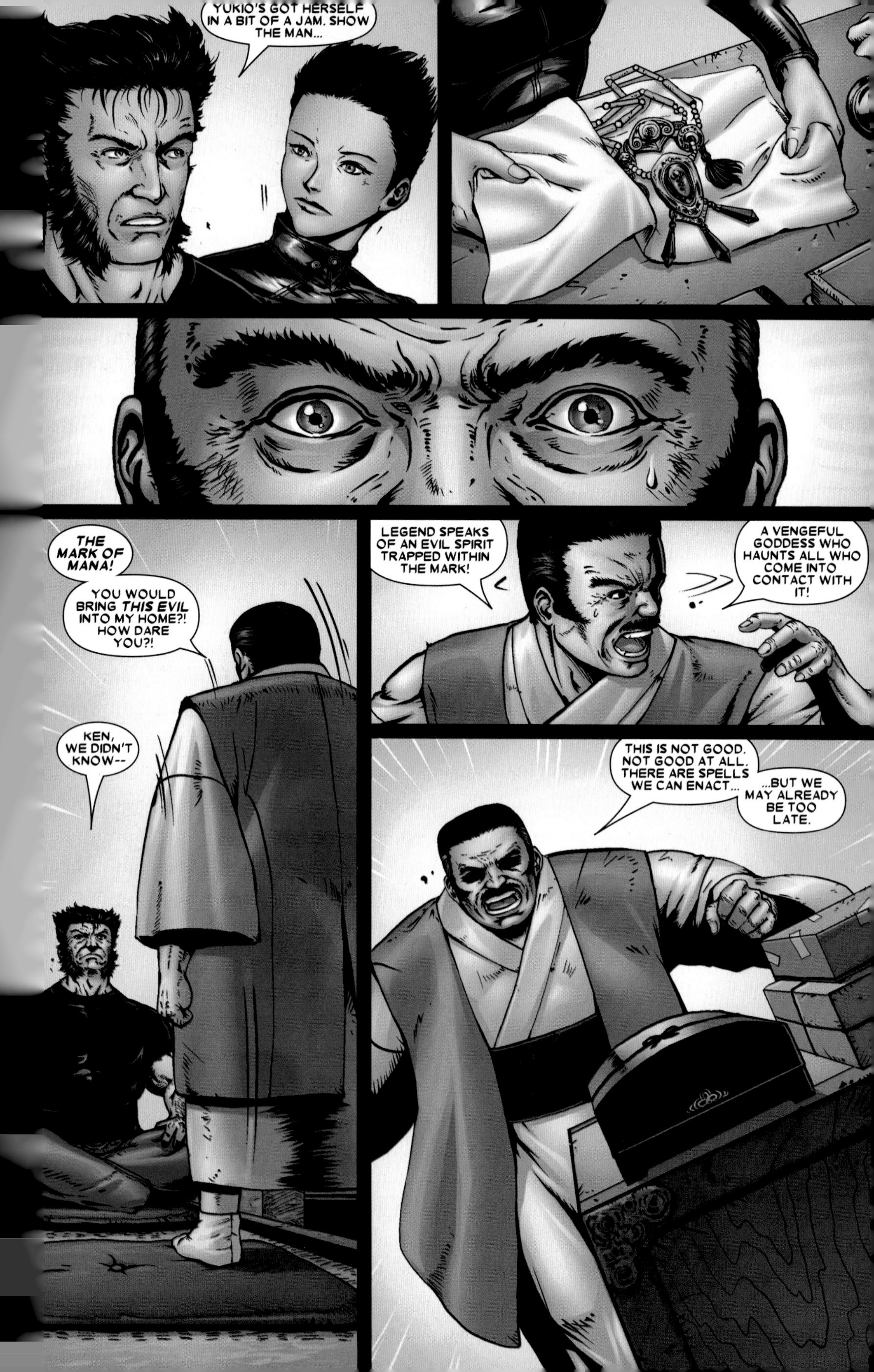
YUKIO'S GOT HERSELF IN A BIT OF A JAM. SHOW THE MAN...
THE MARK OF MANA!
YOU WOULD BRING THIS EVIL INTO MY HOME?! HOW DARE YOU?!
KEN, WE DIDN'T KNOW--
LEGEND SPEAKS OF AN EVIL SPIRIT TRAPPED WITHIN THE MARK!
A VENGEFUL GODDESS WHO HAUNTS ALL WHO COME INTO CONTACT WITH IT!
THIS IS NOT GOOD. NOT GOOD AT ALL. THERE ARE SPELLS WE CAN ENACT...
...BUT WE MAY ALREADY BE TOO LATE.

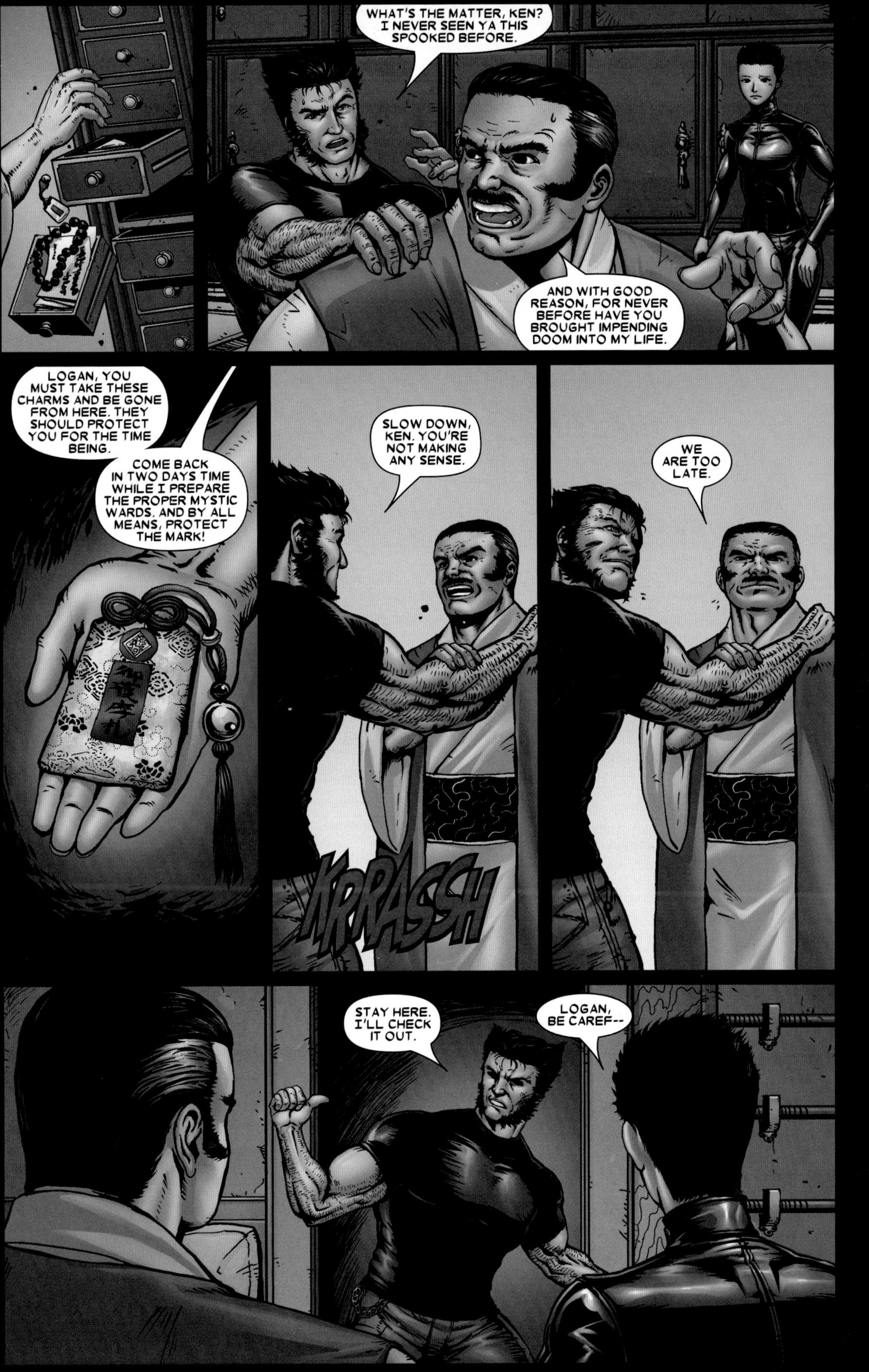

WHAT'S THE MATTER, KEN? I NEVER SEEN YA THIS SPOOKED BEFORE.
AND WITH GOOD REASON, FOR NEVER BEFORE HAVE YOU BROUGHT IMPENDING DOOM INTO MY LIFE.
LOGAN, YOU MUST TAKE THESE CHARMS AND BE GONE FROM HERE. THEY SHOULD PROTECT YOU FOR THE TIME BEING.
COME BACK IN TWO DAYS TIME WHILE I PREPARE THE PROPER MYSTIC WARDS. AND BY ALL MEANS, PROTECT THE MARK!
SLOW DOWN, KEN. YOU'RE NOT MAKING ANY SENSE.
KRRASSH
WE ARE TOO LATE.
STAY HERE. I'LL CHECK IT OUT.
LOGAN, BE CAREF--

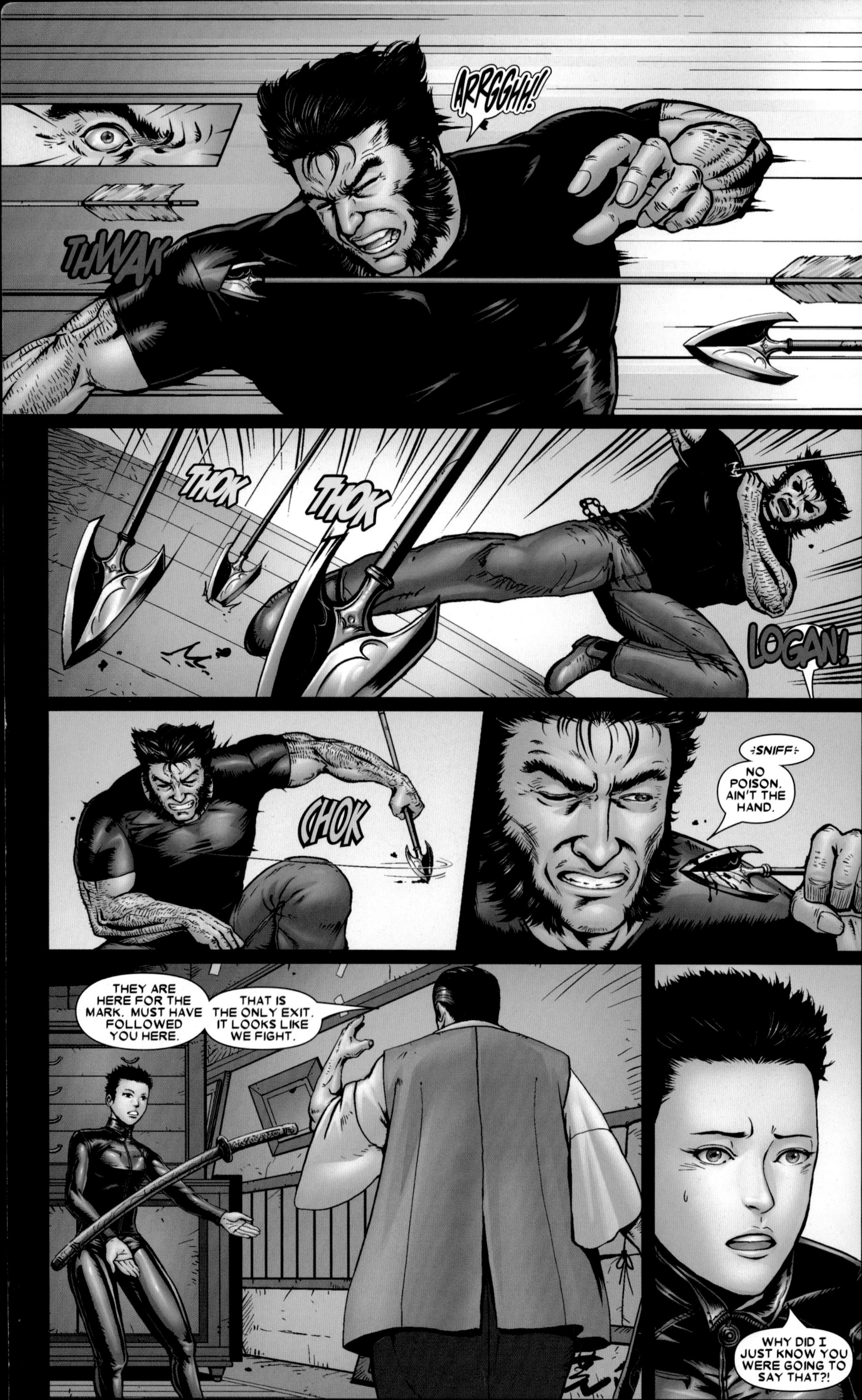
ARRGGHH!
THWAK
THOK
THOK
LOGAN!
CHOK
SNIFF
NO POISON. AIN'T THE HAND.
THEY ARE HERE FOR THE MARK. MUST HAVE FOLLOWED YOU HERE.
THAT IS THE ONLY EXIT. IT LOOKS LIKE WE FIGHT.
WHY DID I JUST KNOW YOU WERE GOING TO SAY THAT?!

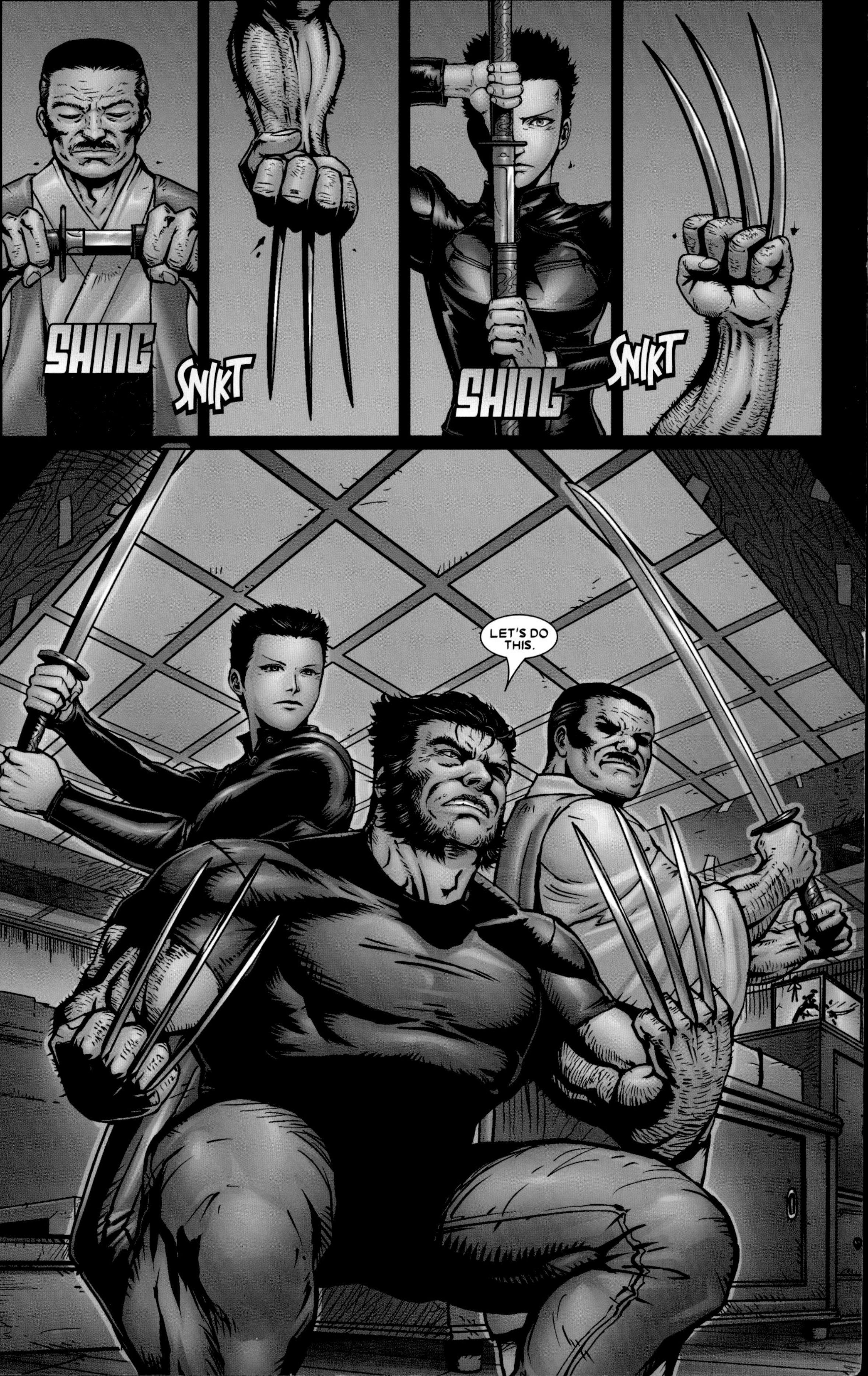
SHING
SNIKT
SHING
SNIKT
LET'S DO THIS.

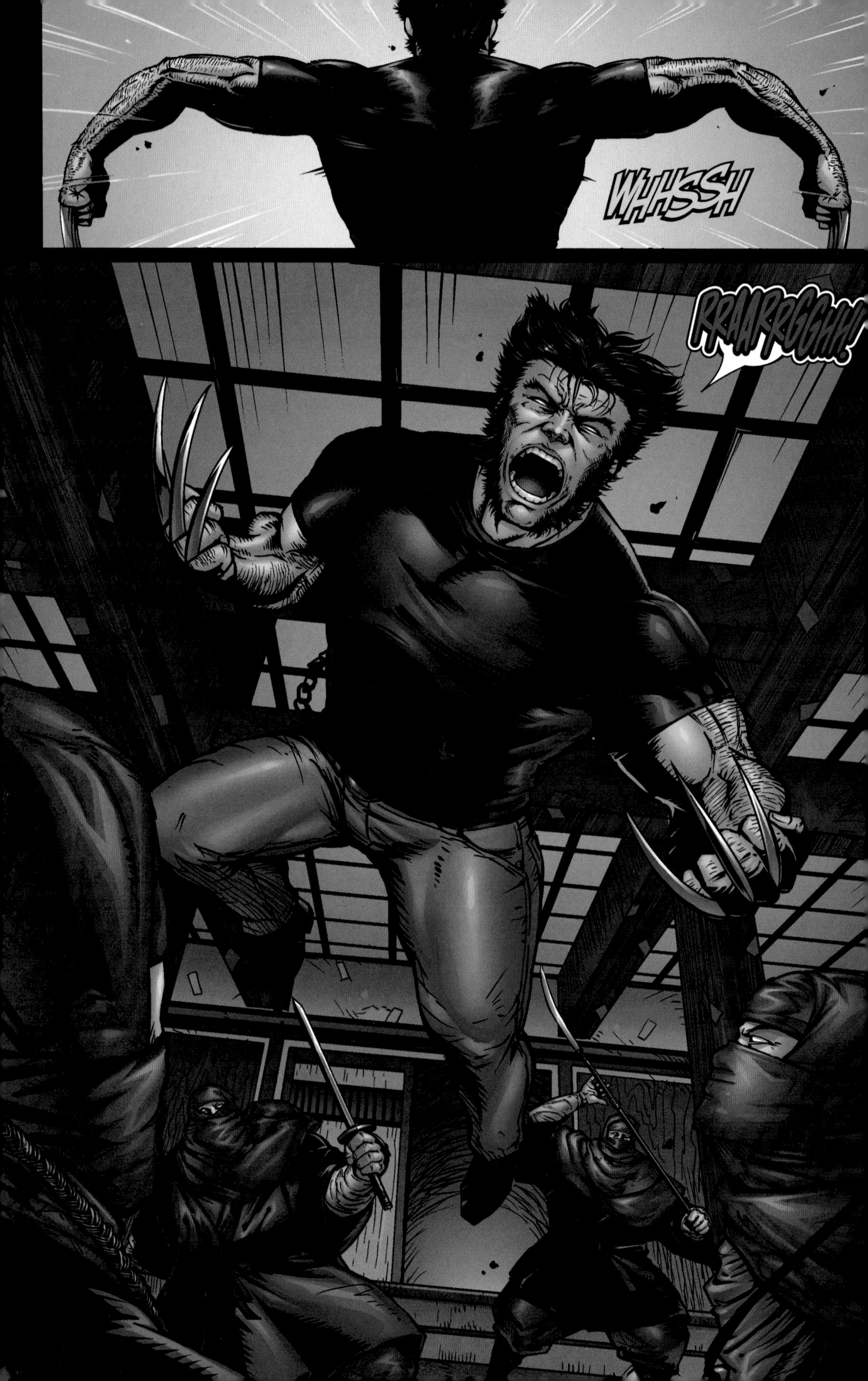
WHHSSH
RRAAARRGGHH!

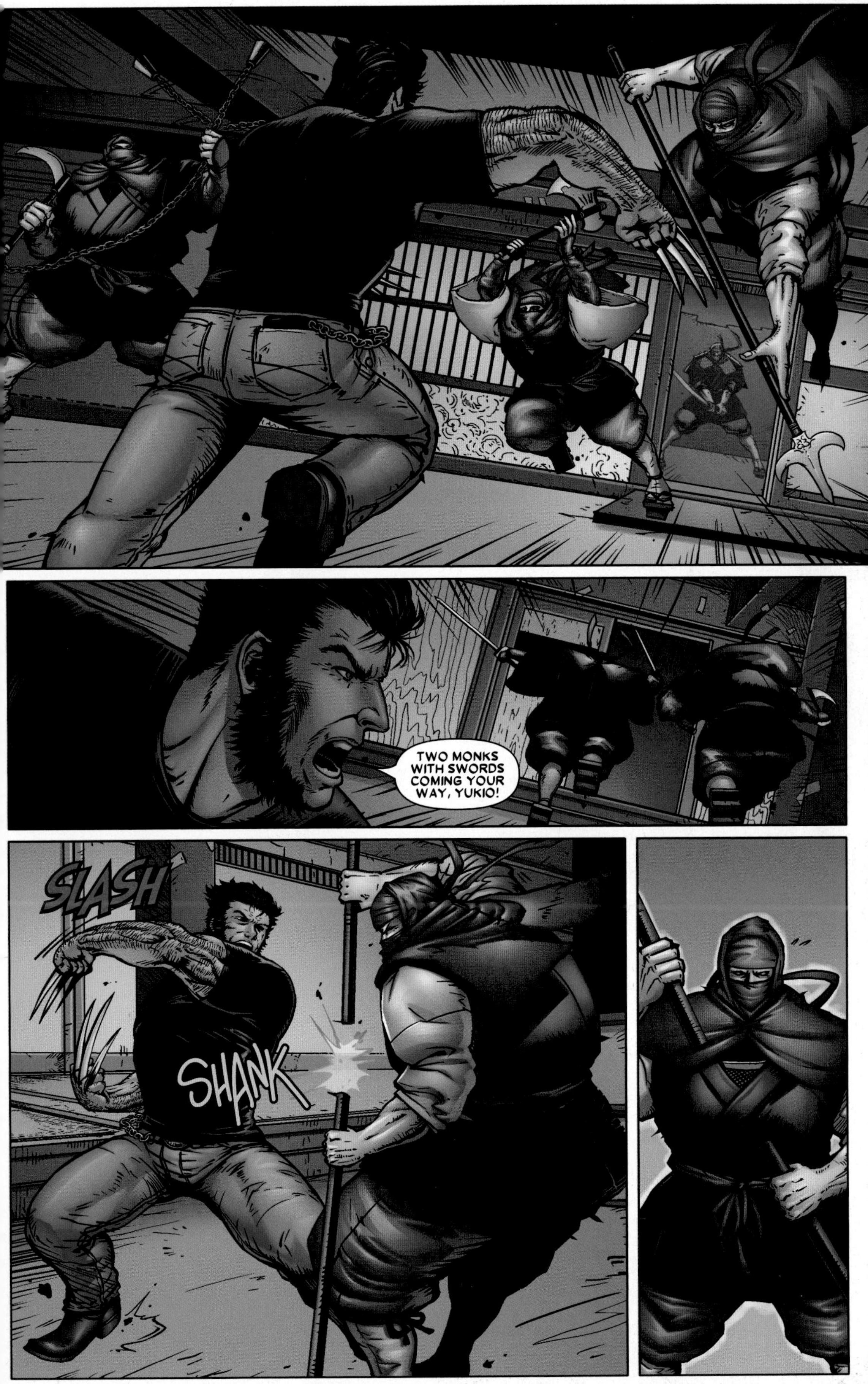
TWO MONKS WITH SWORDS COMING YOUR WAY, YUKIO!
SLASH
SHANK

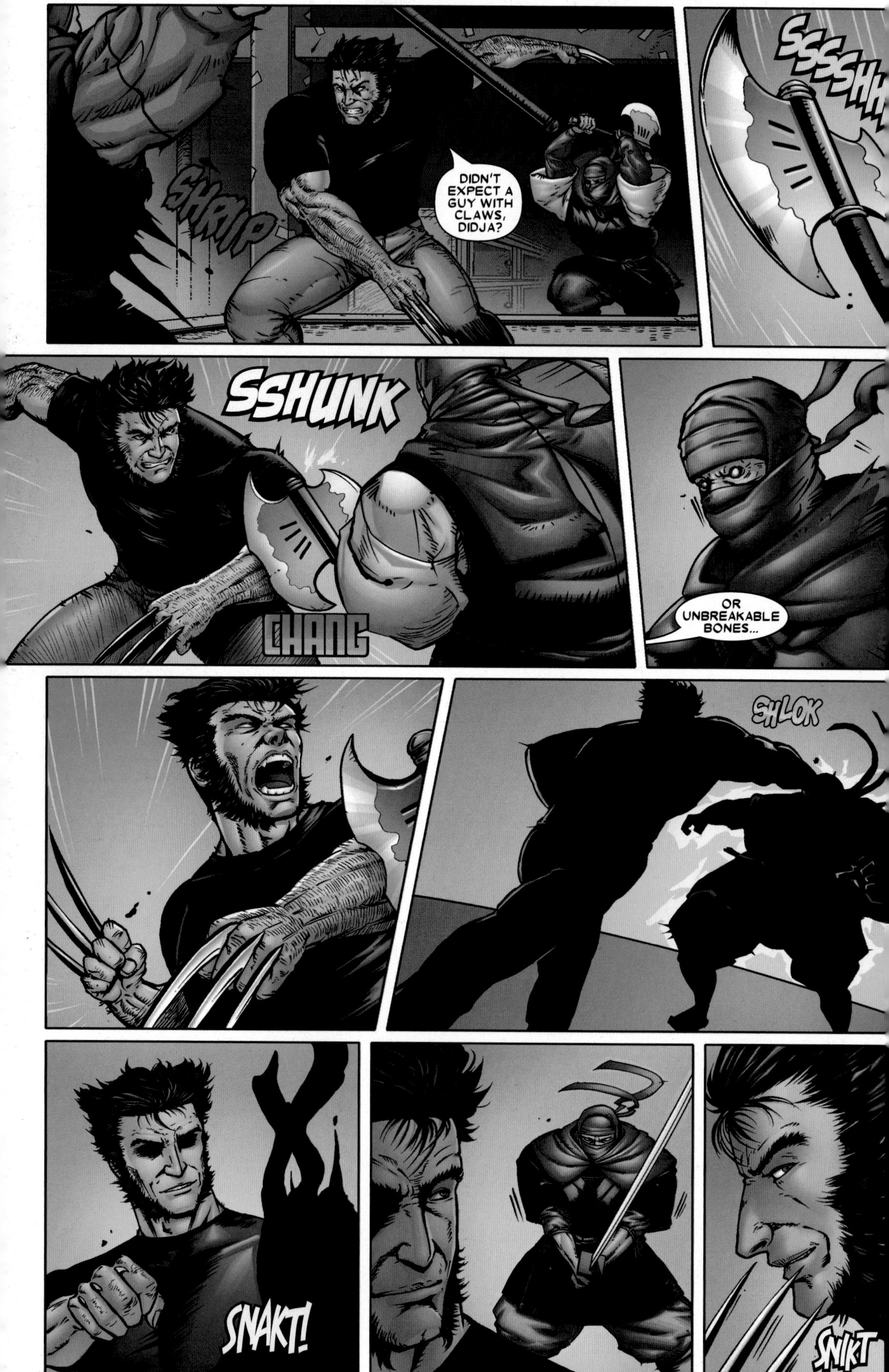
DIDN'T EXPECT A GUY WITH CLAWS, DIDJA?
SHRIP
SSSSHH
SSHUNK
CHANG
OR UNBREAKABLE BONES...
SHLOK
SNAKT!
SNIKT

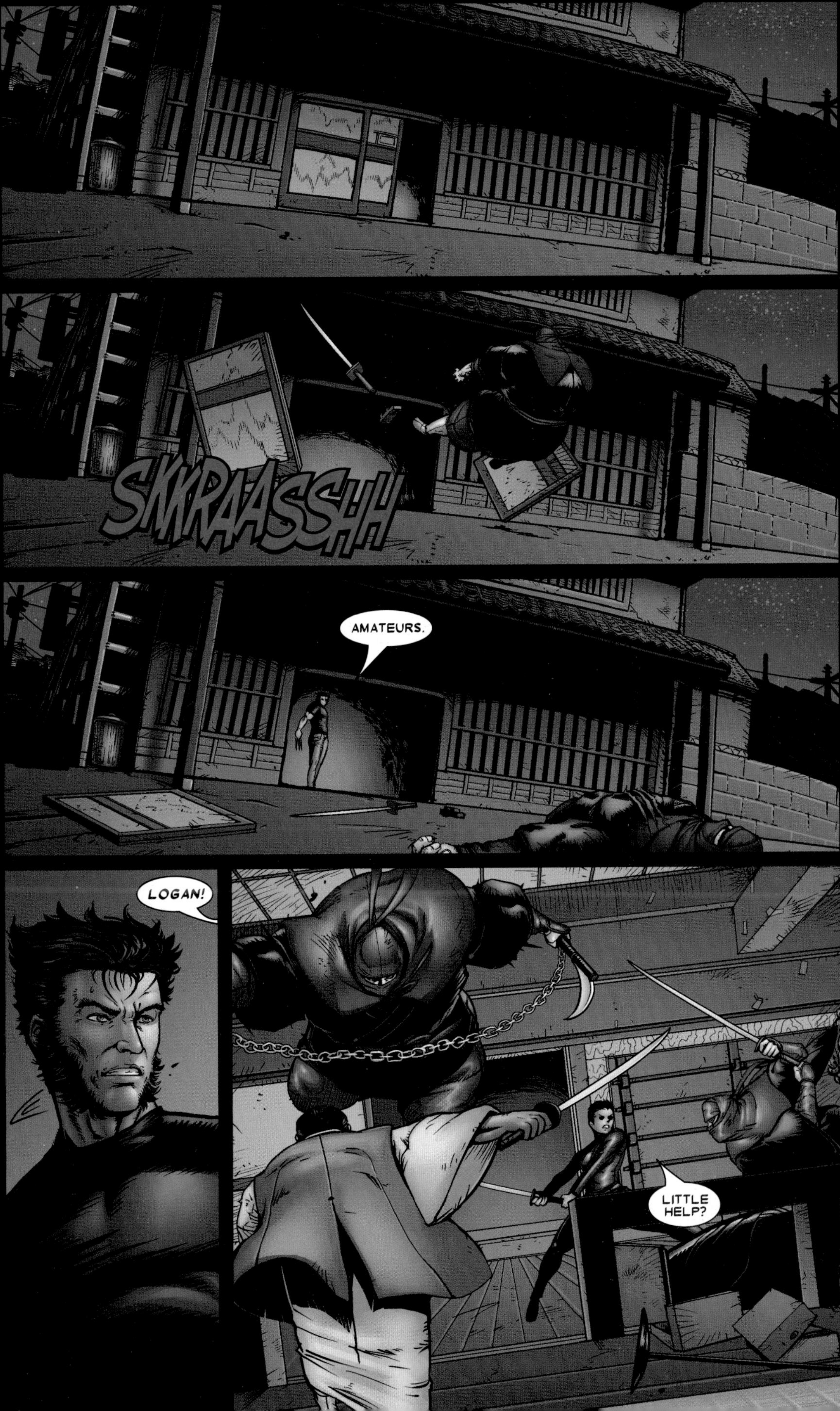
SKKRAASSHH
AMATEURS.
LOGAN!
LITTLE HELP?

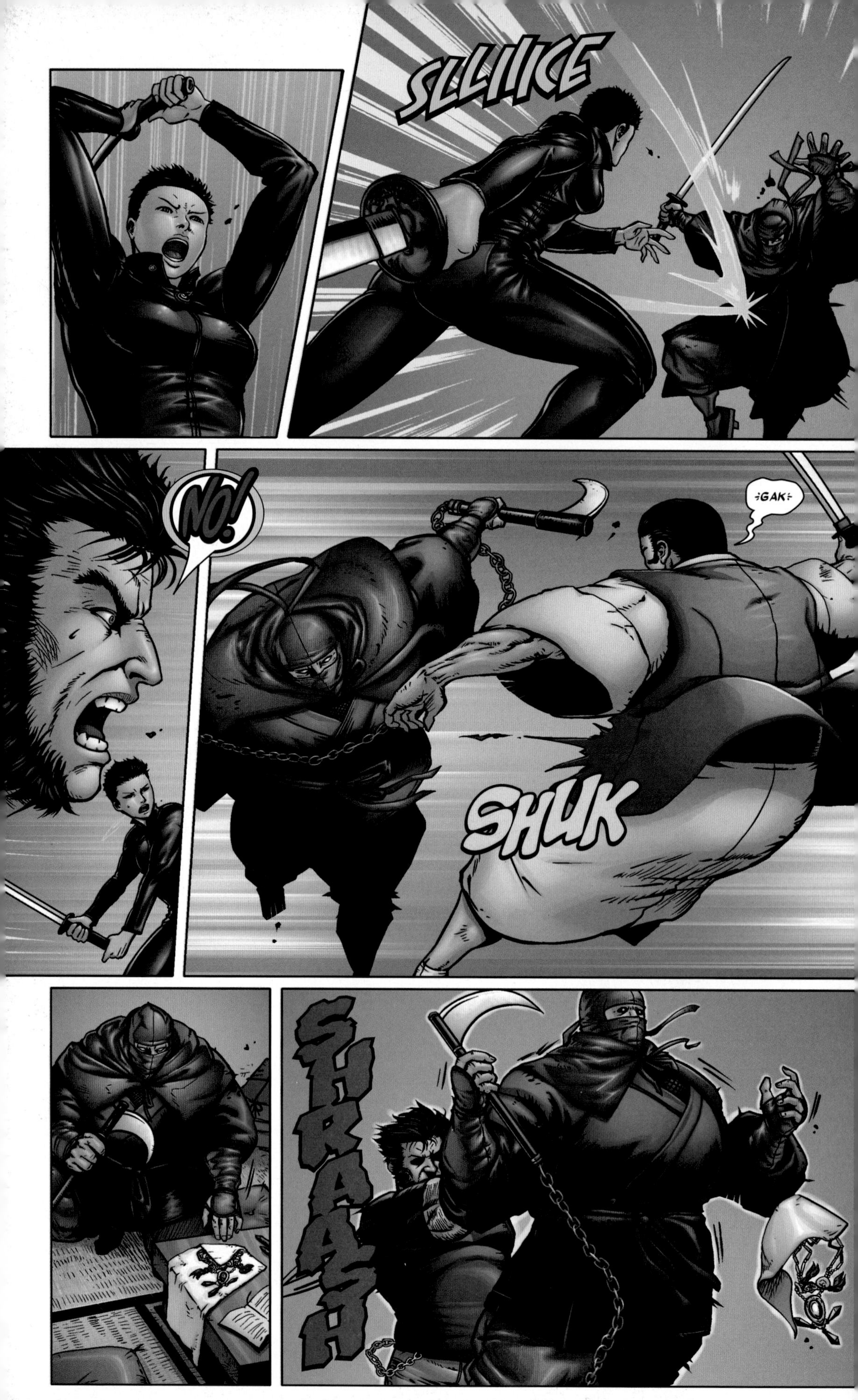
SLLIIICE
NO!
GAK
SHUK
SHRAASH

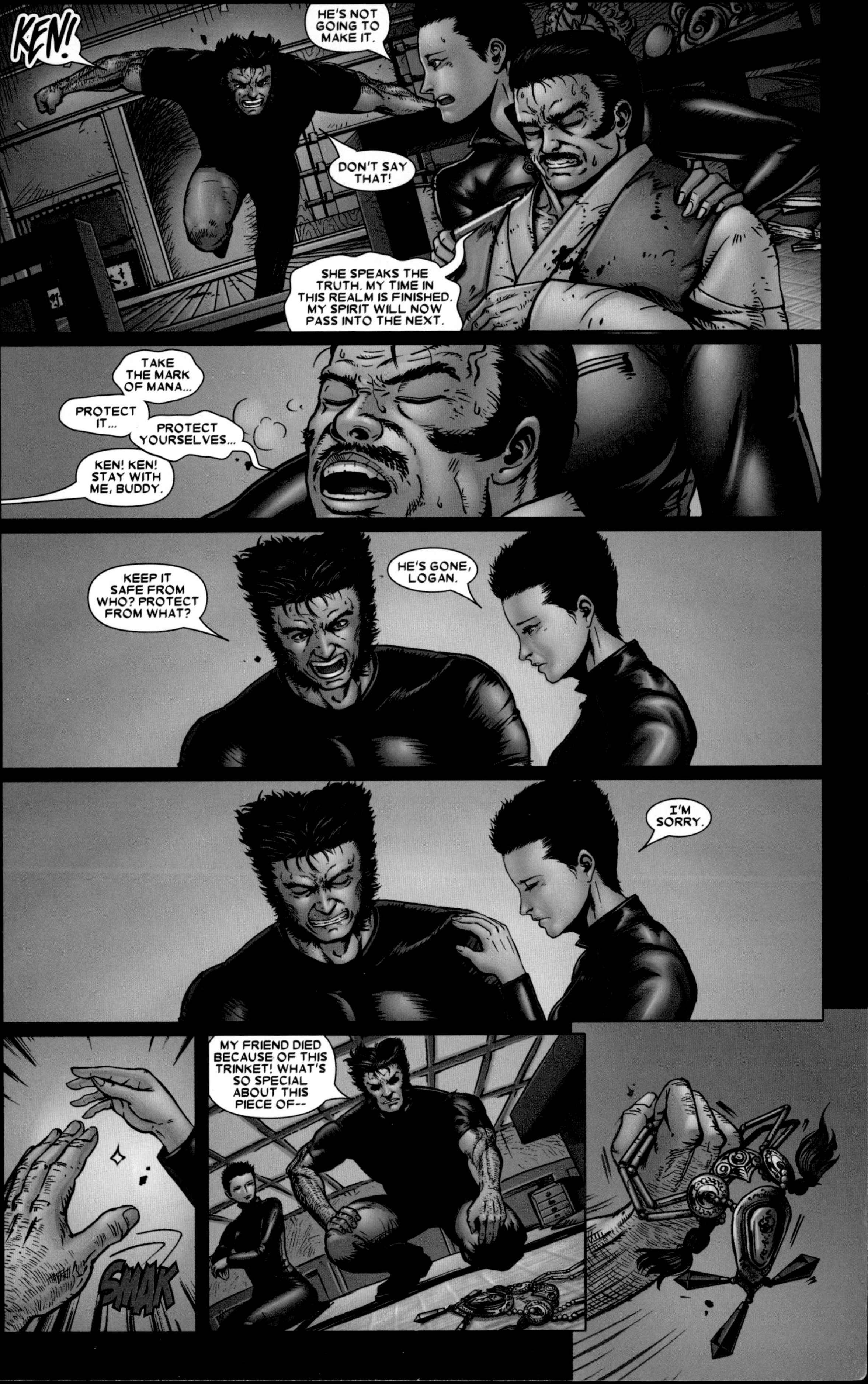
KEN!
HE'S NOT GOING TO MAKE IT.
DON'T SAY THAT!
SHE SPEAKS THE TRUTH. MY TIME IN THIS REALM IS FINISHED. MY SPIRIT WILL NOW PASS INTO THE NEXT.
TAKE THE MARK OF MANA...
PROTECT IT...
PROTECT YOURSELVES...
KEN! KEN! STAY WITH ME, BUDDY.
KEEP IT SAFE FROM WHO? PROTECT FROM WHAT?
HE'S GONE, LOGAN.
I'M SORRY.
SMAK
MY FRIEND DIED BECAUSE OF THIS TRINKET! WHAT'S SO SPECIAL ABOUT THIS PIECE OF--

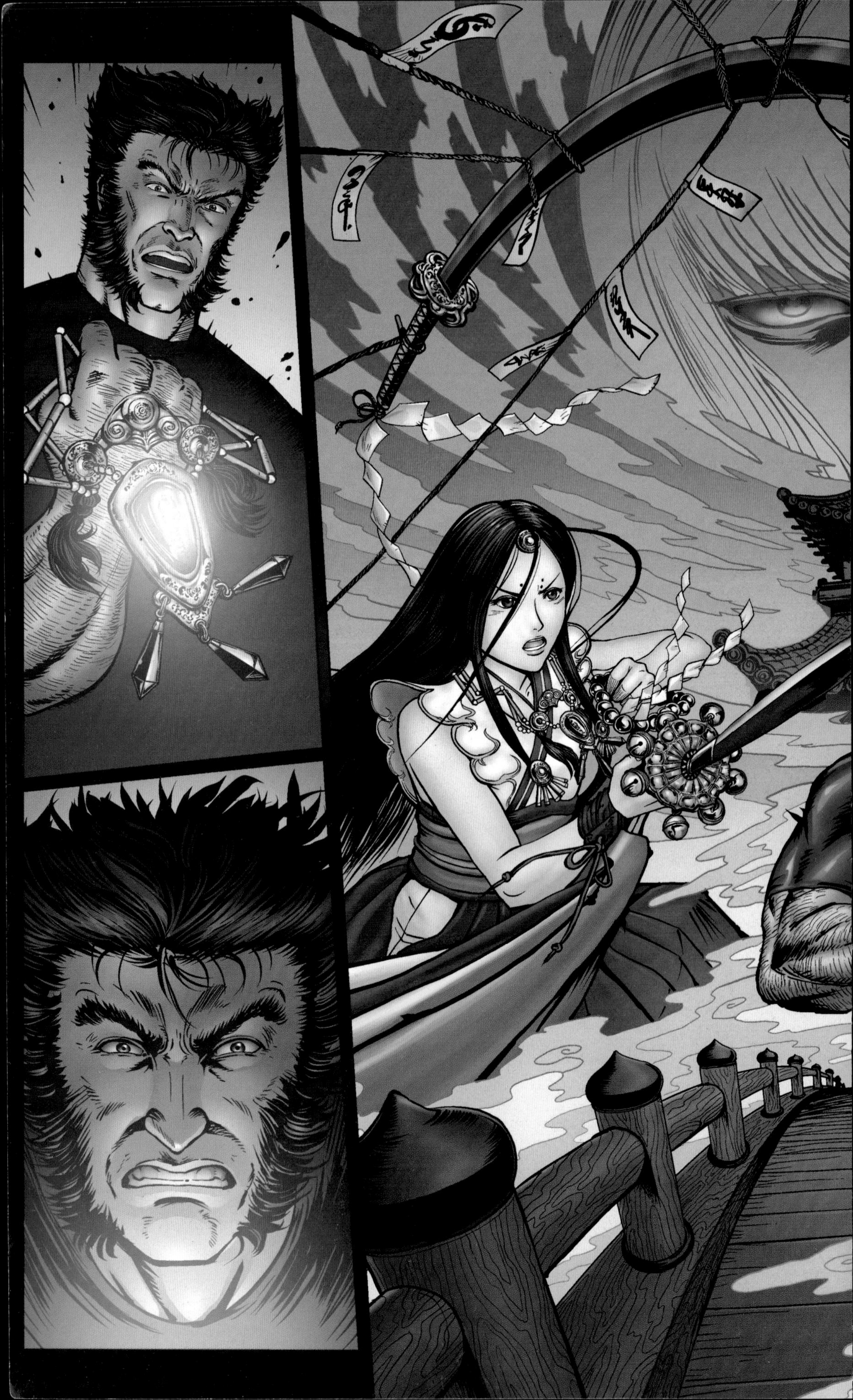

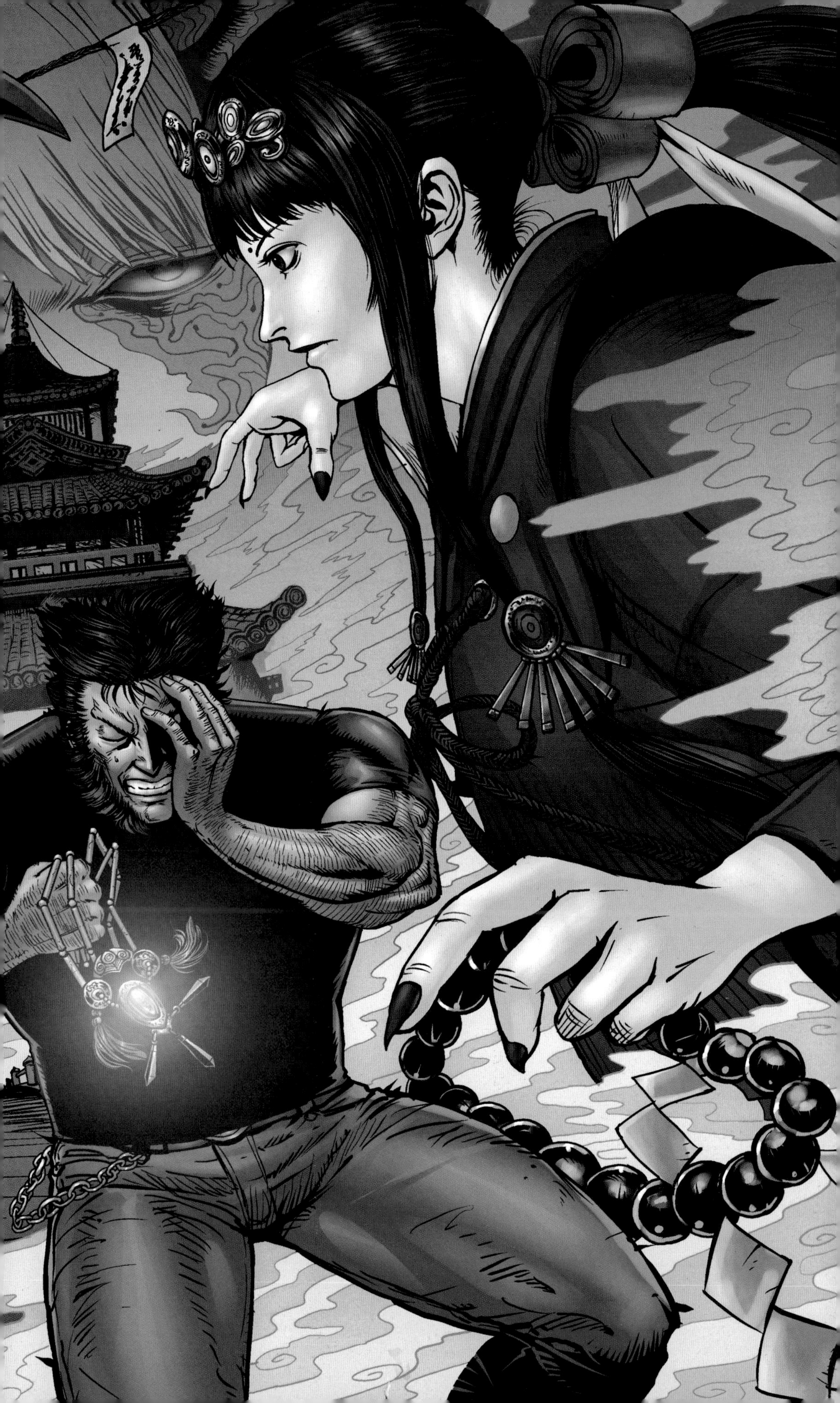

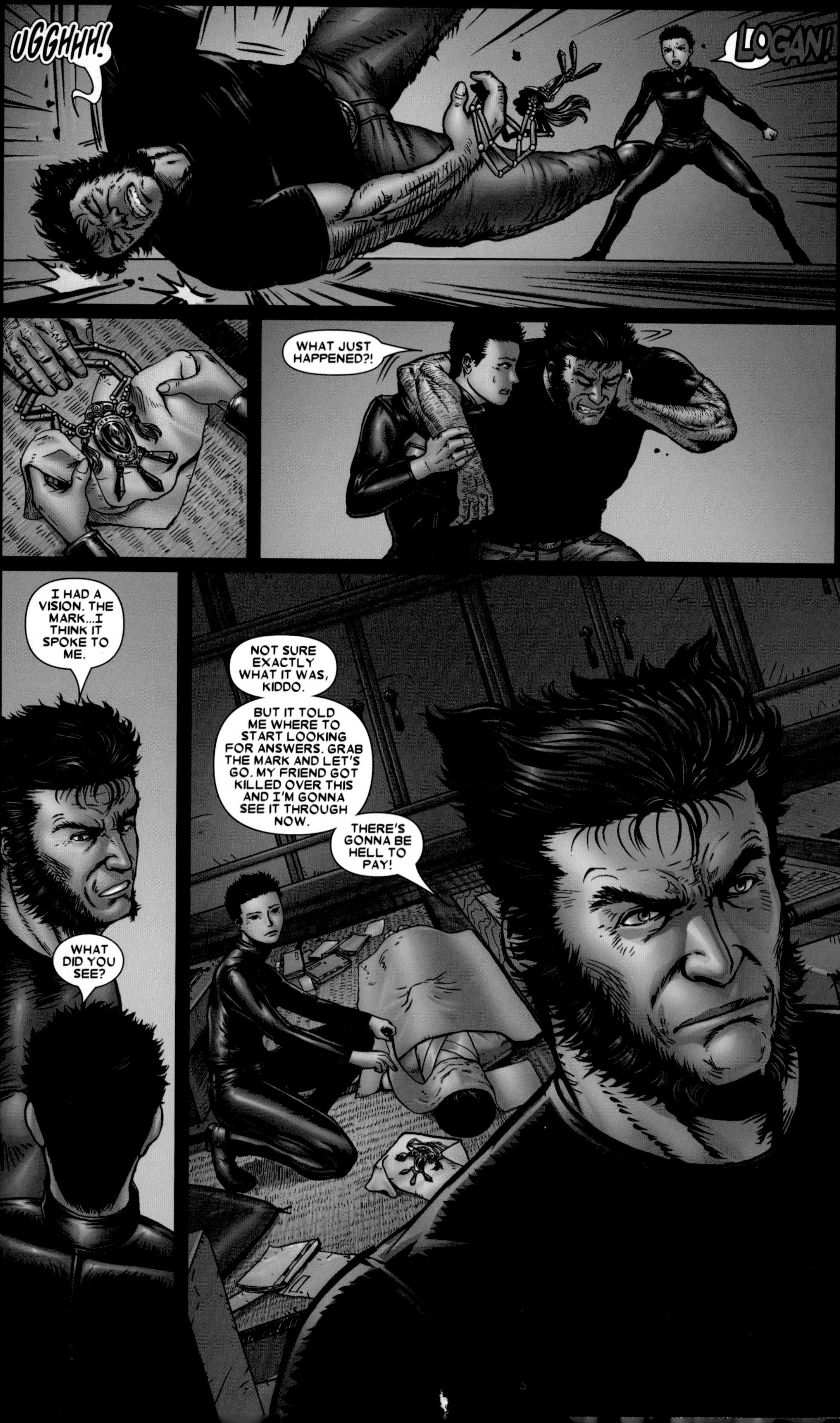
UGGHHH!
LOGAN!
WHAT JUST HAPPENED?!
I HAD A VISION. THE MARK...I THINK IT SPOKE TO ME.
WHAT DID YOU SEE?
NOT SURE EXACTLY WHAT IT WAS, KIDDO.
BUT IT TOLD ME WHERE TO START LOOKING FOR ANSWERS. GRAB THE MARK AND LET'S GO. MY FRIEND GOT KILLED OVER THIS AND I'M GONNA SEE IT THROUGH NOW.
THERE'S GONNA BE HELL TO PAY!

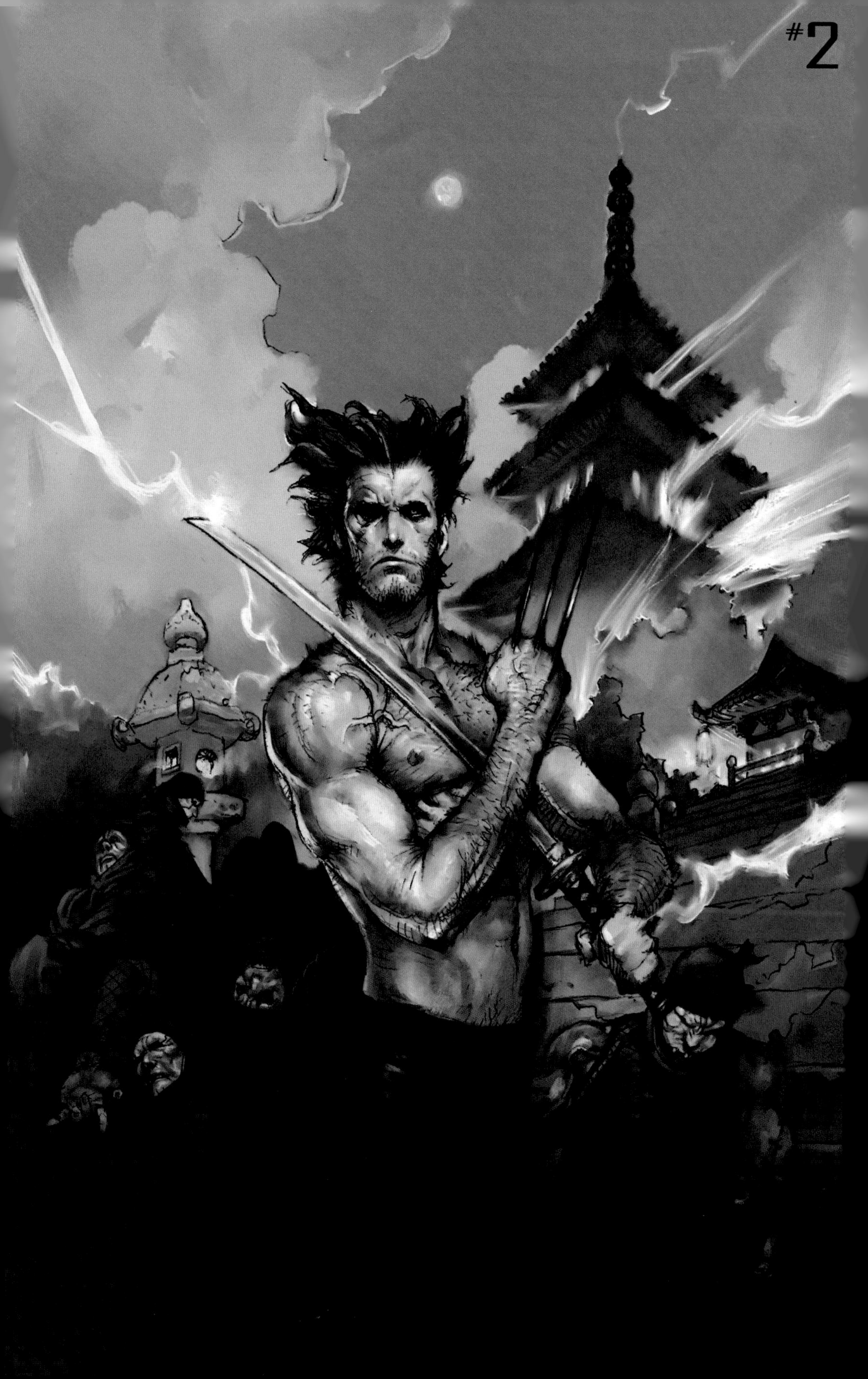
#2

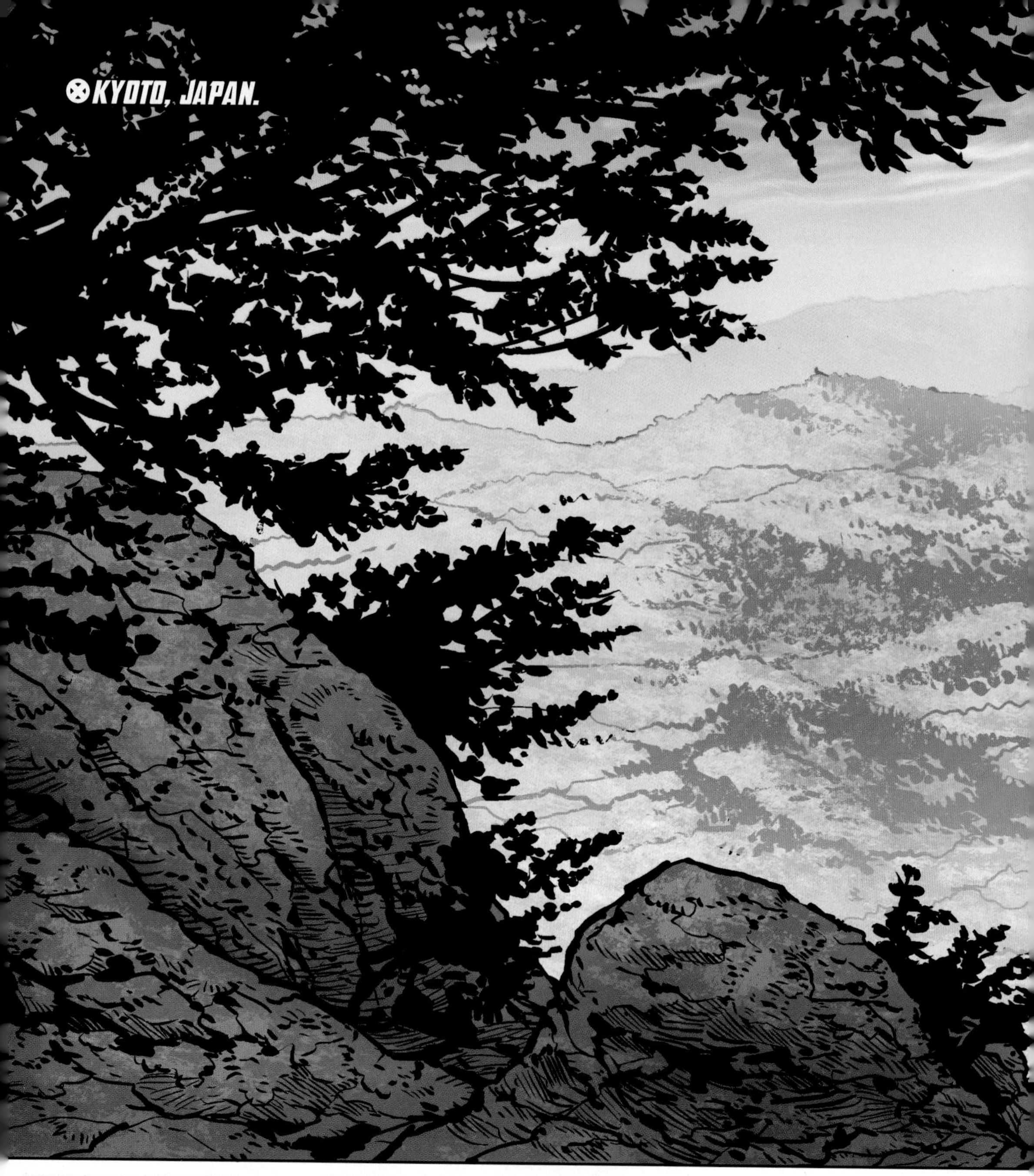
KYOTO, JAPAN.

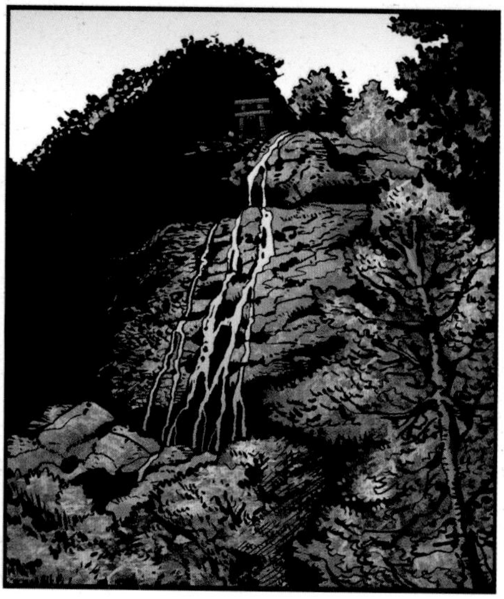

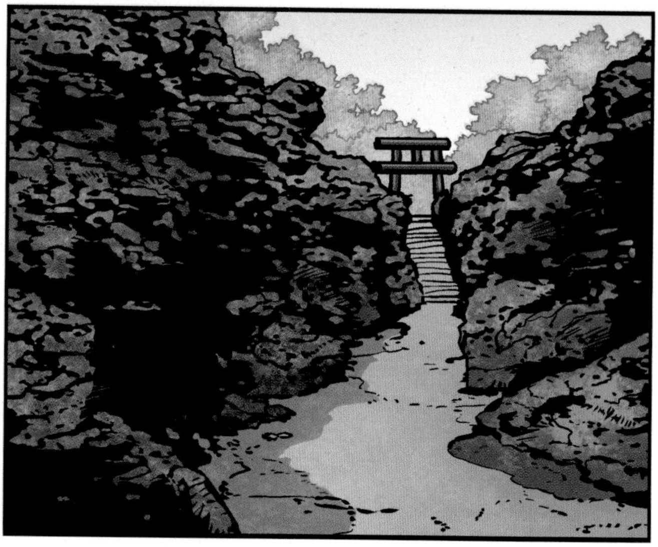

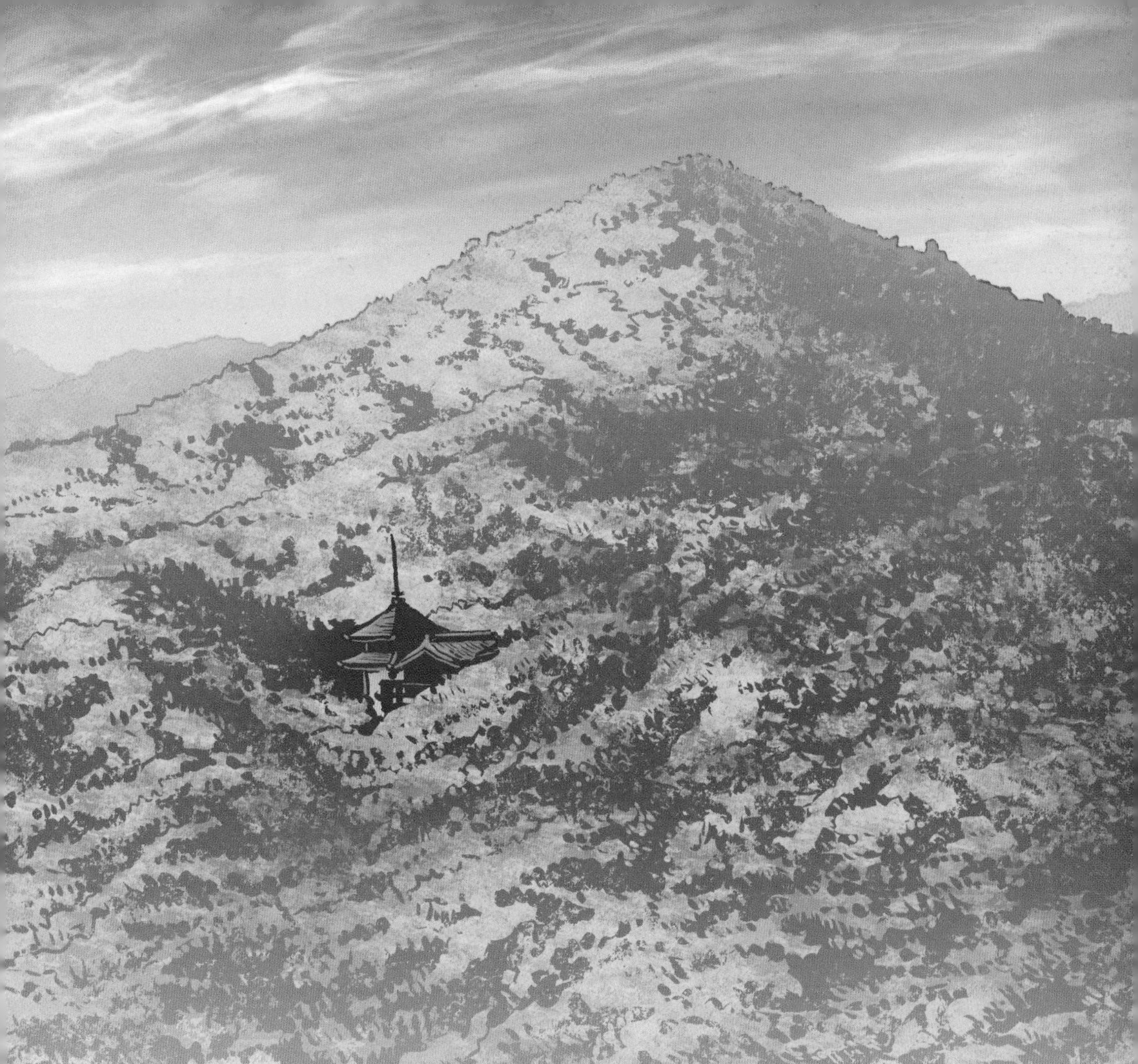

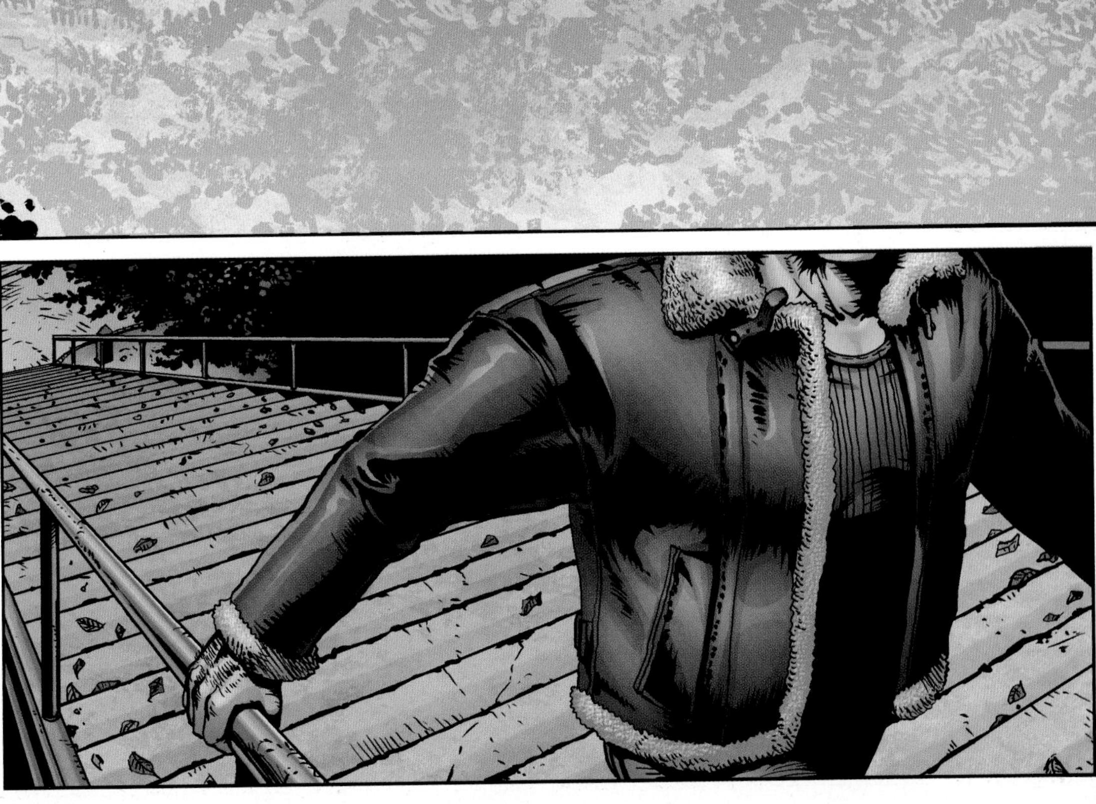

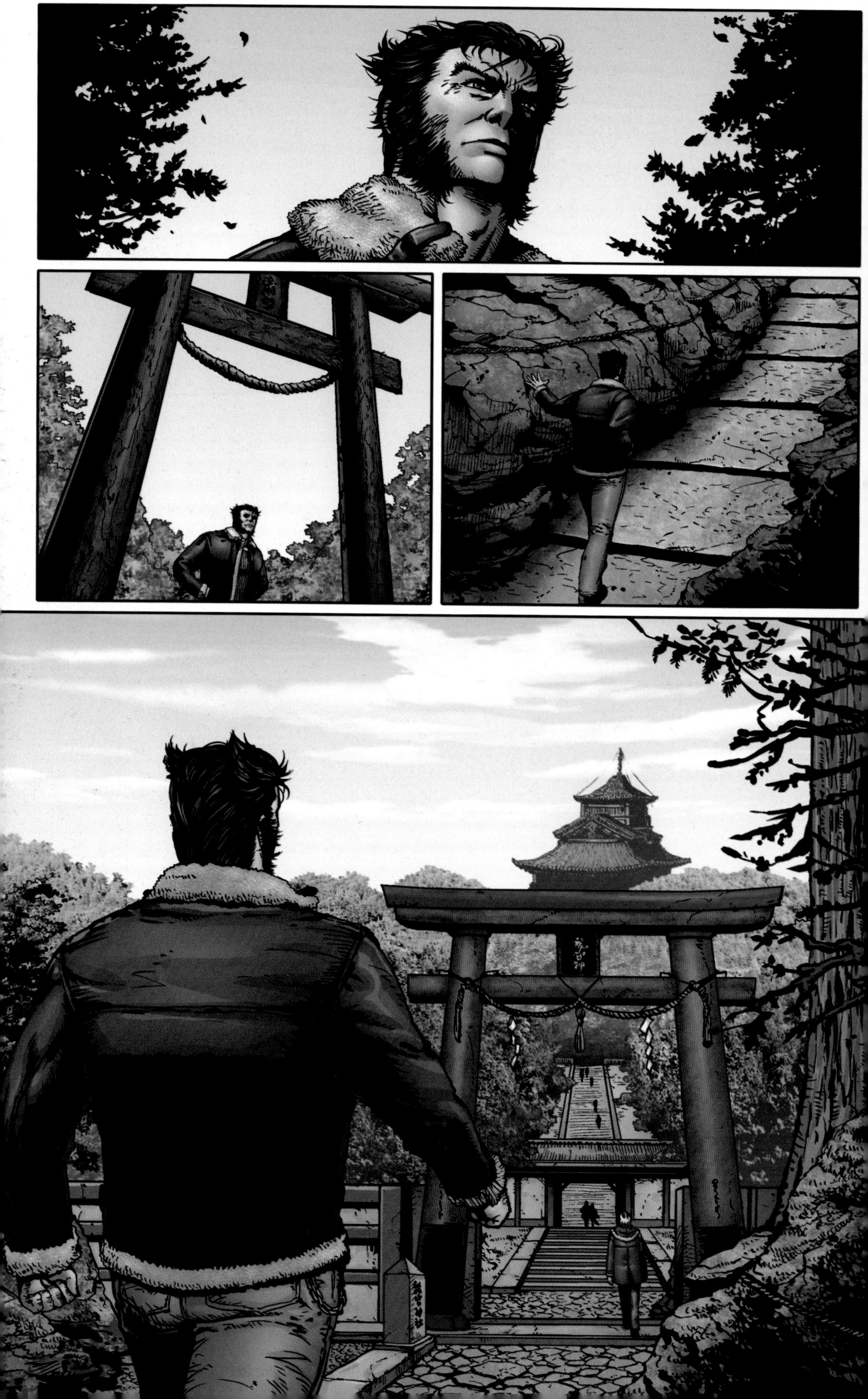

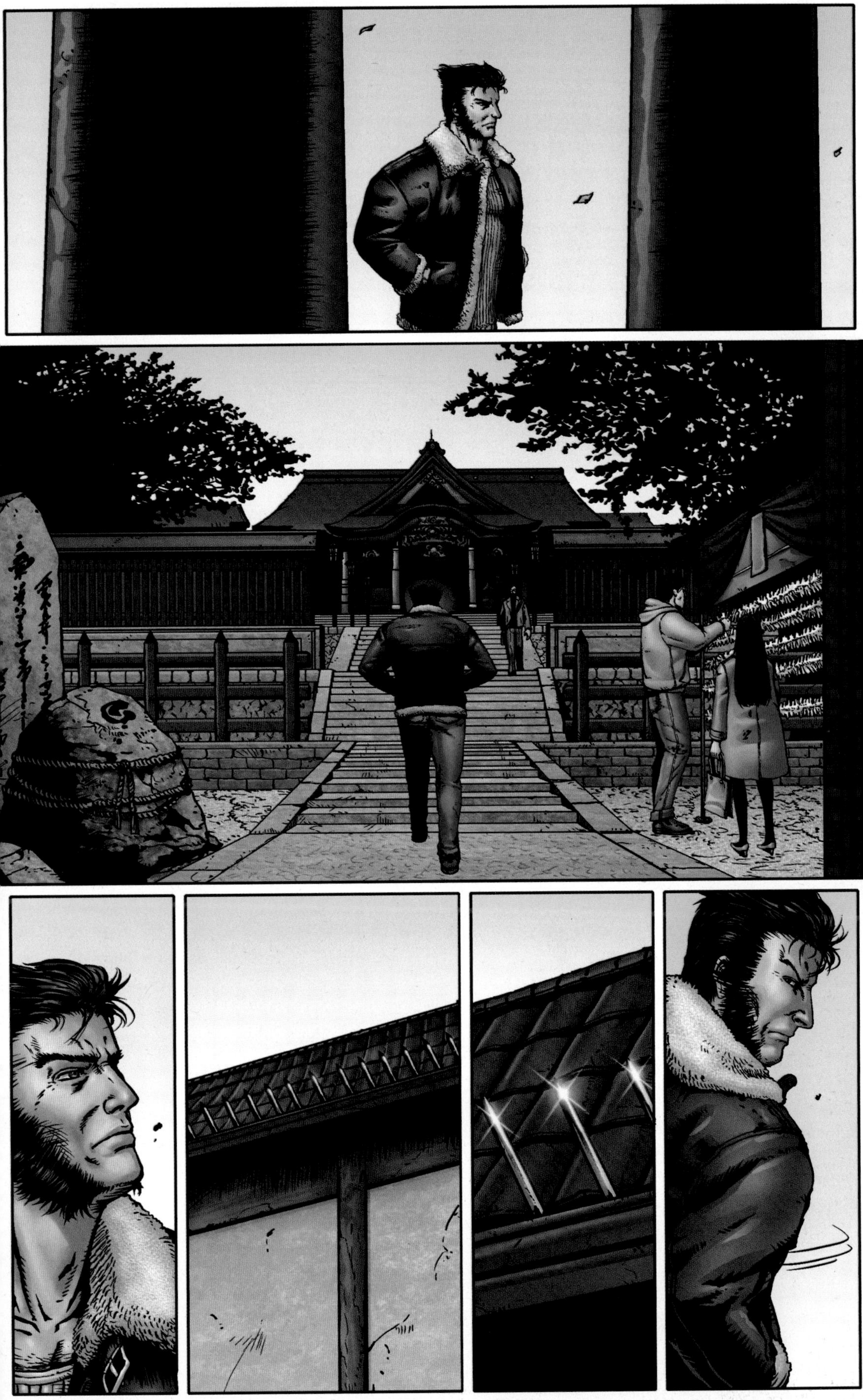

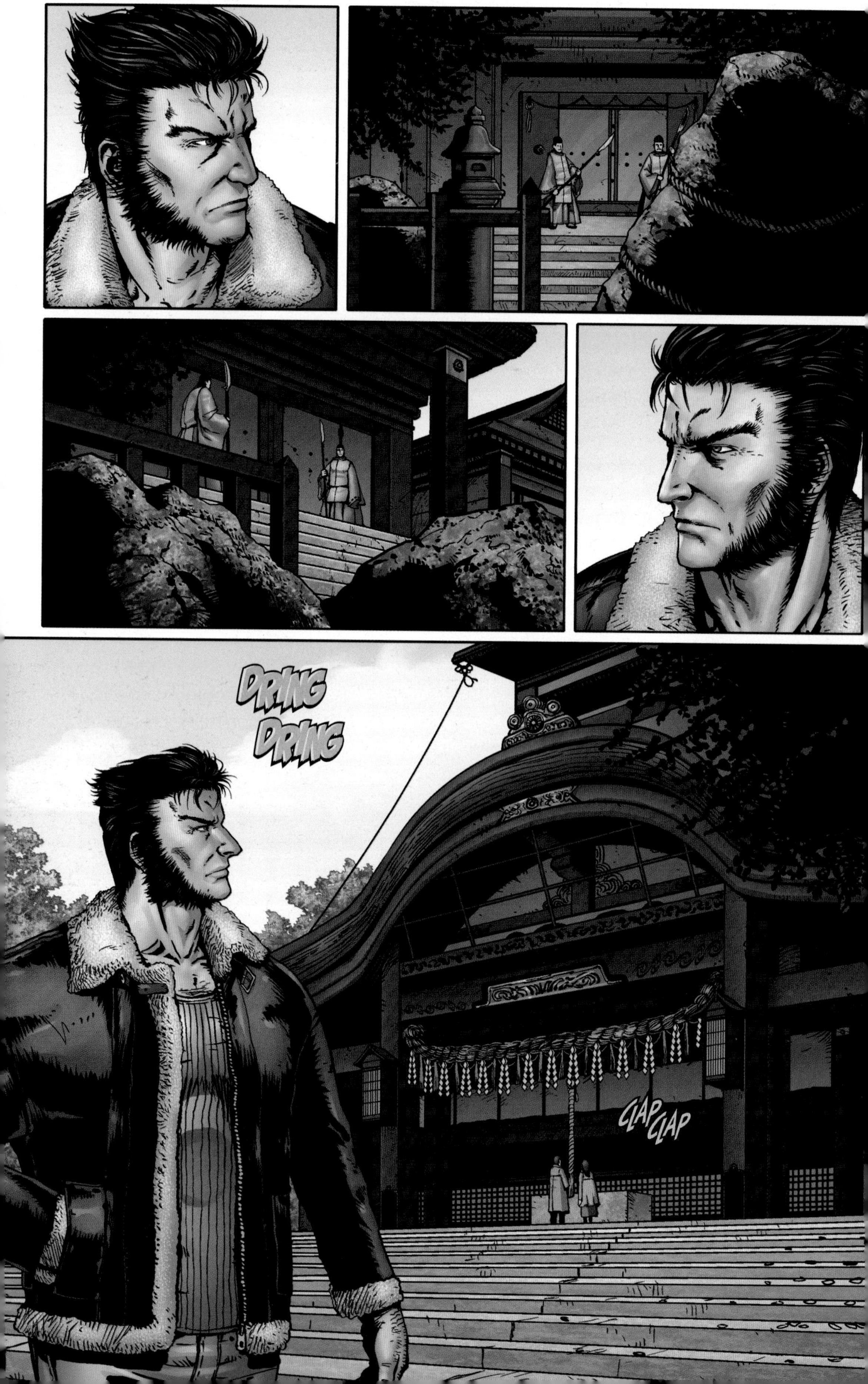
DRING
DRING
CLAP CLAP

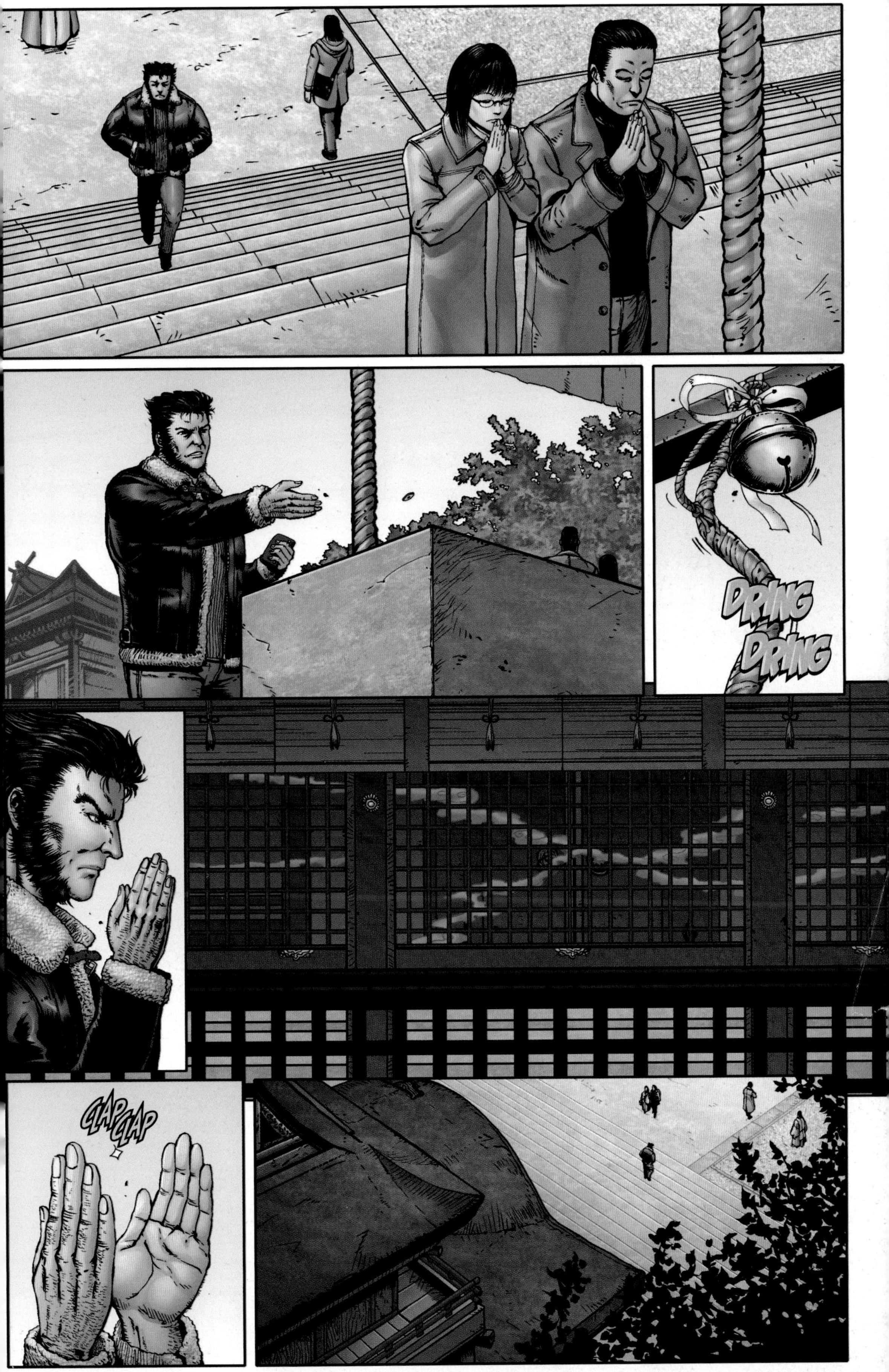
DRING
DRING
CLAP CLAP

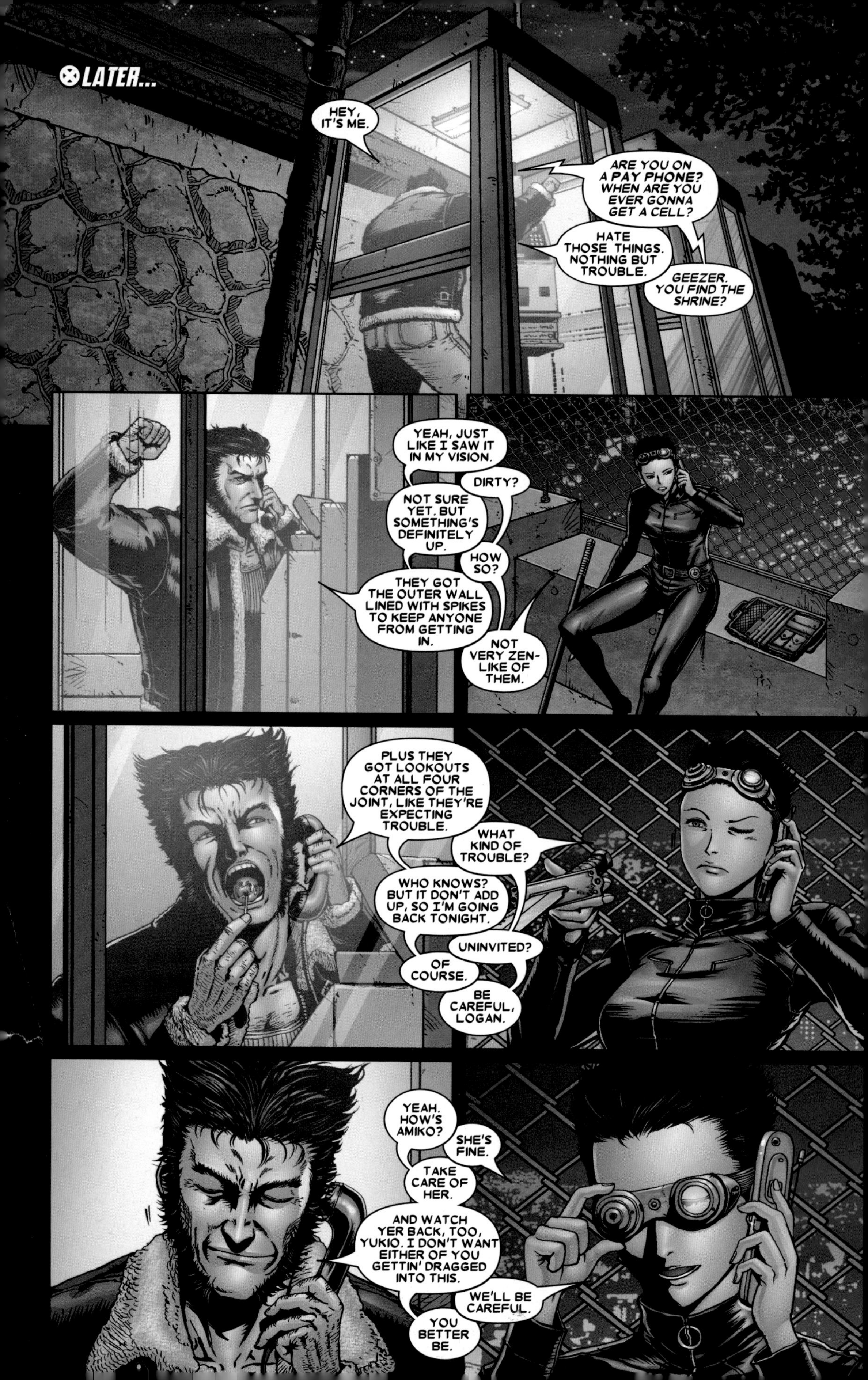
LATER...
HEY, IT'S ME.
ARE YOU ON A PAY PHONE? WHEN ARE YOU EVER GONNA GET A CELL?
HATE THOSE THINGS. NOTHING BUT TROUBLE.
GEEZER. YOU FIND THE SHRINE?
YEAH, JUST LIKE I SAW IT IN MY VISION.
DIRTY?
NOT SURE YET. BUT SOMETHING'S DEFINITELY UP.
HOW SO?
THEY GOT THE OUTER WALL LINED WITH SPIKES TO KEEP ANYONE FROM GETTING IN.
NOT VERY ZEN-LIKE OF THEM.
PLUS THEY GOT LOOKOUTS AT ALL FOUR CORNERS OF THE JOINT, LIKE THEY'RE EXPECTING TROUBLE.
WHAT KIND OF TROUBLE?
WHO KNOWS? BUT IT DON'T ADD UP, SO I'M GOING BACK TONIGHT.
UNINVITED?
OF COURSE.
BE CAREFUL, LOGAN.
YEAH. HOW'S AMIKO?
SHE'S FINE.
TAKE CARE OF HER.
AND WATCH YER BACK, TOO, YUKIO. I DON'T WANT EITHER OF YOU GETTIN' DRAGGED INTO THIS.
WE'LL BE CAREFUL.
YOU BETTER BE.

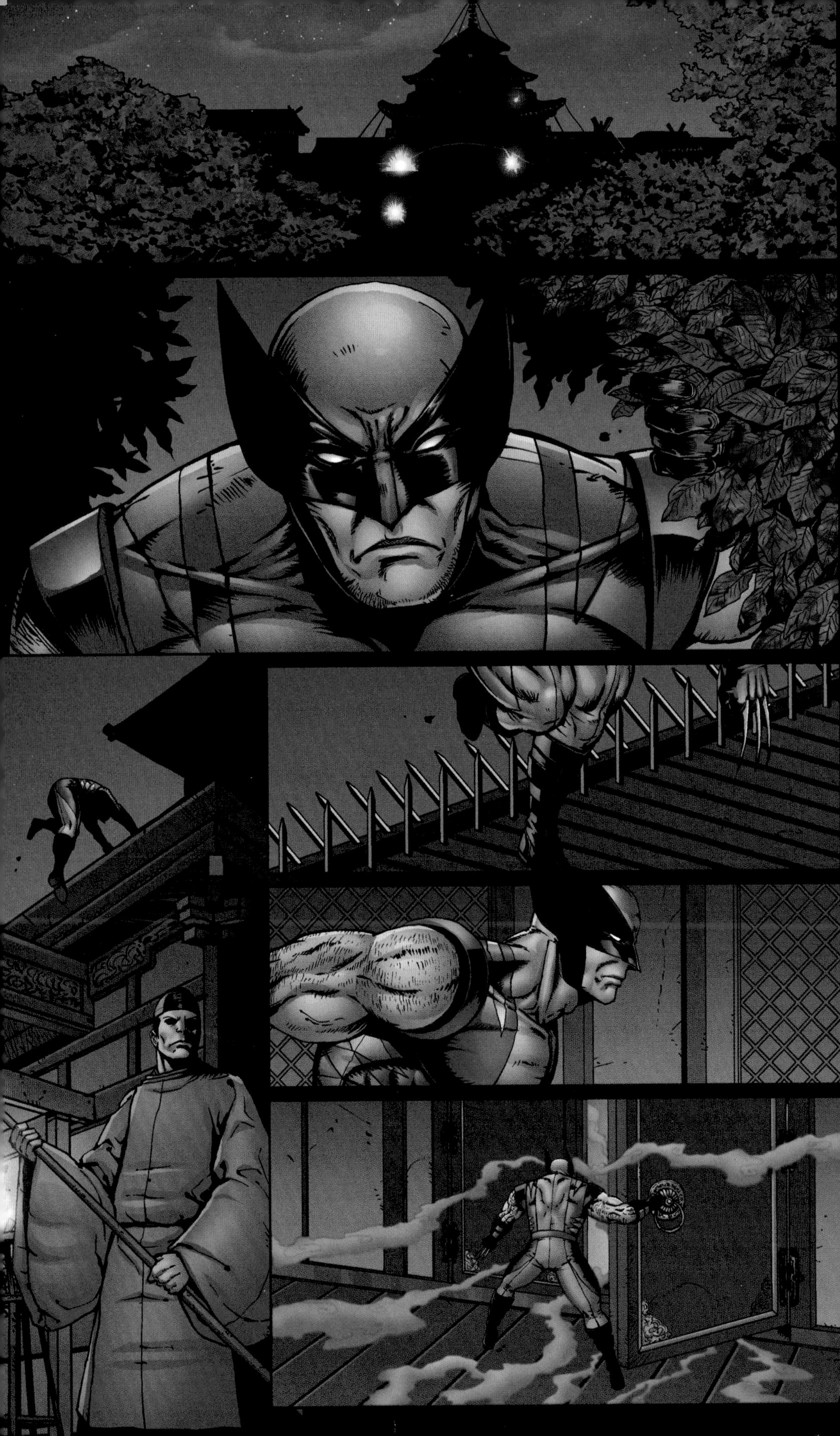

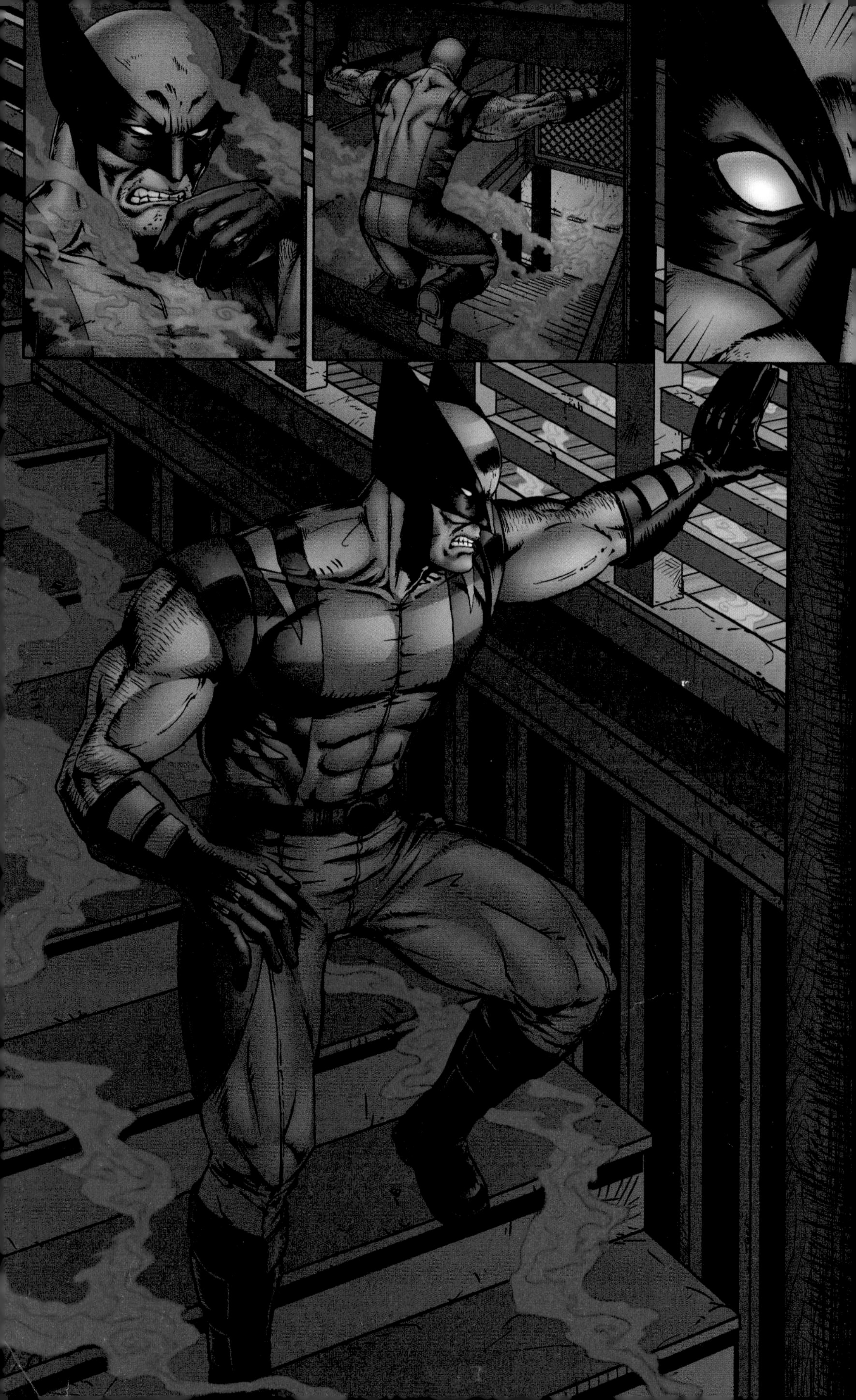

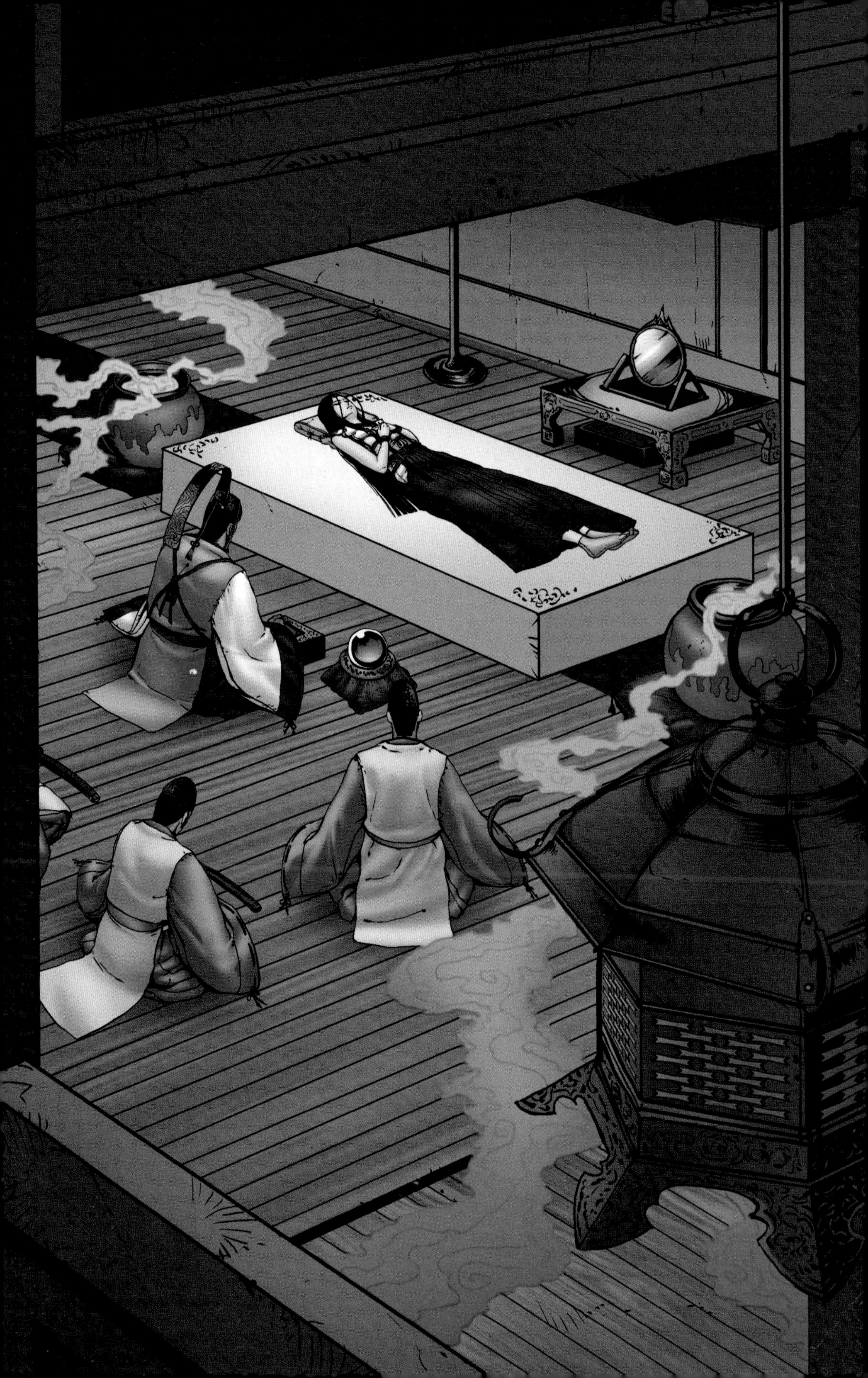

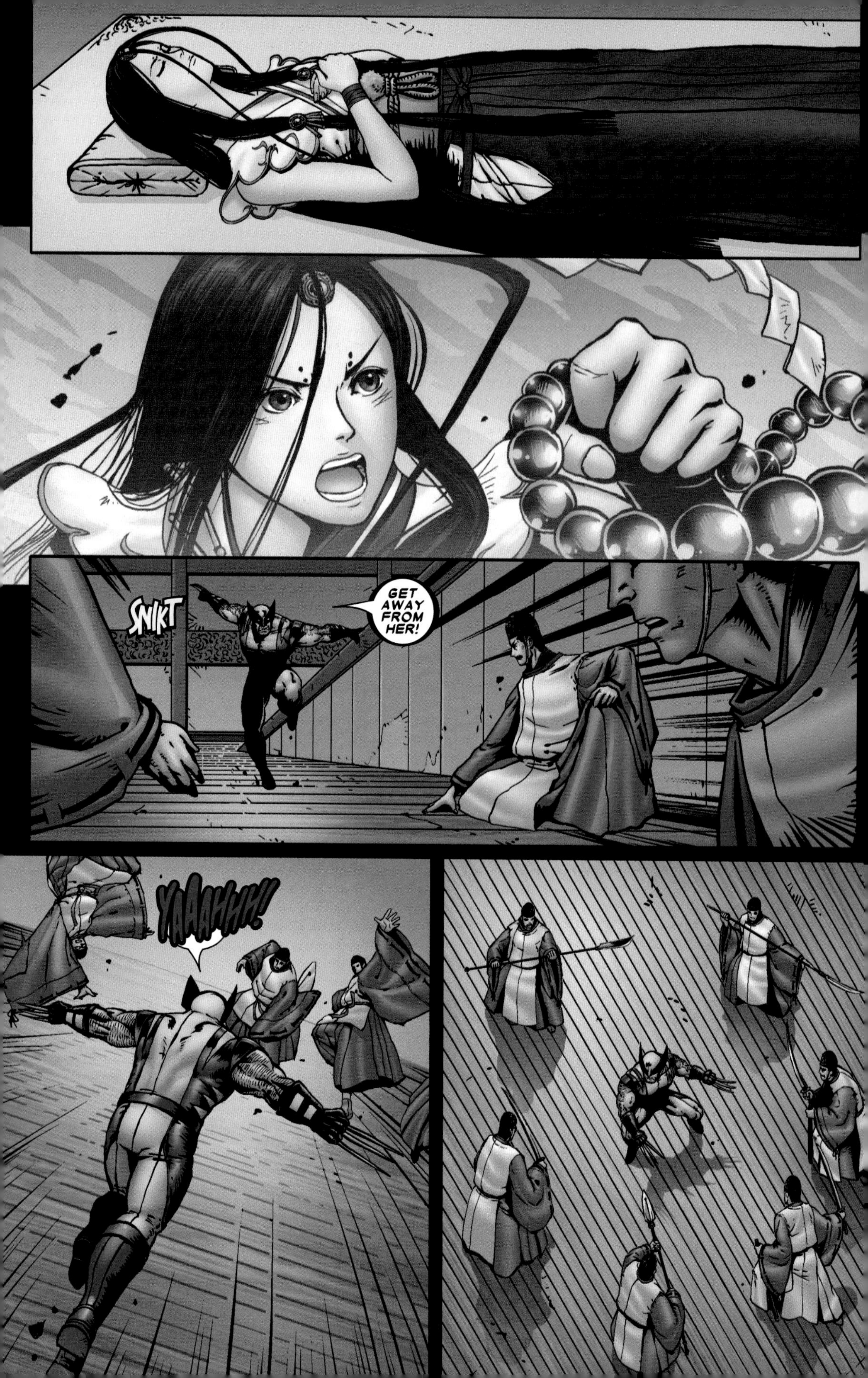
SNIKT
GET AWAY FROM HER!
YAAAHHH!!

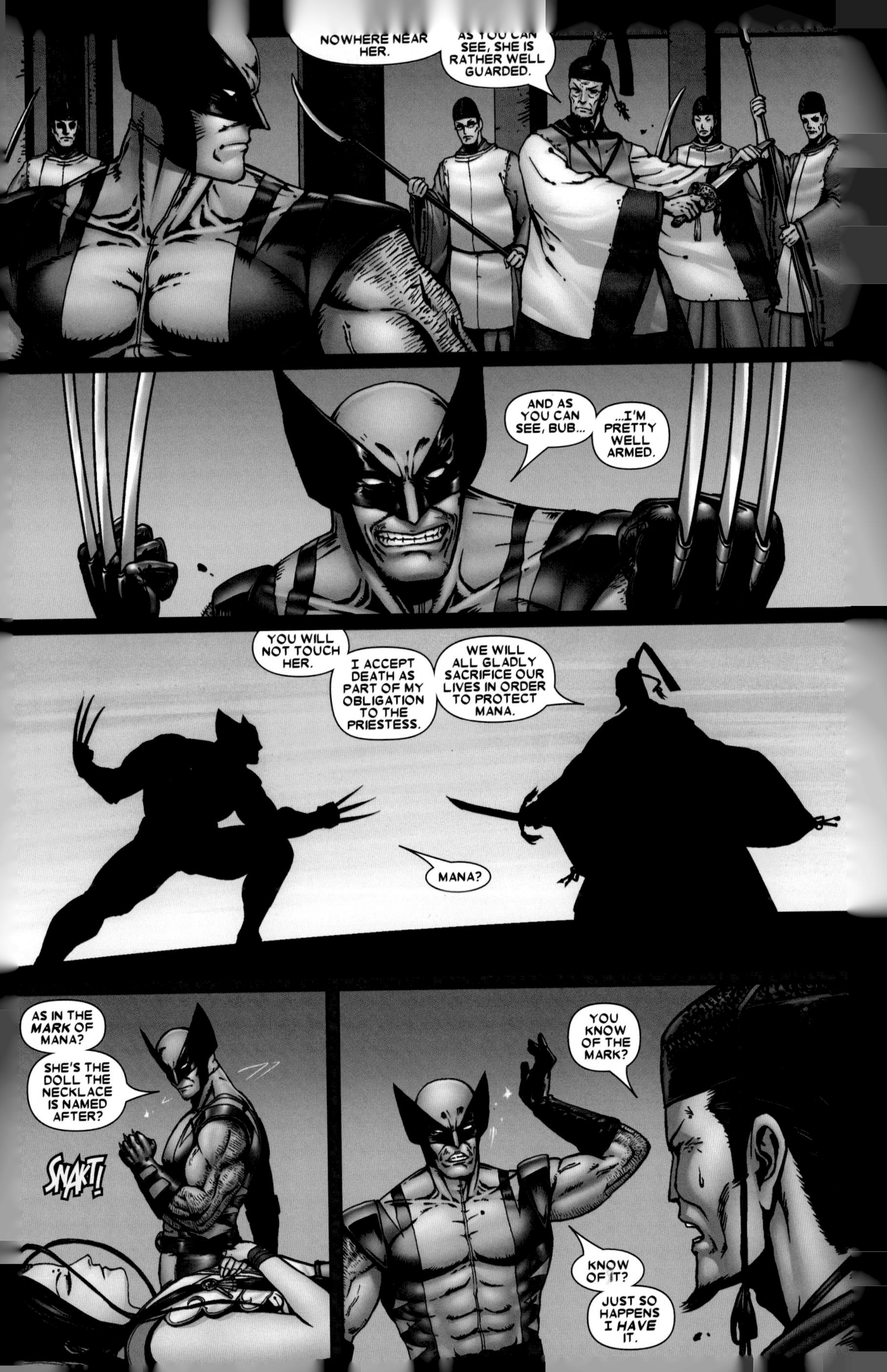
NOWHERE NEAR HER.
AS YOU CAN SEE, SHE IS RATHER WELL GUARDED.
AND AS YOU CAN SEE, BUB...
...I'M PRETTY WELL ARMED.
YOU WILL NOT TOUCH HER.
I ACCEPT DEATH AS PART OF MY OBLIGATION TO THE PRIESTESS.
WE WILL ALL GLADLY SACRIFICE OUR LIVES IN ORDER TO PROTECT MANA.
MANA?
AS IN THE *MARK* OF MANA?
SHE'S THE DOLL THE NECKLACE IS NAMED AFTER?
SNAKT!
YOU KNOW OF THE MARK?
KNOW OF IT?
JUST SO HAPPENS I *HAVE* IT.

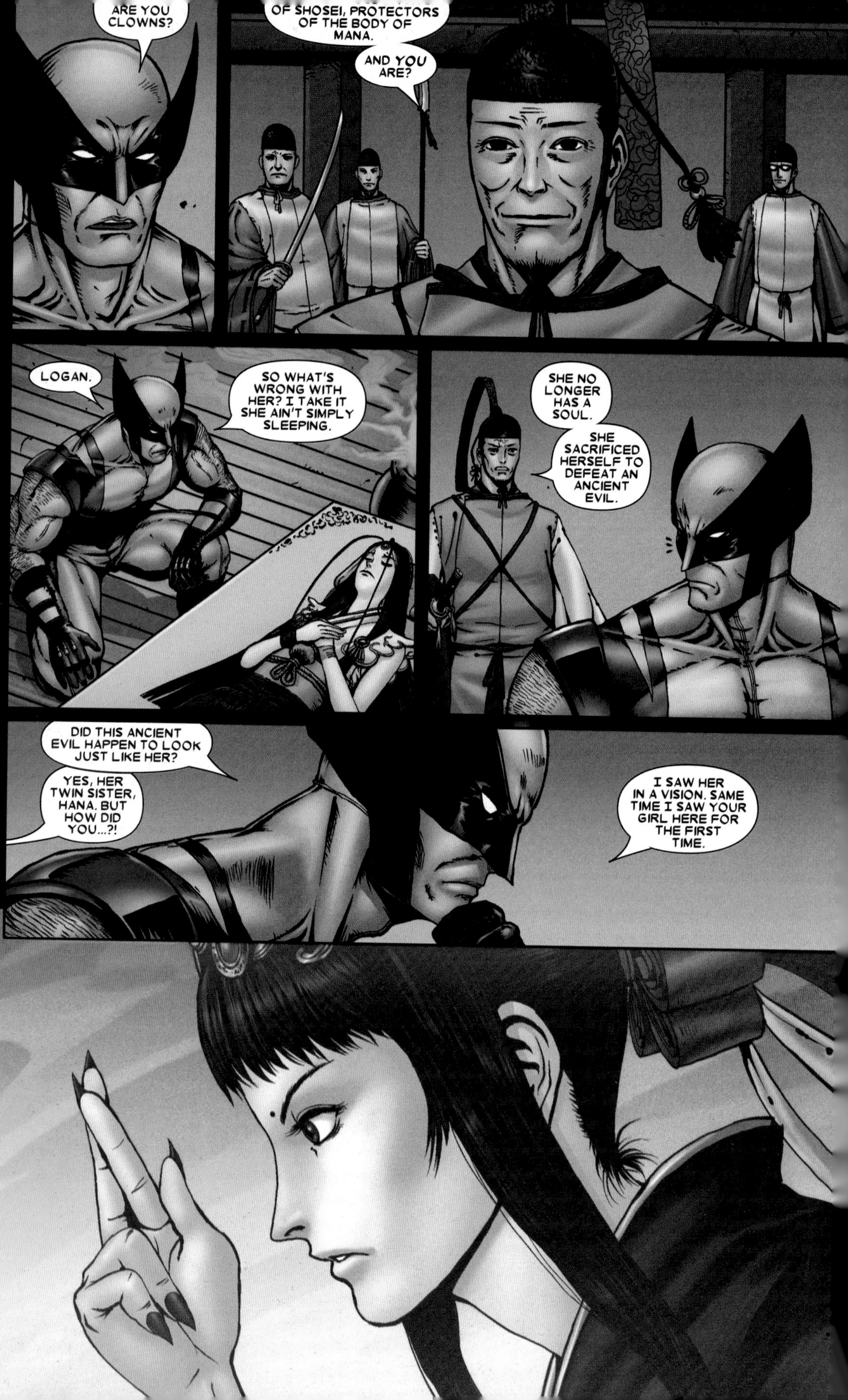

ARE YOU CLOWNS?
OF SHOSEI, PROTECTORS OF THE BODY OF MANA.
AND YOU ARE?
LOGAN.
SO WHAT'S WRONG WITH HER? I TAKE IT SHE AIN'T SIMPLY SLEEPING.
SHE NO LONGER HAS A SOUL.
SHE SACRIFICED HERSELF TO DEFEAT AN ANCIENT EVIL.
DID THIS ANCIENT EVIL HAPPEN TO LOOK JUST LIKE HER?
YES, HER TWIN SISTER, HANA. BUT HOW DID YOU...?!
I SAW HER IN A VISION. SAME TIME I SAW YOUR GIRL HERE FOR THE FIRST TIME.

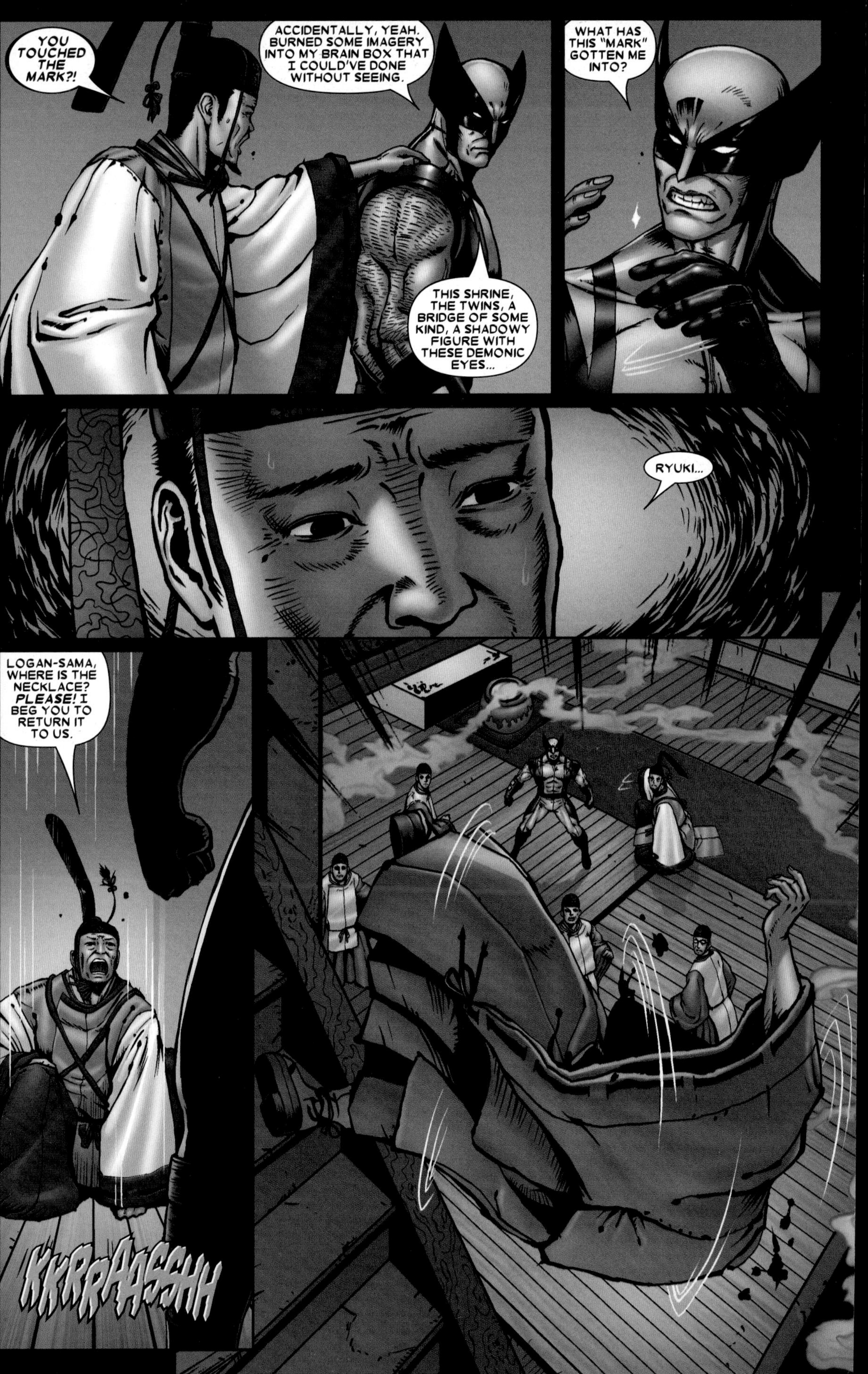
YOU TOUCHED THE MARK?!
ACCIDENTALLY, YEAH. BURNED SOME IMAGERY INTO MY BRAIN BOX THAT I COULD'VE DONE WITHOUT SEEING.
THIS SHRINE, THE TWINS, A BRIDGE OF SOME KIND, A SHADOWY FIGURE WITH THESE DEMONIC EYES...
WHAT HAS THIS "MARK" GOTTEN ME INTO?
RYUKI...
LOGAN-SAMA, WHERE IS THE NECKLACE? *PLEASE!* I BEG YOU TO RETURN IT TO US.
KKRAASSHH

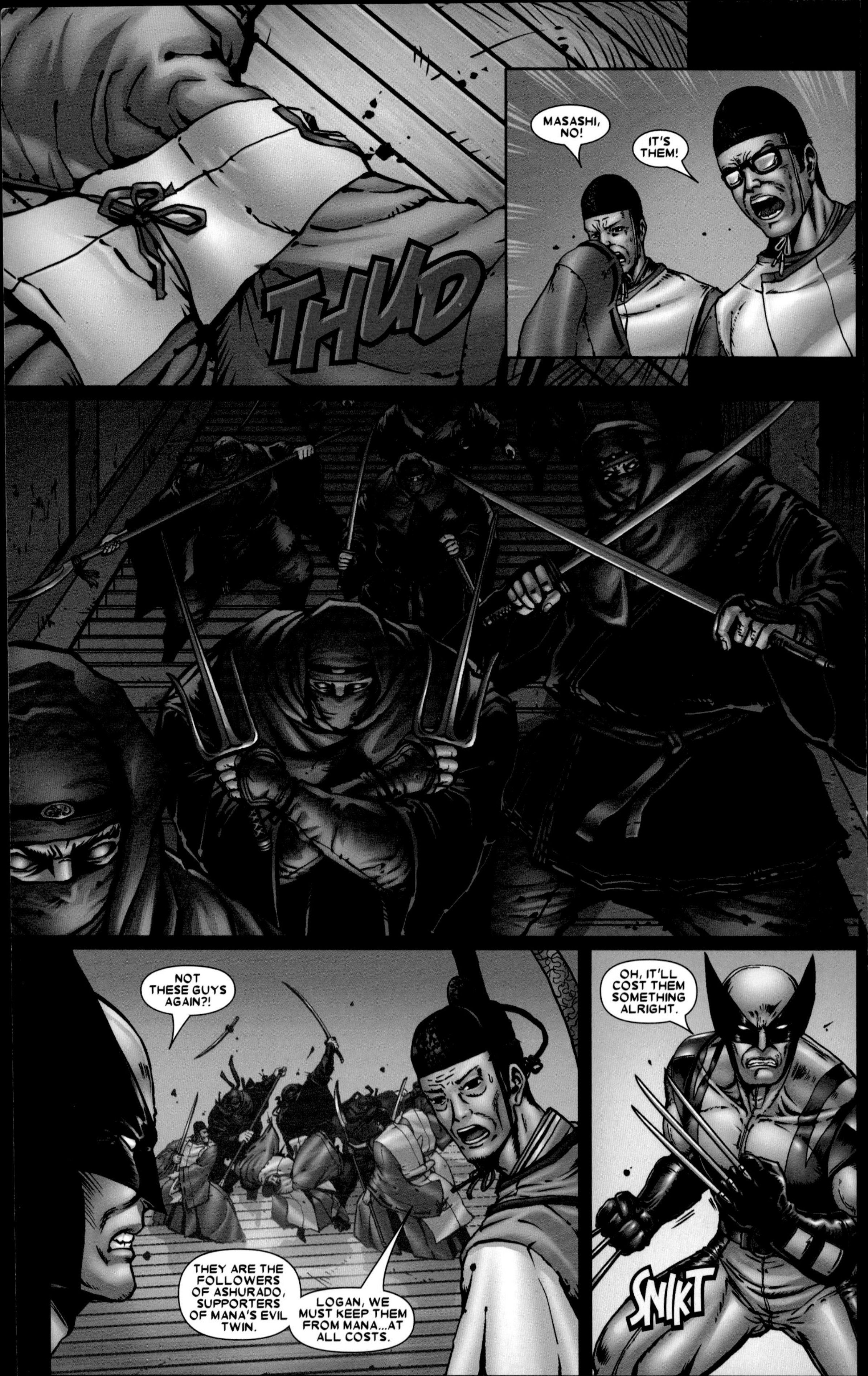
THUD
MASASHI, NO!
IT'S THEM!
NOT THESE GUYS AGAIN?!
THEY ARE THE FOLLOWERS OF ASHURADO, SUPPORTERS OF MANA'S EVIL TWIN.
LOGAN, WE MUST KEEP THEM FROM MANA...AT ALL COSTS.
OH, IT'LL COST THEM SOMETHING ALRIGHT.
SNIKT

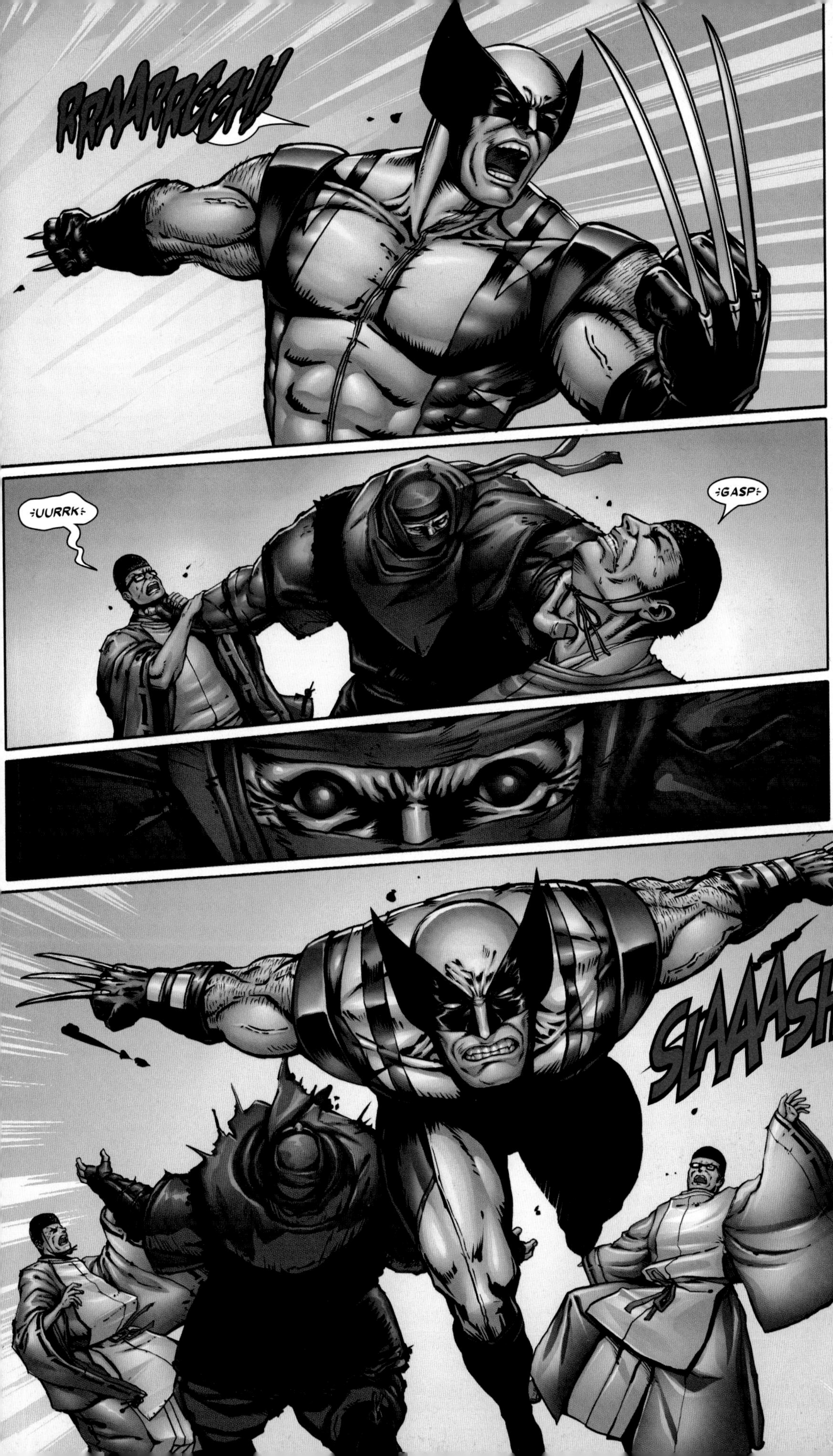
RRAARRGGH!!
UURRK
GASP
SLAAASH

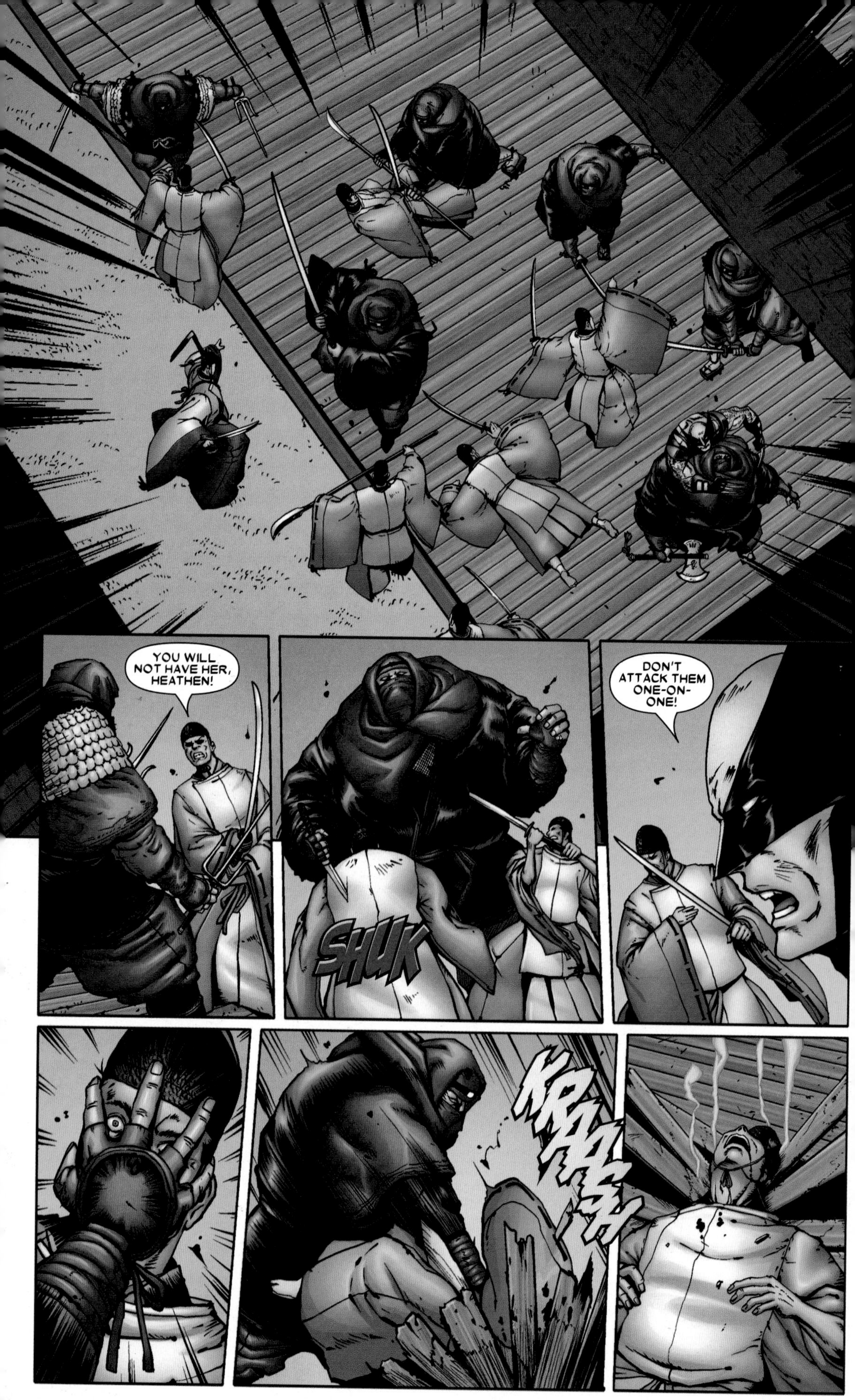
YOU WILL NOT HAVE HER, HEATHEN!
SHUK
DON'T ATTACK THEM ONE-ON-ONE!
KRAKKK

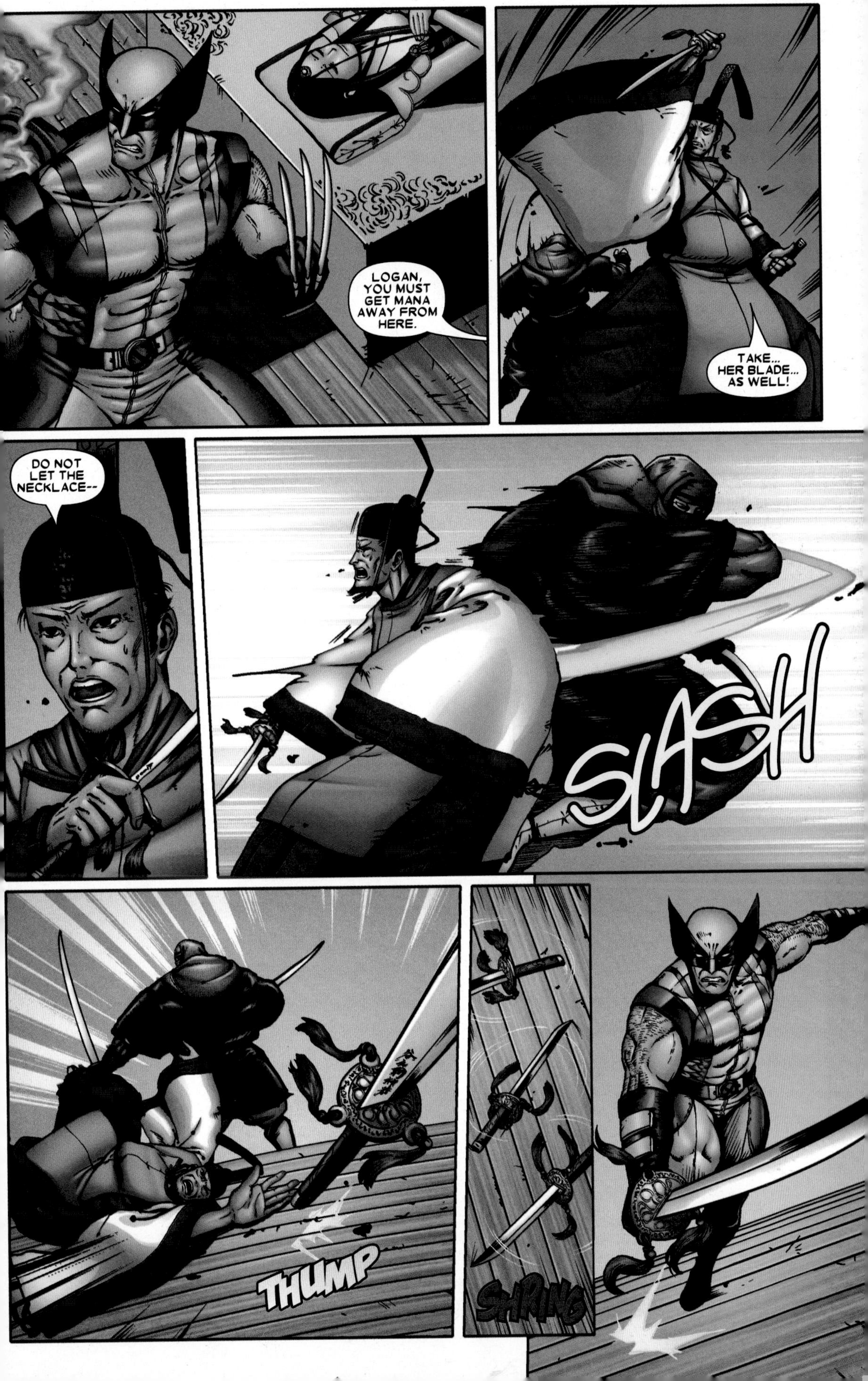
LOGAN, YOU MUST GET MANA AWAY FROM HERE.
TAKE... HER BLADE... AS WELL!
DO NOT LET THE NECKLACE--
SLASH
THUMP
SHING

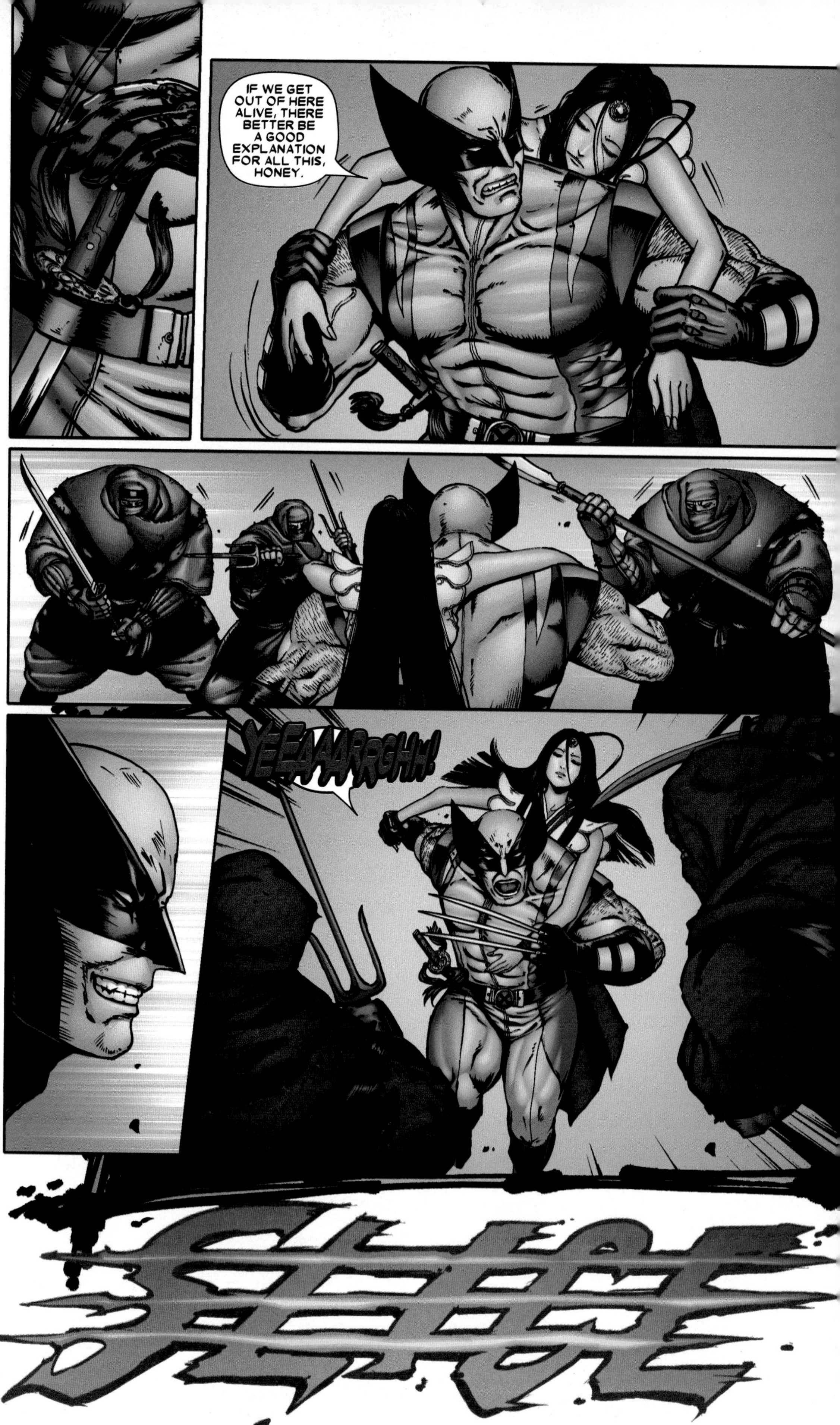
IF WE GET OUT OF HERE ALIVE, THERE BETTER BE A GOOD EXPLANATION FOR ALL THIS, HONEY.
YEEAAARRGHH!

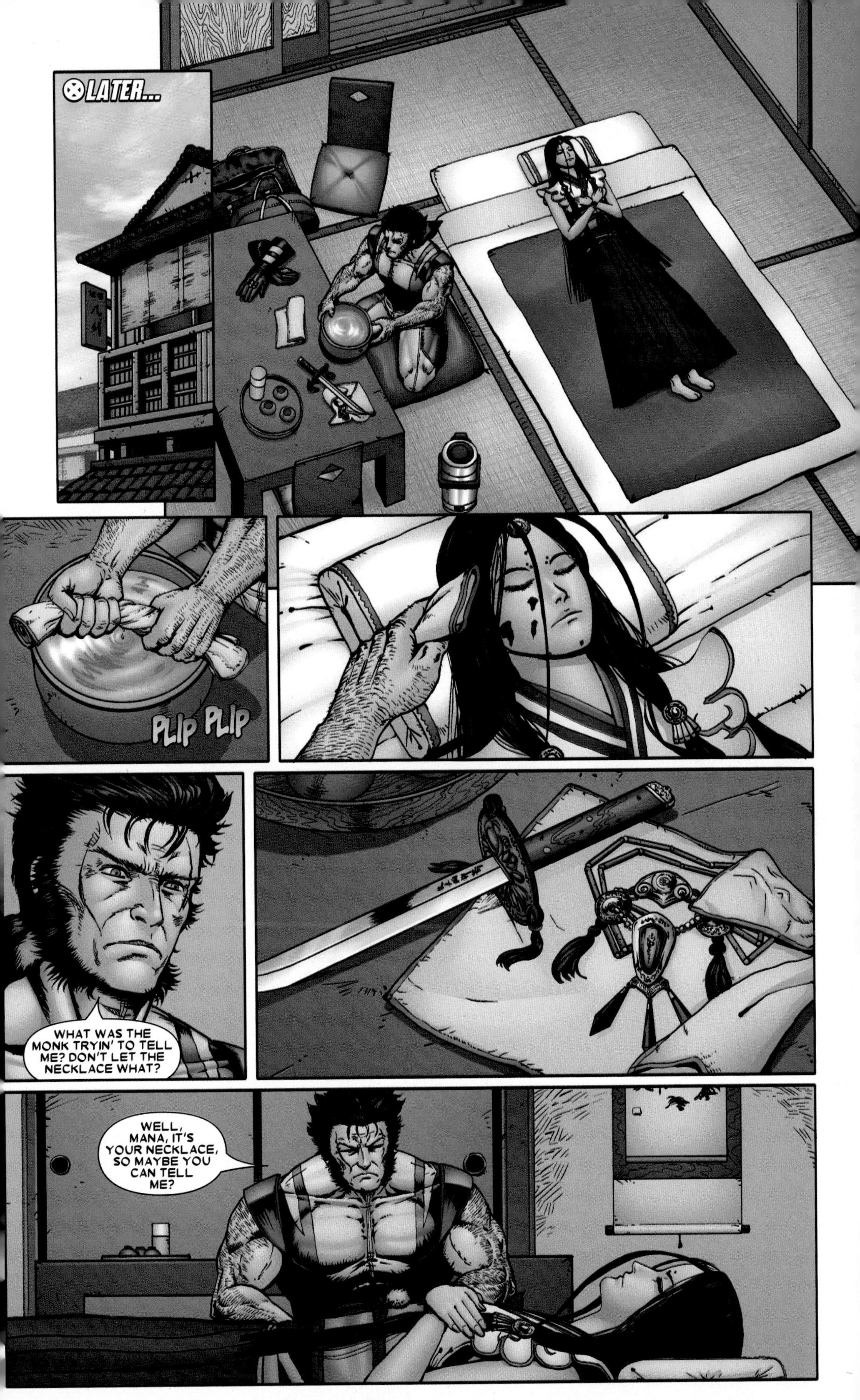
LATER...
PLIP PLIP
WHAT WAS THE MONK TRYIN' TO TELL ME? DON'T LET THE NECKLACE WHAT?
WELL, MANA, IT'S YOUR NECKLACE, SO MAYBE YOU CAN TELL ME?

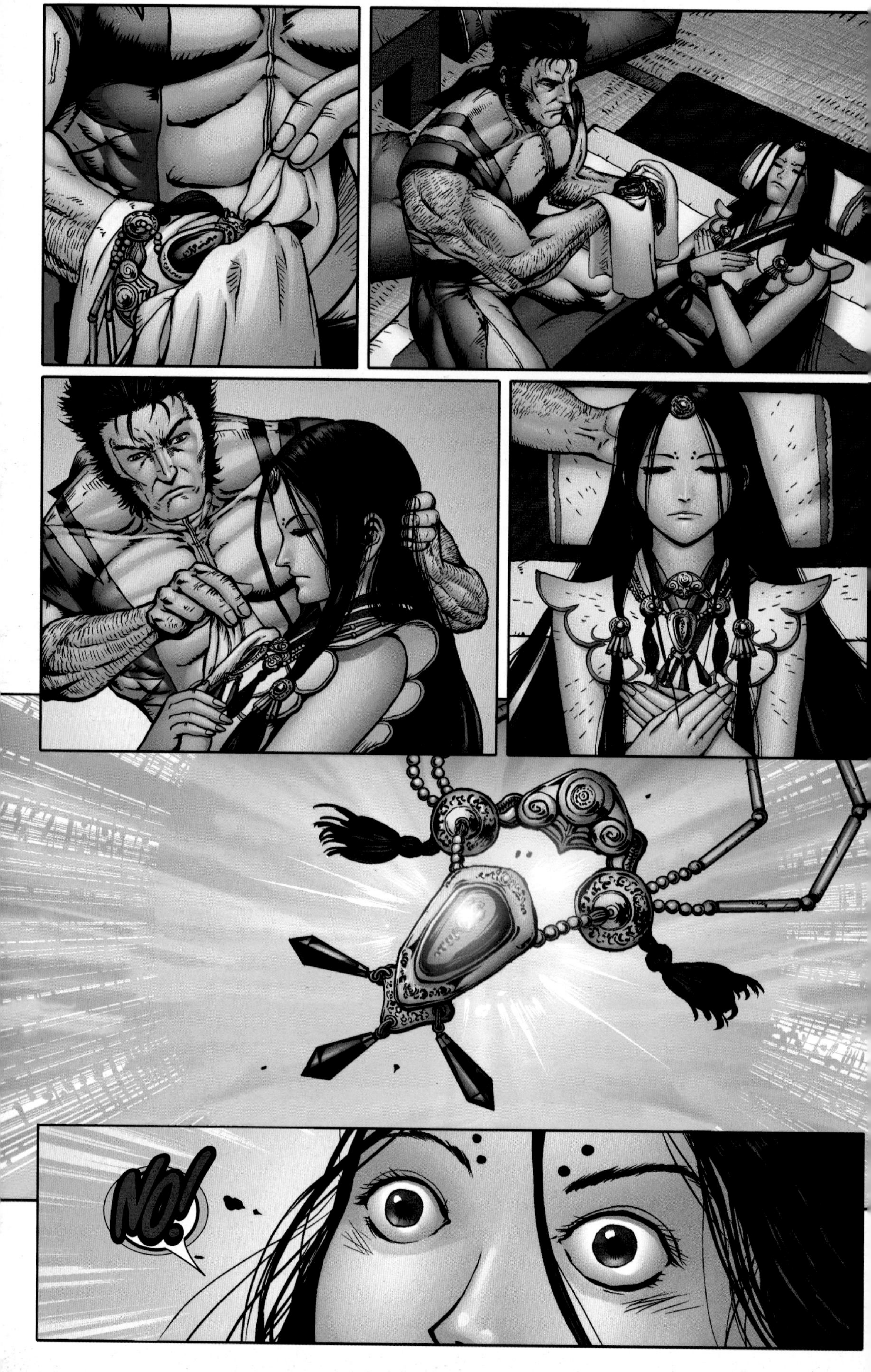
NO!

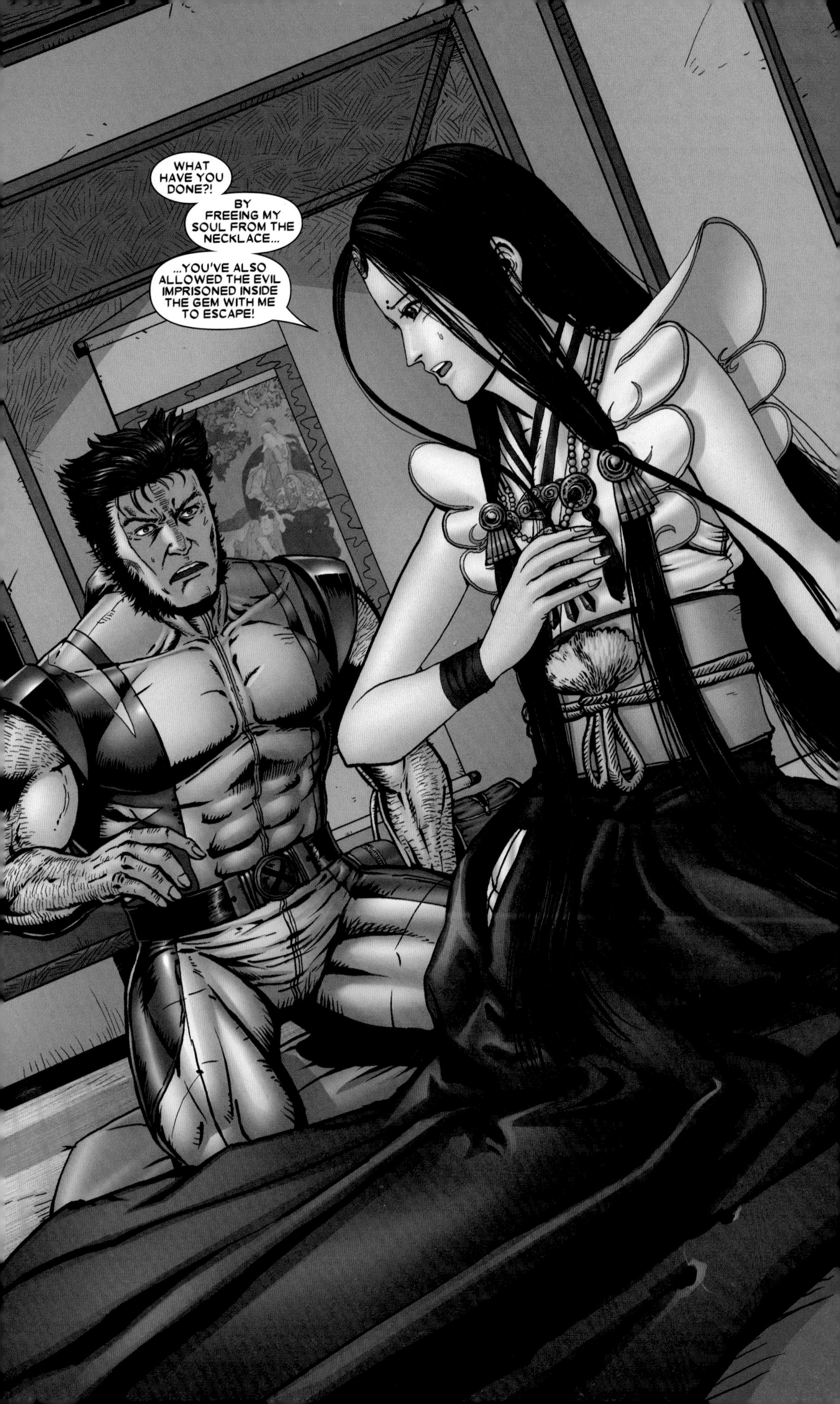
WHAT HAVE YOU DONE?!
BY FREEING MY SOUL FROM THE NECKLACE...
...YOU'VE ALSO ALLOWED THE EVIL IMPRISONED INSIDE THE GEM WITH ME TO ESCAPE!